# THE
# THINKER'S
# DICTIONARY

## SECOND EDITION

### A HANDBOOK FOR PHILOSOPHY AND SIMILAR INTELLECTUAL ENDEAVORS

J.A. VAN DE MORTEL
CHAIR, PHILOSOPHY DEPARTMENT
CERRITOS COLLEGE

McGraw-Hill, Inc.
College Custom Series

New York  St. Louis  San Francisco  Auckland  Bogotá
Caracas  Lisbon  London  Madrid  Mexico  Milan  Montreal
New Delhi  Paris  San Juan  Singapore  Sydney  Tokyo  Toronto

McGraw-Hill's College Custom Series consists of products that are produced from camera-ready copy. Peer review, class testing, and accuracy are primarily the responsibility of the author(s).

*Acknowledgements*

First, I wish to thank my family, especially my wife, for the time to work on this project. Working on a manuscript of this sort is like living in the style of a cave-dwelling hermit, selfishly seeking nirvana.

Also, I am very grateful to Cerritos College for a teaching environment wherein research, convivial disagreement, and creativity are supported. In particular my colleagues Douglas Wessell, Edward Bloomfield, and Ana Torres-Bower, as well as Ken Samples, Clayton Kradjian, and James Mahoney, have provided a philosophical consonance conducive to writing.

On a scholarly level, I am indebted to many of the philosophers and theologians I have had the opportunity to learn from over the years including Max Wildiers, Vernon Ruland, S.J., Hamilton Hess, James P. Mackey, John H. Elliott, Anthony de Mello, S.J., William Alamshah, John B. Cobb, jr., Charles Hartshorne, Vishwanath Naravane, Paul Shepard, Herbert W. Schneider, Peter Hess, Claudio Luna, Craig Ihara, J. Michael Russell, Charlene McCarthy, John H. Hick, Jan Potting, and Robert Evans. Through their example I have become a better philosopher.

In my own work, I am grateful for those students whose exuberance gives me confidence in the goodness of humanity. Without their desire to acquire wisdom and knowledge this book would not be necessary. I hope that they appreciate this work as much as I have appreciated their interest in the subject, whether in the classroom or in many beautiful miles of sailing in *symposia at sea*.

Finally, my ways are also the product of years spent in the trades, where the spirit and ideals of pragmatism never allowed my mind to drift too far from the redemptive effects of a skillfully crafted earthly life. This is in part a reflection of a set of parents who encouraged each of their sons to pursue an expertise in the techniques and principles of light, heavy, and finish construction.

*Cover design*

Plato's life was spent with philosophy on horseback. As a youth, he was raised in the equestrian class. This allows us to infer certain facts about his character and interests. Both the horse and the hunt were a part of Plato's life. Plato's discussion with

Glaucon in the *Republic* compares philosophers to a "ring of huntsmen".   Young Greeks hunted the boar and the lion to promote self-mastery, courage, and a robust physical condition.  Plato's equestrian life included such a regimen.

The philosopher is a hunter of ideas, and perhaps an intellectual atavist.  The same awareness one acquires in the venatic art is found in the soul of the philosopher.  Vigilance characterizes the philosopher's way, looking in all directions for insights, not knowing from which places they will come, not knowing when the truth will be captured.

The Greek youth and the horse symbolize the challenge and adventure of earthly  life.  Plato himself used the horse as a metaphor for the soul.  Its energy and power require guidance in order to produce a happy journey through this world.

*In Memoriam:*

Juan Garcia Camacho
(1918-1993)

A man who offered each of his children a university education.

# Preface

**To the Student:**

*The Function of this Handbook*

This handbook is written for the student who wants to make dramatic improvements in the way she or he thinks, writes, and speaks.

Topically, it is designed to eliminate the problems of acquainting one's self with the general layout of philosophy and religion. It uses a dictionary format to outline the main features of Eastern and Western thought, especially with regard to key figures and movements in philosophy. Entries for figures include life dates, the titles of major writings, and selected quotes. This format gives you easy-access to the principal facts and, thus, a better feel for what in going on in the discussion of philosophical topics.

Pedagogically, an important feature of this dictionary is the inclusion of what can be labelled *the intellectual's vocabulary*: words which are often found in the work of philosophers, poets, and other intellectual writers; having an uncommon but crucial usage. The idea of including these words in a special dictionary became apparent to me years ago while making my own way through the university. The study of these special and sometimes very unusual terms is propaedeutic to the reading of advanced primary sources and will help you master beforehand the vocabulary of the world's intellectual literature.

The brevity of definitions is functional. They are short to facilitate easy memorization. This makes casual study of the text immediately rewarding. For additional help on pronunciation and etymology, the reader is advised to consult the unabridged *Webster's New International Dictionary, 3rd Edition*. Many of the words here are <u>not found in the average college dictionary.</u>

*Why There Is Ideological Conflict*

The work of intellectuals is a history of ideological conflict. In many ways, this conflict is important to the advancement of human understanding. The world's religions themselves, owe much of their refinement to the existence of heretics, individuals who were driven by their own philosophical conscience to protest the often ridiculous assumptions of the past.

There are really no two thinkers who concur in the details of their theoretical understanding of reality. This has often caused people to despair about the utility and validity of philosophy, where disagreement seems more widespread than in the philosophies of science proper. The common sense needs of most people do not accomodate a situation of endless analysis. This, in part, accounts for the unpopularity of philosophy. The average person's temperament and outlook is predominantly pragmatic, seeking definite connections between knowledge and action. There is great merit to this kind of critical awareness. The world is always pressing in around us, requiring the application of what we believe to be best in our choices. Yet, a close examination of any two 'common-sense' advocates will uncover areas of disagreement as well. The simple desire, and pragmatic preference, for ideological concurrence does not create such concurrence. The fact remains that, whether one is a serious contemplative or a common-sense realist, the philosophy each person forms about life is marked by a degree of subjectivism.

*The Egocentric Predicament*

The subjective character of human thought, and the consequential existence of disagreement, is explained by a type of tactical limitation which philosophy refers to as *the egocentric predicament*. This means it is not possible to see the world exactly from anyone else's point of view. Each person is egoistically positioned in a finite domain of experiences. These experiences include the presence of other persons who are, likewise, external to the consciousness of each self and who provide us with their own views as data.

This *egocentric predicament* handicaps all human judgment and cannot be traded existentially. An awareness of this handicap softens the handicap. It makes a refinement of philosophical methods necessary and obvious. Philosophical thought is then more carefully directed toward the creation and use of effective methods of judgment which aid us in acquiring an alethic view of life.

The *egocentric predicament*, as a condition, limits and supports the importance of sound philosophical reflection. It limits this reflection by the inherent subjectivity of our opinions, and it supports it through the conscious effort to transcend the subjective nature of our ideas. This is accomplished by considering, using, and advocating the best methods of reasoning.

*A One Percent Approach*

Think about spending 1% of your time with this text, if you'd like to get the most out of it. One percent of life doesn't seem like much to commit, and yet it is. It breaks down to about 15 minutes each day. If you make that kind of commitment, you'll see a marked improvement in your vocabulary over a year's time. In fact, even a few words from this dictionary can help you impress people with your new habits of thought. This is because words are the public proof of one's knowledge, and it isn't how much you say, rather its what you say that makes people listen.

A person's vocabulary tends to level off at about 25 years of age. This is called *rational leveling*. (*Rational leveling* represents an equilibrium of intellectual content, meaning there is a tendency to rest at the intellectual level of one's surroundings.) Unfortunately today, mental life has become somewhat merdivorous. The general pre-occupation with social *pathos* means that people often have little to say that is hooked up to self-improvement and a wholistic spiritual life. The encounter with new ideas seems retarded and the mind fixated on a finite banausic content. New 'material' is not acquired because the people one regularly sees may lack the vital reflective habits which prevent a *rational leveling*.

Going to college is the usual means of producing a new level of intellectual awareness. However, that's no guarantee either. There are quite a few college students who are completely indifferent to their educational opportunities. (Beer-drinking fraternities and sororities need members too.) So, initiating a 1% commitment to the text, in solitude, will give you exposure to a vocabulary that might take 10-15 years to acquire under normal academic circumstances. I began constructing the notes and collecting the terms for this manuscript a long time ago. Even then, a lot of material has been excluded for economic reasons.

*Your Instructor*

Your instructor's commitment to the field of philosophy affords you an obvious opportunity to enlist her or his encouragement in mastering the subject. Your instructor's own training has involved serious and sustained contact with most of the ideas in this handbook and can provide you with the necessary guidance to make correct interpretations of controversial views.

*Wisdom and Youth*

To make a harsh observation, it is both charming and useless to become wise in old age. The opportunities of life are past, and one can only wonder what might have been. All too often, people begin meaningful pursuits when it is too late. Our society even promotes a false sense of optimism by pointing to extraordinary individuals who make good on their projects late in life, whereas I recommend the assumption that one will run out of both time and opportunities sooner than one thinks. The fact is that the time-resistant champion also had a lion's will in youth. So, how much mental suffering is represented in the old because they were unimpressed with wisdom in youth can only be guessed at. I guess with Buddha; it is a lot. Each generation seems to produce its own failure of judgment to some degree. Failure of judgment is something philosophy is designed prevent.

The study of philosophy benefits the young. It sharpens the mind in its quest for purpose, and purpose is what we seek. To apply wisdom in youth is difficult, because there are so many attractions which seem both pleasing and harmless. But, even roses have thorns, and by karmic effects, we reap what we sow. As John Stuart Mill observed, "the rational individual discriminates not only as to the quantity of pleasures but also their quality."

Philosophy emphasizes a mental seeing of reality. It is both a skill and a body of knowledge. Youthful acquaintance with its variety and depth improves decision-making skill in the young practitioner. It recommends us toward a rational and spiritual self-sufficiency. It sets us apart from the unreflective masses and gives direction to the creative vitality that exists in the young. It encourages a creative rebelliousness against jaded ways of thought. It insures that society will progress in its policies, values, and physical existence.

Philosophy should be studied and then practiced, because wisdom has no purpose if it is not put into action. The durability of youth allows us to make mistakes, and the message of evolution is clear: *improve or perish*. A serious mistake can be viewed as a specific instance of evolutional pressure. It is nature's demand on the individual to assess the risks in a certain point of view. Subsequently, you might say wisdom is an emergent power of judgment bleeding out of the individual's adjustments to mistakes and nature's teachings.

## To the Instructor

### The Socratic Method

This text assumes an interest in the traditional Socratic approach to instruction. It will be of interest to the instructor whose style fosters philosophical talk in the classroom and who enjoys the maieutic expansion of ideas through definition. The variety of terms and quotes will offer quick remedies to stalled classroom investigations. This is especially important for the beginning student whose level of confidence and philosophical inexperience are often obstacles to dialectical work.

### Compatibility

The topical coverage of this text will fit well with texts requiring an *historical* or *problems* familiarity of the student, without superceding the detail which is found in texts using the *historical* or *problems* approach. For the instructor who agrees the foundational nature of testing the students knowledge of the basic facts, this book offers an easy means of listing requirements while making rigorous intellectual demands. After all, we know that the student who does not master the relevant philosophical vocabulary is often a chronic recycler of useless street jargon.

### The Problem of Post-Literacy

Today the average person is more often found in the local video store than the library. In essence, we have entered an age where reading is taught and not practiced. Amusement has more popular value than knowledge. (Some etymology: *'Amusement'* derives from the Latin *'muse'*, which means 'to think'. The prefix *'a'* means not. Thus, *'amusement'* means 'not to think').

Never before has so much knowledge been available to so many, while so many default on its use. The number of people who do not read seems inversely proportional to the amount of knowledge available. Soon, no one while be reading everything. Even our palliative substitute, the computer, does not really represent a true questing, since most people use computer equipment for 'amusement'.

Anyway, vocabulary building provides direct access to the necessary *material* for the synthetic creation of thoughts, papers, and discussions. Thus, the *material* provided here should be viewed as a means to an end: resurrecting the habit of investigative reading.

The problem of post-literacy is compounded by the nature of modern life. Nearly 20 years of professing philosophy has convinced me that heavy reading is not something to be imposed on people who have given up their freedom to a bogus hedonism. Yet no one can become an expert without aggressive reading habits. This point is not lost on the older returning student who has already been hammered by reality, but the younger counter-part is often unconvinced. With this in mind, the presentation of compact ideological *material* is a valuable tool in getting the attention of the student who needs the sudden encounter with dense facts to transcend post-literacy.

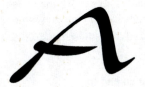

**Abelard, Peter** (1079-1142) - a French philosopher and theologian, condemned as a heretic by Pope Innocent II at the Council of Sens in 1141. At one time the Abbot of St. Gildas (1125), Abelard had a strong confidence in reason and chose to emphasize this over simple-minded faith.

Abelard became involved in the philosophical controversy over 'universals' (words which refer to groups of things, e.g., 'horse' refers to all (universal)horses, whereas 'Silver', as a name, refers to one horse.). Basically, he concluded that a universal is a word and a concept based in some reality; that words are not a reality in themselves. Thus, Abelard opposed 1) the nominalist position that words are not real in the world or in the mind, and 2) a conceptualism which argued that words are a reality in themselves.

Abelard's love of reason led to work in logic, where his thoughts led to the theory of substitutions (*suppositio terminorum*). Overall, this focus and reputation was very important to a new intellectual climate, helping to undermine the dogmatic and moralistic attitude toward knowledge advocated by the Church.

Principal works: *Yes and No,* 1122, *Theologia Christiana,* 1124, and *Logical Glosses.*

> "*By doubting we are led to inquire, by inquiring we are able to perceive the truth.*"
>
> -Peter Abelard, <u>Yes and No</u>

**abiogenesis** - n. reference to a process of generating life from non-living elements [of interest in the theory of evolution and discussions on the creation of life].

**ablation** - n. from Latin 'ablatus' meaning a wearing away or removal; a process of gradual elimination.

**abrade** - v. another word for 'wearing away,' specifically, a wearing of the surface; to roughen by rubbing or friction.

**Abreaction** - n. (German, *abreagieren;* Spanish, *abreaccion*)in the philosophy of psychology, the equivalent of spiritual catharsis or release. It recognizes the influence of negative emotions and operates to eject these pressures from the self. Traumatic events often account for a genesis of hysterical phenomena. The patient may be carrying an unconscious awarenessof trauma into the course of daily life. As such it remains isolated and unrecognized butactive.

In Freud, *abreagieren* is a recollection and 'working out' of the traumatic event. Through words and discovery, the patient is able to lift the weight of events which have produced pathological complications in carrying on with one's life.

Texts to Consult: *Studies on Hysteria* and *The Psychopathology of Everyday Life*, S. Freud.

**abrogate** - v. to terminate as in putting an end to.

**abscond** - v. to depart or escape, especially secretly.

**absonant** - adj. without reason or logic.

**abstemious** - adj. to be marked by moderation in eating and drinking; control of the mouth.

**absterge** - v. to clean off, especially by wiping.

**Abstinence, Rule of** - n. (German, *Abstinenz*; Spanish, *abstinencia*) in the philosophy of psychology, the realization that the patient must not become reliant on the counselor's or patient's ability to create substitute satisfactions. The creation of substitute satisfactions blocks the 'working out' of psychological problems, reassigning them to new manifestations.

Suffering is involved in the elimination of weaknesses. If this suffering is mitigated or compromised when it must take place, the cause of difficulties will not be eliminated.

Text to Consult: *The Complete Psychological Works of Sigmund Freud* (24 vols.)

**Absurd, The** - n. in existentialism, a reference to the absence of meaning. In philosophical-moral terms, absurdity announces the disconnectedness between the members of modern society. It is life marked by alienation and estrangement. This includes the degradation of personhood, often through the suffocating effects of bureaucratic social organization.

In the philosophy of Louis Lavelle (1883-1951), *the absurd* is the absence of love. Love alone can lay a meaning over life that reduces the chronic existence of meaninglessness. Love creates joy in the sense that it emphasizes the importance and meaning of 'the other.'

Text to Consult: *The Meaning of Holiness*, Louis Lavelle, 1950.

**abulia** - n. reference to the loss of will; pertaining especially to inability to act or decide; choosing by not choosing; a sign of mental confusion and inability to commit.

**abysmal** - adj. like an abyss or chasm; also meaning 'profound' or 'immeasurable'.

2

**acatalepsy** - n. in Greek 'katalepsis' means understanding. The term acatalepsy originates in the philosophy of Skepticism, especially the views of Pyhrro (360-270 B.C.). It refers to an inability to understand or the impossibility of gaining knowledge.

**accinge** - v. to bolster, prepare, or brace.

**acclivity** - n. an upward slope; especially from the observer's point of view.

**accouter** - v. to equip; to furnish or provide.

**accretion** - n. an increase by natural process; growth, especially by addition to external parts.

**acescent** - adj. to be sour.

**acosmic** - adj. literally 'not cosmic'; in philosophy, a reference to the unreality of the external world. Hegel advocated an idealism which was 'acosmic'.

**Act deontology** - n. in ethical theory, the view that with respect to *duty* the agent must consider each act as a unique ethical situation in which to conclude right or wrong. In theory, the act possesses inherent goodness, thus it merits participation.
    Text to Consult: *Ethics*, Louis Pojman, 1995.

**actinism** - n. the tendency or property of radiation to produce chemical changes.

**actuary** - n. an expert on life expectancy and the statistics of risk.

**Act utilitarianism** - n. in ethical theory, the view that an act is morally correct if and only if it provides as much good as any other available act. In theory, the act is judged for its effectiveness in getting to desireable consequences.

**adelphogamy** - n. the practice of sharing a wife or wives between brothers.

**adephagous** - adj. gluttonous; having a voracious appetite.

**Ashesiveness of the Ego or Libido** - n. (German, *Klebrigkeit der Libido*; Spanish, *adherencia de la libido*) in philosophy of psychology, a reference to the way the libido sticks to an object or phase. Carl Jung used the term 'psychic enertia' to mean the same thing. It is the recognition of limits in the effectiveness of counseling to free the individual from troubling psychic objects.
    On the other hand, this theory also sees problems in being too detached or mobile in one's interests. In such instances, the advice of counseling will not stick.
    Text to Consult: *Three Essays on the Theory of Sexuality*, Sigmund Freud.

**adiaphoresis** - n. lack of perspiration.

**adipopexia** - n. storage of fat in the body.

**Adler, Alfred** (1870-1937) - a philosopher of psychology, trained at the University of Vienna as an M.D.  His medical training had a light influence on his philosophical conclusions, which were put forth in several important essays, including *Uber den nervosen Charakter* (*The Neurotic Character*), 1912, and *Inferiority and Its Psychical Compensation,* 1927.  An opponent of psychological determinism, Adler argued that each person is born with feelings of inferiority and works to compensate for this by creating a life plan which will bring about a healthy adjustment to the external world.  Adler tried to study the effects of such things as age-rank, excessive affection, neglect, and physical constitution in the understanding of development of the young.  Exaggerated feelings of inferiority, 'the inferiority complex', leads to over-compensation in a pathological development of arrogance or 'the superiority complex'.  Adler was convinced of the power of creative reason to organize the life of the individual, and though influenced by some psycho-genetic elements in Freud's philosophy, he believed most human problems stem from the incorrect development of a life-plan.

Adler's theory of the 'aggressive-drive' is reminiscent of Nietzsche's 'will to power', but he regarded an exaggerated drive as evidence of neurosis.  The healthy individual finds a balanced way of creating a place in the world.  This is validated by the social interests of the individual, especially the concern for social well-being.  The psychotic insists on making the fictions of the mind reality, attempting to make life fit the subjective images of one's inner world, simultaneously ignoring the social dimensions of life.

Adler also presupposed a type of personalism, claiming that each individual is unique. This uniqueness is, however, often compressed by societal influences, which are often destructive.  This seems consistent with Adler's analysis of the human movement from inferiority to superiority.  Society as a 'superiority' presence can work against the 'superiority' of the individual by corrupting the authentic life plan or "guiding fiction", as Adler calls it.

Principal works: *The Neurotic Character,* 1912, *Practice and Theory,* 1920, *Understanding Human Nature,* 1927, and *Superiority and Social Interests,* 1933-37.

> *"Anyone who wants to understand Individual Psychology correctly must orient himself by its clarification of the unitary purposefulness of thinking, willing, and acting of the unique individual.  He will then recognize how the stand the individual takes and the life style, which is like an artistic creation, are the same in all situations of life, unalterable until the end - unless the individual recognizes what is erroneous, incorrect, or abnormal with regard to cooperation, and attempts to correct it.  This becomes possible only when he has comprehended his errors conceptually and subjected them to the critique of practical reason, the common sense - in other words, through convincing discussion."*
>
> *Alfred Adler, <u>Superiority and Social Interests</u>*

**adscititious** - adj.  supplemental; additional; unessential.

**advalorem** - L.  according to the value.

**Adventism** - n.  in religion, the views of William Miller (1782-1849).  Miller tried to predict the Second Coming of Christ in 1843.  Miller was of course wrong.  However, he revised his predictions to the immediate future. Near the end of his life, he was very reluctant to make further predictions. Modern Seventh Day Adventists have their roots in the views of William Miller.

**adventitious** - adj. casually or accidentally acquired; especially in the sense of 'good fortune'.

**aesthete** - n. a lover of beautiful objects; one who appreciates the sensory qualities of things.

**Aesthetics** - n. in philosophy, the study of beauty (Greek 'aisthesis', meaning sensation). Logically then, aesthetics is also the study of that which is ugly, for the study of the beautiful is conditioned by a knowledge of the ugly. Oddly enough, people are just as interested to see, for example, the ugliest person in the world as they are to see the most beautiful person in the world.

Beauty is often connected with 'value', and value is derived from scarcity versus interest. The scarcity of gold or diamonds accounts for value, combined with our interest in their appearance as found substances.

In aesthetics there is also a linkage with ethics in the concern for the relationship between happiness and beauty, i.e., "Is it possible to be happy in an ugly world?" Thus, we are concerned with the way appearances contribute to our own sense of order and harmony. Creative actions, as ethics-aesthetics, build appearances in paintings, sculpture, architecture, landscapes, and various other mediums which are the products of individual and collective genius.

There is the question, also, whether beauty is subjective or objective. If beauty is not always noticed, it can sometimes be explained as a consequence of lower awareness. Likewise, if an object or event is not perceived as ugly, it may be connected to analytic weaknesses. The wide differences of opinion regarding the beautiful and the ugly can be explained as difficulties of discernment. After all, the sensory object, e.g., the Mojave Desert, is a relatively steady reality. It would reveal different meanings to different observers depending on their knowledge and interest in it.

The needs of everyday life may also dictate what is beautiful. In fact, the need to work out physical survival represents a non-aesthetic influence on the aesthetic way of looking at the world. The pure aesthetic concern with reality is, in essence, a luxury that is possible because the everyday needs of life have been fulfilled.

**Agapism** - n. in ethical theory, the view that *love* constitutes the highest virtue. Thus, love becomes a principle of decision-making. It is especially concerned with altruistic feeling.

**ageusia** - n. the state of not having taste sensation; the state of lacking good taste.

**Aggressive Instinct** - n. (German, *Aggresionstrieb*; Spanish, *instinto agresivo*) in the philosophy of Alfred Adler, the tendency of humans to act destructively rather than simply dropping a concern or interest which is not meeting the wishes of the ego.

It is related to the 'death instinct' and has much to do with the research into aggression. An underlying assumption is that all human behavior is in some fashion aggressive.

**agnosia** - n.  the mental condition of not being able to recognize ordinarily common objects.

**Agnosticism** - n.  in philosophy and theology, view which emphasizes skepticism about the existence of God.  Agnostics are sometimes said to be 'sympathetic' to the idea of God, however they are unable to make a mental commitment to belief in such a metaphysical reality.  Instead agnostics hold that all real knowledge can only be knowledge of a material world.  The term 'agnosticism' is attributed to Thomas Henry Huxley (1825-1895), *Man's Place in Nature,* 1864, *Essays Upon Controversial Questions,* 1889.  Huxley believed consciousness to be epiphenomenal, a by-product of physical biological processes.  He was an advocate of Darwinism and a rather strict form of empiricism.

Technically, it possible to equate agnosticism with atheism, since it is the failure to affirm a belief in God.  Moreover, it is often regarded as a turning point to or from atheism.

> *"It is wrong for a man to say that he is certain of the objective truth of any proposition unless he can produce evidence which logically justifies that certainty.  This is what Agnosticism asserts."*
> - *T.H. Huxley,* <u>Essays Upon Controversial Questions</u>

**alacrity** - n.  a state of being vitally ready, even cheerful with regard to required actions.

**alethic** - adj.  having a connection to fact or truth.

**algolagnia** - n.  in psychology, pathological sexual enjoyment or pleasure derived from the existence of pain.  Passively, algolagnia is the sexual satisfaction in suffering pain *(masochism)*.  Actively, algolagnia is the sexual satisfaction derived from inflicting pain *(sadism)*.

**algophobia** - n.  in psychology, a morbid or disproportionate fear of pain.

**allocentrism** - n.  in ethical theory, the view that one should center interest and concern on other persons rather than one's self.

**alloeroticism** - n.  making another person the object of sexual excitement, feeling, and action; as opposed to *auto-eroticism.*

**allopsychic** - adj. characterized by being related mentally to the external world.

**allotheism** - n. the adoration of gods outside a recognized theological system.

**alter-ego** - n.  in psychology, a second self;  someone who is deeply trusted.

**altrigendristic** - adj.  being interested in the opposite sex without specific sexual goals or aims.

**Altruism** - n. in ethical theory, the view that life should be lived in such a manner as to use one self up for the good and well-being of others. Essentially, it is a concern for others that overrides the concern for one self. In the West, Christ is the paradigm.

Altruism exists in animals as well as in humans, and it has long presented a puzzle in understanding individual self-preservation. Some philosophers argue that altruism is a disguised form of egoism and is enacted to produce advantages indirectly.

Texts to Consult: _Sociobiology, E.O. Wilson_, 1975, _Die Frohliche Wissenschaft_ (_The Gay Science_ being the unfortunate translation), Friedrich Nietzsche, 1882., _Complete Psychological Works of Sigmund Freud_, "The Economic Problem of Masochism", vol. 19.

**ambosexual** - n. or adj. having characteristics of both sexes; somewhat of a hermaphrodite.

**amensa et thoro** - adj. in marital ethics, a reference to a conjugal relationship in which the man and woman are married but no longer sleep together.

**anaclitic depression** - n. (German, _Anlehnungsdepression_; Spanish _depresion anaclitica_) in psychology, a downward turn in the psychic life of the child who is deprived of its mother after having a good relationship for the first six months of life. Manifestations include weight loss, changed facial expression, and withdrawal.

Text to Consult: _The First Year of Life_, Rene Spitz, 1965.

**anaclitic focus** - n. in psychology, a mental or libidinal dependence on a love object which represents infantile needs, e.g., the father or mother.

**anagogic** - adj. having a spiritual or uplifting effect; relating to inner psychic forces which move one toward lofty ideals. Referring to a universal ethical meaning, this term is contrasted with psychological analysis which points toward sexual meaning.

**anal character** - n. in psychology, a personality characterized by excessive devotion to neatness, self-discipline, pedantry, acquisitiveness, miserliness, and control. These are seen as the symbolic manifestations of anal eroticism.

**Anarchism** - n. from the Greek 'an' (without) and 'archos' (head). In political philosophy, it is the view that organized government is the source of social injustice and the slaughter of liberty. Thus, anarchists typically call for the dissolution of the state. Anarchists come in violent and non-violent varieties. Some, like William Godwin (1756-1836), _The Inquiry Concerning Political Justice_, 1793, argue for its emergence through gradual moral progress, emphasizing a kind of evolution of society and confidence in the goodness of persons. Others, like Max Stirner (1806-1856), _The Ego and One's Own_, 1845, advocate radical individualism and open rebellion. In the case of Stirner, individual freedom, as a principle of virtue and a withdrawal into one's creativity, implies the respect of every other individual and thus would not increase conflict. Still others, like Mikhail Bakunin (1814-1876), _The State and Anarchy_, 1873, advocate a mission of destruction on the assumption that privileged society is depraved in heart and mind.

_"The state is the sum of all the negations of the individual liberty of all its_

*members . . . . . negation of the liberty of each in the name of the liberty of all or of the common right - that is the State. Thus, where the State begins, individual liberty ceases, and vice versa."*
*- Mikhail Bakunin, <u>The State and Anarchy</u>*

**Anaxagoras** (500-428 B.C.) - a friend of Pericles, Anaxagoras was highly regarded for his knowledge of mathematics and astronomy. The main elements of his thought are left to us in a fragmented work entitled *On Nature*. Like the philosopher, Empedocles, Anaxagoras was interested to solve the puzzle of how and why things change. He disagreed with Empedocles, however, on the existence of four basic elements: earth, air, fire, and water. Anaxagoras argued that there must be some absolute and unchangeable foundation to reality, but that this foundation was composed of more than four basic elements. Change was said to be the result of relative adjustments in the arrangement of the foundational elements. Consequently, Anaxagoras held the view that nothing comes into existence or passes away. Change is primarily a cosmetic re-organization of matter.

*"It is the sun that endows the moon with its brilliance."*
*Anaxagoras, <u>On Nature</u>*

**Anaximander** (611-546 B.C.) - a student of Thales, Anaximander was well-schooled in the astronomy, geography, and cosmology of his time. Certainly one of his greatest insights into the nature of life was his belief that all living things evolved from the sea, including humanity. In the process, he advocated a kind of alternation of worlds theory. This meant that all worlds recur in a cyclical fashion: a separation from and return to a primordial substance, a substance referred to by Anaximander as the "Boundless Indeterminate".

**Anaximenes** (588-524 B.C.) - a pupil of Anaximander, Anaximenes was the last important natural philosopher of the Milesian school. His main contribution to primitive science was an adjustment in the theories of his teacher. He proposed that 'air' is the principal substance and that all changes are the result of rarefaction and condensation. Fire is a type of rarefaction, and stone, ice, water, and clouds are examples of degrees of condensation.

**ancillary** - n. or adj. subordinate.

**animism** - n. the view that all matter has 'soul'. It stems from attempts to explain 'change' in the physical world. In Greek philosophy this view was called 'hylozoism'.

**anoesis** - n. the mental condition of vacant organization in which any content of the mind is not understood or coherently assimilated.

**anoia** - n. pure idiocy.

**Anselm, St.** (1033-1109) - a Christian philosopher and Archbishop of Canterbury, Anselm is known primarily for his philosophical creation of the ontological proof for the existence of God. While his book *Monologium* contains a cosmological proof inherited from St. Augustine, *Proslogium* makes use of Platonic elements to show how one deduces the existence of God from the concept of God: God is that being greater than which nothing can be thought of. The ontological argument uses the perfection of God to imply existence, especially a highest existence or being. This logical move is achieved on the Platonic introduction of the Theory of Forms, which are said to have existence apart from and superior to the existence of material objects. The effect of this argument on the wider thought of Anselm is obvious: to reveal the relationship between divine reality and physical reality. Further, it is used to demonstrate the implications for human existence, especially human conduct. God is equated with the supreme Good, self-existent, eternal, and the source of absolute truth.

> *"It is one thing for an object to be in the understanding, and another to understand that the object exists. . . . even the fool is convinced that something exists in the understanding, at least, than which nothing greater can be conceived. For when he hears of this, he understands it. And whatever is understood, exists in the understanding. And assuredly that, than which nothing greater can be conceived, cannot exist in the understanding alone. For, suppose it exists in the understanding alone: then it can be conceived to exist in reality; which is greater.*
>
> *"Therefore, if that, than which nothing greater can be conceived, exists in the understanding alone, the very being, than which nothing greater can be conceived, is one, than which a greater being can be conceived. But obviously this is impossible. Hence, there is no doubt that there exists a being, than which nothing greater can be conceived, and it exists both in the understanding and in reality."*
>
> -St. Anselm, <u>Proslogium</u>

**anthropomorphism** - n. a philosophical view which attributes human qualities and characteristics to God or things which are not human. It is regarded as a fallacy of reification in the study of logic.

**anthropopathism** - n. a philosophical view which projects human feelings onto nature, especially feelings of cruelty or sympathy. Particularly evident in the work of some poets, as in Shelley and Tennyson. In logic, it is considered an error in reasoning, close to the fallacy of reification.

**antithesis** - n. counter-argument or counter-theory. In epistemology (the study of theories of knowledge), *antithesis* is a central feature of dialectical process. Without counter-theory, there can be no real progress in the development of ideas. Ideas must be attacked in order to be validated or remodeled. Thus, Western thought is a history of *antithesis*.

**aphanisis** - n. the disappearance of sexual desire; the consequence of a deep fear.
     Article to Consult: *'Early Development of Female Sexuality'*, Earl Jones, 1927.

**apologia** - n. a defense, usually of a philosophical or theological position.

9

**a posteriori** - Latin meaning 'from the latter'; in reasoning this phrase refers to knowledge that comes after experience or the encounter with fact; connected to inductive reasoning.

**a priori** - Latin meaning 'from before' or 'from the preceding'; in reasoning this phrase refers to statements which are true independent of experience; connected to deductive reasoning.

**Aquinas, Thomas** (1224-1274) - an Italian philosopher and theologian, Aquinas became the dominant theological voice for Catholicism. Aquinas' thought reflects a strong Aristotelian influence which he used creatively to construct his philosophy. A true systematician, Aquinas' thought is laid out in great abstract description, almost defying adequate summation.

God is both pure actuality and pure form. A knowledge of God can be acquired by faith or reason, but God's existence is variously inferred from creation: a) everything has a cause, b) it is not necessary that natural objects exist; they exist because of some necessary ground; c) there are graded forms of being starting from a lowest to the highest; d) everything exists for a purpose, implying an intelligent designer; e) matter cannot create itself, thus God created it *ex nihilo* (out of nothing).

Aquinas defines man as pure spirit and substance, a higher being in the chain of being ascending toward God. The human soul is an immaterial and subsistent form. It possesses an eternal nature in that it is also actual form. So, it features an immortal condition which succeeds in the absence of the body. Moreover, he argues that the union of body and soul is partial, with the soul retaining a type of independence, especially with regard to destiny.

The highest good is the realization of the true self. This is accomplished by living a contemplative life, with God as the meditative object. Reason and faith contribute to an understanding of the best life in God, but it is finally a type of intuitive knowledge acquired in the afterlife that completes our understanding. Preparing for one's positive eternal destiny (*salvation*) requires a commitment to asceticism and ethical-spiritual development through the Sacraments of the Church and the message of the Gospels.

Principal works: *On Being and Essence*, 1243, *On Truth*, 1259, *Summa Contra Gentiles*, 1260, and *Summa Theologica*, 1272.

> *"A certain participation of Happiness can be had in this life, but perfect and true Happiness cannot be had in this life . . . Since happiness is a perfect and sufficient good, it excludes every evil, and fulfills every desire. But in this life every evil cannot be excluded. For this present life is subject to many unavoidable evils: to ignorance on the part of the intellect, to disordered affection on the part of the appetite, and to many penalties on the part of the body. . . . Likewise neither can the desire be satiated in this life. For man naturally desires the good which he has to be abiding. Now the goods of the present life pass away, since life itself passes away, which we naturally desire to have, and would wish to hold abidingly, for man naturally shrinks from death. Therefore, it is impossible to have true Happiness in this life."*
> Thomas Aquinas, <u>Summa Theologica</u>

**ardhamagadhi** - n. a northern Indian language used in the canon of Jainism.

**Aretaic ethics** -n. in ethical theory, the view that *character* of the agent is an essential part of the measurement of goodness. Thus, the concern with acts and duties becomes secondary to the personality or spiritual disposition (meaning character) of the agent.

**argot** - n. special vocabulary used by an underworld group to communicate privately.

**Aristotle** (384-322 B.C.) - a student of Plato and the teacher of Alexander the Great, he had the most decided effect on Western thought outside of his teacher. He invented the field of formal logic, including the starting points of reason, the syllogism, and the foundation of causal analysis for events in the natural world.

      Aristotle argued for substance as the primary essence of reality and deepened the Platonic reference to matter and form by showing their interdependence. As a teleological thinker, Aristotle worked out strong explanations of the potentiality of being vs. the actuality of being, including sophisticated arguments for design and the processes of change.

      In coming to an understanding of things Aristotle recognized four types of cause to aid in the explanation of being and change:

    1) *formal cause* - the design of a thing.

    2) *material cause* - the substance from which a thing is made.

    3) *efficient cause* - the forces which bring a thing into empirical existence.

    4) *final cause* - the purpose or function for which a thing is created.

His conviction that all things possess a design permeates his entire understanding of reality, including psychology, ethics, biology, politics, physics, cosmology, and even art. For Aristotle, the problem of happiness and a successful life are dependent on how well each thinker is able to master and benefit from an understanding of the design of the cosmos. This assumption has had a direct influence on the entire development of knowledge in the Western world.

      Principle works: *Organon; On the Soul; The Metaphysics; Nicomachean Ethics;* and *Politics.*

> *"All men by nature desire to know. An indication of this is the delight we take in our senses; for even apart from their usefulness they are loved for themselves; and above all others the sense of sight."*
>            *-Aristotle, <u>Metaphysics</u>*

> *"It is no easy task to be good. For in everything it is no easy task to find the middle, e.g. to find the middle of a circle is not for everyone but for him who knows; so, too, anyone can get angry - that is easy - or to give or spend money; but to do this to the right person, to the right extent, at the right time, with the right motive, and in the right way, 'that' is not for everyone, nor is it easy; therefore goodness is both rare and laudable and noble."*
>            *-Aristotle, <u>Ethics</u>*

**arriviste** - n. one who has acquired success by dubious methods.

**arrogate** - v. to seize without permission or right to do so.

**Asceticism** - n. from the Greek 'askesis' meaning training. In philosophy and religion, it refers to the practices which aid self-mastery. It represents a type of moral science which seeks to eliminate vices and encourage personal excellence. In both Eastern and Western religious traditions it is a type of denial of body in order to keep the work of salvation or enlightenment clearly focused on spiritual goals. In Hinduism, asceticism is emphasized in the later stages of life with a renunciation of worldly interests. And, while Buddhism produced the 'Middle Way", it retains certain ascetic practices as central requirements for proof of inner liberation from desire. In the West and in the East, asceticism has sometimes been practiced to excess, leading away from enlightenment in a kind of negative focus on the body to the detriment of the spiritual life. Overall, the principles of asceticism offer a method for renewed personal unity. Typical restrictions and recommendations of asceticism include:

> 1) A commitment to non-violence.
> 2) Minimal contact with physical wealth.
> 3) Simplicity of habitat, including only the possessions necessary for the most basic physical survival, e.g., a begging bowl, a razor, a robe, sandals, a candle, a cup, the simplest furniture (if any).
> 4) Non-involvement in various kinds of sensual entertainment.
> 5) Dietary laws: strict limits on how much and what one eats; often including no food after mid-afternoon.
> 6) No use of intoxicants of any kind.
> 7) Transcendence of sexual desires and activities.
> 8) A daily routine of prayer, meditation, and simple but often demanding physical work.
> 9) Progressive and continuous mastery of the Scriptures.
> 10) The cultivation of universal love for humanity and one's community.

> *"When strict with one's self, one rarely fails."*
> > *- Confucius (551-479 B.C.), The Analects*

> *"It is a great grace of God to practice self-examination. But, too much is as bad as too little."*
> > *- St. Theresa of Avila (1515-1582), The Interior Castle*

> *"Everyone should enjoy a quiet soul and be free from every type of passion. Then will strength of character and self-control shine through in all their brilliance. But, when appetites are unleashed to run wild, either in desire or aversion, and are not reined by reason, they exceed all restraint and measure. They throw off obedience and leave it behind."*
> > *- Marcus Tullius Cicero (106-43 B.C.), On Duties*

**ascribe** - v. to attribute

**aseptic** - adj. though normally a reference to being 'not poisonous' or 'not infectious', it also implies a lack of attachment; also, the absence of vitality.

**ashram** - n. in religions of India, a place to meditate; a religious retreat house.

**askance** - adj. to be turned to the side.

**asomatous** - adj. without body; incorporeal; a condition beyond lifelessness.

**asperity** - n. roughness or sharpness, especially of manner.

**asperse** - v. to slander or attack, especially with damaging claims or charges of moral wrong.

**asperulous** - adj. to possess a slight roughness.

**asseverate** - v. to affirm with sincerity and earnest, especially with regard to truth.

**assiduous** - adj. with regard to a project or business, the quality of paying very close attention; being persistent in the completion of work.

**assignation** - n. an arrangement to meet; especially a secret lover's meeting.

**assuage** - v. to soften intensity.

**astatize** - v. to make unstable or active.

**asthenia** - n. a condition of lessened strength.

**asthenic** - adj. relating to or denoting a tall, lean build; a lightly muscled athletic physique.

**ataraxia** - n. in philosophy, an ideal mental state; characterized by an almost euphoric sense of pleasure and calm with regard to the life of the philosopher.

**Atavism** - n. in philosophy, the view that one should go back to a more primitive lifestyle; the re-creation of an ancestor's lifestyle. Hunting with the bow is an example of atavism. In such an action, one attempts to recover values and perceptions which may have contributed to a foundational understanding of life. Bow-hunting, as atavism, affords the opportunity to examine the dynamic properties of man as a rational predator; the sensory awareness, the improvisation of needs, and the general spiritual and physical self-sufficiency which enhances the possibility of personal happiness through a wholistic immersion in nature.

> *"Thus the principle which inspires hunting for sport is of artificially perpetuating, as a possibility for man, a situation which is archaic in the highest degree: that early state in which, already human, he still lived within the orbit of animal existence."*
> *-Jose Ortega y Gasset (1883-1955), Meditations on Hunting*

> *"It is surprising to see the insistence with which all cultures, upon imagining a*

*golden age, have placed it at the beginning of time, at the most primitive point. It was only a couple of centuries ago that the tendency to expect the best from the future began to compete with that retrospective illusion. Our heart vacillates between a yearning for novelties and a constant eagerness to turn back. But the latter predominates. Happiness has generally been thought to be simplicity and primitivism. How happy man feels when he dreams of stripping off the oppressive present and floating in a more tenuous and simpler element!"*
*-Jose Ortega y Gasset, Meditations on Hunting*

**atelier** - n. a craftsman's workshop or artist's studio.

**Atheism** - n. in philosophy and religion, the view that God does not exist. A common misconception associated with atheism is the belief that atheists are not religious. This misconception arises from the Judeo-Christian influence, especially the Genesis account of the Garden of Eden which identifies reason without faith as the source of alienation from God. Buddhism is, for example, a religion without God.

Hostility toward atheism has a long history. In fact, even certain novel interpretations of God have been treated as atheism. Benedict Spinoza's (1632-1677) claim that God and nature are one brought about an assassination attempt on his life, making it clear that pantheists are often considered as dangerous as atheists. This hostility exposes the emotional basis of belief in God, which is, in philosophical terms, evidence of irrational formulations and superstition at work.

Atheism has often been an expression of social protest. Take the example of Ludwig Feuerbach (1804-1872) who believed that the love of God often inspires a hatred of one's neighbor. Feuerbach abandoned his theological beginning, in part, as a protest against a seemingly hypocritical Christian society.

*"Atheism is sometimes inspired by great-hearted dreams of justice and progress. . . . and impatience with the mediocrity and self-seeking of so many contemporary social settings."*
*- Pope Paul VI, Ecclesiam Suam, 1964*

Paul Tillich (1886-1965), *Shaking of the Foundations*, 1948, *The Dynamics of Faith*, 1957, argued that atheism was a spiritual symptom, since it holds that life has no depth beyond a material scene. For Tillich, anyone who believes this must be an atheist since only the reality of God provides the possibility of depth so obviously missing in the ontology of many atheists. Tillich, however, did not embrace the traditional metaphysical definition of God, believing it to be too simplistic.

*"Atheism can only mean the attempt to remove any ultimate concern, to remain unconcerned about the meaning of one's existence."*
*Paul Tillich, Dynamics of Faith*

In a simplistic fashion, the problem of evil has been an ancient source of atheism. If God is good, why is there so much misery and suffering in this world? Where is the mercy and justice of God so commonly implied in the definition of God?

*"Behold, I cry out, 'Violence!' but I am not answered; I call aloud, but there is no justice."*
*-The Book of Job, 19:7*

The anthropomorphic view of God is sometimes attacked as a fallacy of reification. It is illogical to give attributes to God which are clearly a projection of human nature. The atheist argues that there is no verifiable evidence for an anthropomorphic theology.

*"My atheism, . . . is true piety towards the universe and denies only gods fashioned by men in their own image, to be servants of their human interests."*
*-George Santayana (1863-1952), Soliloquies*

The linguistic argument against God employs the verification principle. Language philosophers point out that the sentences which talk about God are filled with pictures that have no external context, that God talk cannot be meaningful without a clear reference in reality.

*"In its metaphysical use . . . the word "God" refers to something beyond experience. The word is deliberately divested of its reference to a physical being or to a physical being that is immanent in the physical. And as it is not given a new meaning, it becomes meaningless. To be sure, it often looks as though the word "God" had a meaning even in metaphysics. But the definitions which are set up prove upon closer inspection to be pseudo-definitions. they lead either to logically illegitimate combinations of words or to other metaphysical words (e.g. "primordial basis," "the absolute," "the unconditioned," "the autonomous," "the self-independent," and so forth), but in no case to the truth conditions of its elementary sentences. An elementary sentence would here have to be of the form "x is a God"; yet, the metaphysician either rejects this form entirely without substituting another, or if he accepts it he neglects to indicate the syntactical category of the variable x."*
*-Rudolf Carnap (1891-1970), The Elimination of Metaphysics*

Freud regarded belief in God as an illusion, even evidence of a neurotic temperament. God, in his view, is merely a conceptual refuge from reality. It allows the individual to escape from the problems of this life in a highly fantasized creation of an alternate reality.

*"Religious phenomena are to be understood only on the model of the neurotic symptoms of the individual."*
*-Sigmund Freud (1856-1939), Moses and Monotheism*

**atrabilious** - adj. morose, gloomy, pessimistic, sad.

**attenuate** - v. to reduce in force or value; to make thin; to threaten non-existence.

**attrahent** - adj. quality of drawing toward; attracting.

**audacity** - n.  a quality of great boldness;  a condition of fearlessness, especially with regard to limiting authority.

**audient** - adj.  hearing.

**au fait** - Fr., expert in something.

**augur** - n. prophet;  (the same in verb form) to prophesize.

**Augustine, St.** (353-430 A.D.) - a Christian philosopher and Bishop of Hippo who brandished the phrase "Understand in order that you may believe, believe in order that you may understand."  The underlying assumption of Augustinian epistemology was that no knowledge outside a knowledge of God and one's self is knowledge worth having. Knowledge of this sort alone will help the individual to secure a happy life.  Ignorance is seen as a type of restlessness or spiritual poverty.  Beauty, truth, and goodness only come about in one's life as a result of a spiritual knowledge of God.

   Augustine's philosophical energy seems to have been driven in part by his youthful alienation from sound moral reasoning.  His early love of pleasure, especially sexual pleasure, reached its final end when he was about 30 years of age.  The psychological features of his transformation through Christian ideas can be found in one of the most important autobiographies in history, *The Confessions*.  There one finds the personal basis of Augustine's rigorous commitment to spiritual purity.  In fact, this attitude was expressed in the official doctrinal position of Christianity for hundreds of years, as a consequence of Augustine's influence on the Christian world-view.

   In *The City of God* Augustine works out the theory of salvation, dividing the human race into 'reprobates' and 'elect', the latter destined for the City of God and the former destined for the fires of hell.  Other works, *On Free Will, On Christian Doctrine,* and *On the Trinity* fill out the main ideas of Augustine on psychology, history, theology, ethics, and the problem of evil.

   Principal works: *Confessions; City of God; On Christian Doctrine;* and *The Trinity.*

> *"I was in love with loving; and I hated security and a life with no snares for my feet.  For within I was hungry, all for the want of that spiritual food which is Thyself, my God; yet I did not hunger for it: I had no desire for incorruptible food, not because I had it in abundance but the emptier I was, the more I hated the thought of it. . . . My longing then was to love and be loved, but most when I obtained the enjoyment of the body of the person who loved me. . . . I wore my chains with bliss but with torment too, for I was scourged with red hot rods of jealousy, with suspicions and fears and tempers and quarrels."*
>
>    -St. Augustine, <u>Confessions</u> , III

> *"I in my great worthlessness . . . had begged You for chastity, saying "Grant me chastity and continence, but not yet." For I was afraid that You would hear my prayer too soon, and too soon would heal me from the sexual craving which I wanted satisfied rather than extinguished."*
>
>    -St. Augustine, <u>Confessions</u> , VIII

16

**Aurobindo, Ghose** (1872-1950) - also known as Sri Aurobindo, was a Hindu philosopher and political leader. Though naturally shy and relatively unknown as a professor at Baroda College in Bengal, he was catapulted into fame by his articles in the English-language weekly *Bande Mataram*. His father's choice to educate him in England from age 7 until age 21 created a deep need to 're-nationalize' himself. His ideology reflects the influence of Ramakrishna, Vivekananda, and Bankim Chandra Chatterjee. It works to liberate India and return the role of Hinduism in politics and national identity.

Metaphysically, Aurobindo defended the view of reality as a graded spectrum of existence, beginning with matter and moving to the Absolute or Brahman. His system offers a bi-polar movement: matter seeks Brahman and Brahman seeks matter, with Brahman guiding the overall dynamic as a kind of integral evolution of being. Aurobindo employs this metaphysic with ethical aims to call for a transformation of mind, life, and body. These principles are implemented in his extremist political philosophy.

Principal works include: *Essays on the Gita*, 1926-44, *The Life Divine*, 2 vols., 1947, and *The Synthesis of Yoga*, 1948.

> *"That which we call the Hindu religion is really the eternal religion, because it is the eternal religion which embraces all others. If a religion is not universal, it cannot be eternal. A narrow religion, a sectarian religion, an exclusive religion can only live for a limited time and a limited purpose. This is the one religion that can triumph over materialism by including and anticipating the discoveries of science and the speculations of philosophy."*
> -Sri Aurobindo, <u>Speeches</u>

**auspicious** - adj. favorable.

**austral** - adj. southern.

**Auto-eroticism** - n. (German, *Autoerotismus*; Spanish, *autoerotisme)* the act of obtaining sexual pleasure from one's own body without recourse to outside cooperatives. It assumes a breaking up of the sexual instinct and deliverance to the realm of fantasy. Theoretically, it has connection to the absence of satisfaction at the beginnng of life.

**Autonomy (thesis)** - n. in ethical theory, the view that moral principles and guidelines can be established without recourse to the Divine revelation. Autonomy emphasizes self-rule.

**avarice** - n. an excessive drive to acquire wealth.

**aver** - v. to declare with confidence.

**Averroes** (1126-1198) - also known as Ibn Roshd, was a principal player in the development of Arabic philosophy. Though himself a Spaniard, Averroes wrote in Arabic. His thought was modeled on the views of Aristotle, as Averroes believed that Aristotle was the perfect human being. Nonetheless, his ideas also revealed strong Neoplatonic tendencies along with a modified Aristotelianism, including the emanation theory of reality and the concept of a universal mind as God. Averroes importance lies in the preservational effects his work had on the transmission of ideas in an age of intellectual stagnation.

Principal work: *Commentaries on Aristotle.*

**Axiology** - n. in philosophy, the study of *worth* or *value*, thus 'value theory' as it has come to be called. It includes the study of value in art, ethics, politics, logic, and the sciences. Moreover, it produces more or less dyadic comparisons: natural vs. non-natural, subjective vs. objective, absolute vs. relative, justifiable vs. unjustifiable, extrinsic vs. intrinsic, religious vs. non-religious, rational vs. non-rational, scientific vs. non-scientific.

Values form in conjunction with human interests. Human interests, in turn, spring largely from the location of one's life, family, friends, teachers, etc. Interests, as values, constitute the domain of actions and are, subsequently, judged as vices or virtues.

**azonic** - adj. not local; not restricted to a local zone; outside an area or zone.

**azygous** - adj. the property of not forming a pair.

**Bacon, Francis** (1561-1626) - an English philosopher and politician who had an odd and contradictory life, perhaps begun by the contrasts of his mother and father. Bacon's mother emphasized the importance of religious purity, while his father advocated the worldly route to success. In the end he defended his political and ethical vices by arguing that it was necessary to acquire power to effect good in the world.

Among his more notable contributions was his view of learning, which included the Idols of the Mind:

1) *Idols of the Den* - each person lives in a kind of den or cave, preferring his or her own ideas to the ideas of others. Bacon advocated careful scrutiny of the ideas one finds most satisfying in order to prevent the egoistic distortion of truth.

2) *Idols of the Tribe* - warns us of the tendency to measure all things by human standards. The human race has anthropomorphic tendencies. We fail to recognize the weaknesses of the senses in determining truth. Man is not the measure of all things.

3) *Idols of the Market* - refers to the likelihood of inferring from mere words that there are actual references in reality. In commerce, we discover that words are ambiguous and many disputes over truth arise from the careless use of language.

4) *Idols of the Theater* - observes the weaknesses of philosophical abstractions. Systems of ideas are like stage plays. They are often barely justified in representing reality.

An advocate of the inductive method, Bacon died as the result of simple winter-time cryogenic experiments. According to history, Bacon tried to prove the preservative effects of snow on chicken. In the process, he contracted a fatal case of bronchitis.

Principal works include: *Novum Organum, The Advancement of Learning,* and *New Atlantis.*

> *"If a child be bird-witted, that is, hath not the faculty of attention, the mathematics giveth a remedy thereunto; for in them, if the wit be caught but a moment, one is new to begin."*
> -Francis Bacon, *The Advancement of Learning*

**bacchant** - n. one given to habits of drunkenness and uncontrolled conduct.

**badinage** - n. playfulness; lightness; good-natured wittiness.

**bagatelle** - n.  something of little or no value.

**bagnio** - n. a place where women are easily had for pleasurable purposes; a brothel.

**baksheesh** - n. a monetary gift;  a tip;  alms.

**balneal** - adj.  connected with baths or bathing, especially as a source of enjoyment.

**balneology** - n.  the study of bathing, especially its therapeutic and hedonistic effects.

**banausic** - adj.  of practical use only;  limited to 'praxis'; also meaning vulgar and damaging with regard to mental development.

**barratry** - n.  fraudulent acts by a captain or crew of a ship at the owner's expense;  also a reference to illegal traffic in ecclesiastical or state promotions of office.

**bathos** - n.  the sudden appearance of the vulgar or the ordinary in the midst of the sublime;  a descent from the sublime to the ludicrous.

**batrachian** - adj.  referring to vertebrate amphibians; toads, salamanders, frogs.

**battologize** - v.  to repeat words or phrases uselessly;  to use the same words to excess.

**battology** - n.  the study of  the tiresome repetition of words.

**Beauvoir, Simone de** (1908-1986) - a French feminist philosopher and the common law wife of Jean-Paul Sartre, Beauvoir became an expert on the role and destiny of women in ancient and modern culture.  Her philosophy of women is profoundly expressed in psychological and philosophical terms.  In her analysis, Beauvoir assembles the pieces to show how woman is essentially preyed upon in a male world.  She also outlines what she believes is necessary for liberating  women from their past and gives men and women new insights into the nature of existence in its sexual manifestations.

She is often credited with broadening the originally narrow rational psychology of Sartre.  This included the introduction of social issues and the experiences of childhood as contributing factors in the formation of the individual.

Principal works include: *The Ethics of Ambiguity*, 1947, and *The Second Sex*, 1949.

*"One is not born, but rather becomes, a woman."*

*"It is not uncommon for the young girl's first experience to be a real rape and for the man to act in an odiously brutal manner;  in the country and wherever manners are rough  -  half consenting, half revolted  -  the young girl loses her virginity in some ditch, in shame and fear.  In any case, what very often happens in all circles and classes is for the virgin to be abruptly taken by an egoistic lover who is primarily interested in his own pleasure."*

*"Man has succeeded in enslaving woman; but in the same degree he has deprived her of what made her possession desirable. With woman integrated in the family and in society, her magic is dissipated rather than transformed; reduced to the condition of servant, she is no longer that unconquered prey incarnating all the treasures of nature. Since the rise of chivalric love it is a commonplace that marriage kills love."*

*-Simone de Beauvoir, The Second Sex*

**bedizen** - v. to dress vulgarly.

**bedlam** - n. a scene or place of complete insanity, madness, or chaos.

**Being** - n. in philosophy, a reference to existence or realness. Awareness of existence leads immediately to the observation that Being stands in contrast to Becoming and Non-Being. In the philosophy of Plato, the material world implies a lesser Being than the spiritual world. This is due to Parmenides' (6th-5th Century B.C.) insistence that true Being implies permanence. Thus, the material world, as a changing world, is not Being or existence in the highest sense. The material world is closer to Becoming and Non-Being. Absolute Being is imperishable, thus it is realness in the highest sense. Much philosophy is an attempt to detail the definition of Being, for it is believed that the successful investigation of Being holds the key to solving the sense of puzzlement human beings have regarding their temporary existence in a material world.

The issue of Being is the basis of ontology. Ontology, the study of being, tries to lay out the tactical possibilities for making sense out of reality as Being. Ontology is then a central project of metaphysics, especially since there is no confidence in matter as ultimate reality. In the East and in the West, the search for a logic of Being accounts for construction of all the various philosophies of life.

**belaud** - v. to praise lavishly, especially with the aim of causing embarrassment.

**Bentham, Jeremy** (1748-1832) - an English philosopher, known as the founder of utilitarianism, a philosophical view which defines the highest moral principle as: the greatest happiness for the greatest number. Bentham developed a novel calculus for the determination of right and wrong based on the pleasure-pain principle. This calculus included seven criteria which are supposedly measured mathematically in plus (+) minus (-) fashion:

1) *intensity* - the acuteness of the pleasure.
2) *duration* - the length of time the pleasure exists.
3) *certainty* - the percentile regarding the pleasure's real occurrence when pursued.
4) *propinquity* - the availability or nearness of the pleasurable experience.
5) *fecundity* - the prospects of a pleasure leading to other pleasures.
6) *purity* - the fractional existence of pleasure vs. pain and misery.
7) *extent* - the number of people who will experience the pleasure.

Bentham spent much of his life pushing the principle of utility into the aristocratic society of his day, which he perceived as an obstruction to the greatest happiness for the greatest number. Logically, he was marked a political radical.

Principal works include: *Introduction to the Principles of Morals and Legislation*, 1798, *A Plea for the Constitution*, 1803, and *Catechism of Parliamentary Reform*, 1809.

> *"The general object which all laws have . . . is to augment the total happiness of the community; and therefore, in the first place to exclude . . . everything that tends to subtract from that happiness . . . "*
>
> -Jeremy Bentham, <u>The Principles of Morals and Legislation</u>

**Bergson, Henri Louis**(1859-1941) - a French philosopher of evolution, he explained evolution as the result of a vital impulse, *elan vital*. This vital impulse operates as a creative force driving all living things toward more complex forms of being. In reasoning this way, Bergson worked against traditional philosophical systems, like Platonism, which defended fixed conceptual models of reality. Bergson emphasized the notion of 'duration' (becoming) in a more rigorous way, pointing out that evolution has no set goal, that the future is open and truly dynamic.

Bergson was critical of science and its analytic emphasis, complaining that thought as analysis is unsympathetic and goes around things, falsifying the object of study. Instead he recommended thought as intuition. Intuition, argued Bergson, does not interrupt the processes which comprise things. Intuition is a sympathy toward things and sees movement or process as reality in itself. Thus, the accurate observation of things depends upon allowing the continuity of change in reality to proceed.

Bergson applied these concepts to moral philosophy, arguing that morality is also an aspiration toward higher forms of being in the Good. Moral and religious systems are of two general types, 1) the static - being closed, dogmatic, self-preservationist systems, and 2) the dynamic - being open, rational, novelty-oriented systems.

Principal works include: *Laughter*, 1900, *Introduction to Metaphysics*, 1903, *Creative Evolution*, 1907, and *Two Sources of Morality and Religion*, 1932.

> *"If we could rid ourselves of all pride, if, to define our species, we kept strictly to what the prehistoric periods show us to be the constant characteristic of man and of intelligence, we should not say 'Homo Sapiens', but 'Homo Faber'. In short, intelligence, considered is what seems to be its original feature, is the faculty of manufacturing artificial objects, especially tools to make tools, and of indefinitely varying the manufacture."*
>
> *"If instinct is . . . the faculty of using an organized natural instrument, it must involve innate knowledge, both of its instrument and of the object to which it is applied. Instinct is therefore innate knowledge of a thing. But intelligence is the faculty of constructing unorganized, that is to say artificial, instruments. . . . The essential function of intelligence is therefore to see the way out of a difficulty in any circumstances whatever, to find what is most suitable, what answers the best question asked."*
>
> -Henri Bergson, <u>Creative Evolution</u>

**Berkeley, George** (1685-1763) - a British philosopher, famous for his contributions to empiricism. "Esse est percipi" (To be is to be perceived.) was the hallmark of his epistemology. Berkeley argued convincingly that nothing exists without being perceived.

A necessary outcome of this logic is that mind or consciousness is primary and objects of perception are secondary in nature. To preserve the role and facticity of things, Berkeley introduces the Mind of God as the master viewer of the so-called objective world. Basically, if there is not a human mind to perceive things and announce their existence, there is always the Mind of God to perceive all things in the absence of human perception. Thus, when a tree falls in the forest and there's no one there to hear it, God hears it. That's why things exist in the absence of our perceiving them.

Principal works include: *Treatise on the Principles of Human Knowledge,* 1710, *Three Dialogues Between Hylas and Philonus,* 1713, and *Alciphron or the Minute Philosopher,* 1733.

> *". . . all those bodies which compose the mighty frame of the world, have not any subsistence without a mind, that their being is to be perceived or known; that consequently so long as they are not actually perceived by me, or do not exist in my mind or that of any other created spirit, they must either have no existence at all, or else subsist in the mind of some Eternal Spirit - it being perfectly unintelligible, and involving all the absurdity of abstraction, to attribute to any single part of them an existence independent of a spirit."*
> -George Berkeley, <u>Treatise on the Principles of Human Knowledge</u>

**binary** - adj. having two parts or elements; in logic, the two-parted nature of logical functions, housing a statement on each side, as in disjunction, conjunction, and implication.

**bisexuality** - n. in philosophy of psychology, the view that every human being is made up of both masculine and feminine characteristics. It represents material for determining conclusions about the conflicts people have in manifesting their own sex. Freud's use of the term was conditioned by the ideas of Wilhelm Fliess.

Text to consult: *<u>Civilization and Its Discontents</u>*, S. Freud.

**Bodhidharma** - n. the legendary founder of Zen Buddhism in the 5th Century who is said to have replied to a monarch's love of reading and good works that "Reading is worthless, and good works gain no merit." Only real meditation admits one to the condition of enlightenment and sainthood.

**Bodhisattva** - n. in Buddhist philosophy, a person aspiring toward enlightenment; a Buddha-to-be; *sattva* meaning existence, and *bodhi* meaning wisdom; a monk or nun who is also committed to the enlightenment of his or her fellows.

**Bonhoeffer, Dietrich** (1906-1945) - a German theologian, executed by hanging in a concentration camp at Flossenburg, Germany, April 9, 1945. Bonhoeffer was an outspoken critic of Nazism who left such a remarkable body of theological work, that many have speculated on the stature of this thinker, had he lived.

Bonhoeffer's thought is characterized by a concern with the non-religious climate of the 20th Century and the challenge to speak about God in non-religious language. He advocated a departure from religious tradition and a return to the primitive vitality of biblical faith.

His views on revelation emphasized its connection to the life of the individual in community.   Revelation occurs in the spiritual communion of souls.

Principal works include: *Die Nachfolge (The Cost of Discipleship)*, 1937, *Ethics*, 1947, and *Letters and Papers from Prison*, 1953.

> *"Cheap grace is the preaching of forgiveness without requiring repentance, baptism without church discipline, communion without confession, absolution without personal confession.  Cheap grace is grace without discipleship, grace without the cross, grace without Jesus Christ, living and incarnate.*
>
> *"Costly grace is the treasure hidden in the field, for the sake of it a man will gladly go and sell all that he has. . . . . Such grace is costly because it calls us to follow Jesus Christ.  It is costly because it costs a man his life.  It is costly because it condemns sin, and grace because it justifies the sinner."*
> *- Dietrich Bonhoeffer, The Cost of Discipleship*

**Brahman** - n. in Eastern philosophy, a reference to the Absolute; a type of world-soul; the main character in the Hindu concept of a trinity (*trimurti*) along with Vishnu and Shiva.  Brahman represents the creative principle, while Vishnu and Shiva stand for maintenance and destruction.  The concept of Brahman has an important cosmic and psycho-spiritual role in the harmony of reality.

> *"No one who seeks Brahman ever comes to an evil end."*
> *Bhagavad Gita (ca. 500 B.C.)*

> *"Meditate and you will realize that mind, matter, and Maya are but three aspects of Brahman, the one reality."*
> *Svestasvatara Upanishad, (ca. 600 B.C.)*

**bromide** - n.  a trite or platitudinous remark.

**brook** - v.  to put up with; to tolerate.

**bruit** - v.  to spread a rumor.

**brumal** - adj.  occurring in winter.

**brume** - n. a fog or mist; also, a camouflage.

**Buber, Martin** (1878-1965) - a Jewish existentialist born in Vienna, Buber worked hard to revive Hasidism which helped him discover a special dialogic.  Buber became known for his piercing analysis of human relationships and articulated the profound implications of relating to objects or things (It) and persons (Thou).  The possibility of treating persons as things, the I-It relationship, assumes a profound moral character, in his view,  in that it is the ground for evil.  The I-It relationship does not produce genuine communion between persons, rather it allows for the exploitation of the other. In the I-Thou setting, however, the person is seen in spiritual terms and in conjunction with God.  Thus, ontologically, one recognizes a hierarchy of Being.  Awareness of types of being introduces the moral guidelines for interaction.

Principal works include: *I and Thou*, 1922, *Between Man and Man*, 1947, and *Knowledge of Man*, 1965.

> *"The capricious man does not believe and encounter. He does not know association; he only knows the feverish world out there and his desire to use it. . . . And what he calls his destiny is merely and embellishment of and a sanction for his ability to use. In truth he has no destiny but is merely determined by things and drives; feels autocratic and is capricious."*
> -Martin Buber, <u>I and Thou</u>

> *"Whoever pronounces the word God and really means You, addresses, no matter what his delusion, the true You of his life that cannot be restricted by any other and to whom he stands in a relationship that includes all others."*
> Martin Buber, <u>I and Thou</u>

**Buddhism** - n. from 'Buddha' meaning 'enlightened one'. Among major religions of the East, it is philosophically connected to Hinduism, Taoism, and Jainism. Founded by Siddhartha Gautama Buddha (560-477 B.C.), it is a philosophy of worldly pessimism and spiritual meditation. Moreover, its psychological and spiritual orientation includes a denunciation of the utility of reason. Subsequently, it does not work out a rationalistic or systematic metaphysics.

> *"What have I not elucidated? . . . I have not elucidated that the world is eternal; I have not elucidated that the world is not eternal. I have not elucidated that the world is finite; I have not elucidated that the world is infinite. I have not elucidated that the soul and the body are identical. I have not elucidated that the monk who has attained (the arahat) exists after death; I have not elucidated that the arahat does not exist after death. I have not elucidated that the arahat both exists and does not exist after death; I have not elucidated that the arahat (saint) neither exists nor does not exist after death. And why have I not elucidated this? Because this profits not, nor has to do with the fundamentals of religion; therefore I have not elucidated this."*

> *"What have I elucidated? Misery have I elucidated. The origin of misery have I elucidated. The cessation of misery have I elucidated; and the path leading to the cessation of misery have I elucidated. And why have I elucidated this? Because this does profit, has to do with the fundamentals of religion, and tends to absence of passion, to knowledge, supreme wisdom, and Nirvana."*
> -Gautama Buddha in H. Warren, <u>Buddhism in Translation</u>, 1922

Buddhism is opposed to the Vedas and the caste system. Furthermore, it has developed into two principal schools, Mahayana Buddhism and Hinayana Buddhism:

'Mahayana' means 'great vehicle'. It is compared to a raft upon which many people may cross the river of life to enlightenment. Mahayana Buddhism distinguishes itself with the institution of the *Bodhisattva*, an enlightened one who remains in this world to spread universal love for all beings. Some Mahayanists regard Bodhisattvahood as essential, requiring all to pass through its gates. Other Mahayanists regard it as optional. It is sometimes called "the long easy path."

'Hinayana' means 'little vehicle'. It is compared to a raft upon which one individual at a time crosses the river of life to enlightenment. Hinayana Buddhism emphasizes the absence of God, thus putting full responsibility upon the individual to achieve salvation. It is sometimes called "the short steep path."

The *Dhammapada*, a Buddhist text meaning 'right path of life', contains simple teachings of Buddhism intended to produce contact with nirvana. Its message is built on the Four Noble Truths, i.e. 1) life is suffering, 2) the cause of suffering is desire, 3) desire can be eliminated, 4) the elimination of desire is achieved through the Eightfold Path:

> i) *Right Belief* - belief in the Four Noble Truths.
> ii) *Right Purpose* - the promise or vow to overcome a life of sensual desire.
> iii) *Right Speech* - well-defined talk that is not hurtful or false.
> iv) *Right Conduct* - well-defined actions that bring only harmony to this world.
> v) *Right Livelihood* - choosing a subsistence that is right for one's talents and is consistent with the teachings of the Buddha.
> vi) *Right Effort* - striving in a way that preserves spiritual awareness of that which is wise and that which is foolish.
> vii) *Right Mindedness* - establishing good habits of thought and good topics of thought.
> viii) *Right Meditation* - commitment to the advanced stage of enlightenment so that the soul is prepared for its passage to *Nirvana*, the extinction of re-birth.

*"Better than a hundred years lived in vice, without contemplation, is one single day of life lived in virtue and in deep contemplation." (110)*
> — *The Dhammapada, 500 B.C.*

*"Neither in the sky, nor deep in the ocean, nor in a mountain cave, nor anywhere, can a person be free from the evil they have done." (127)*

*"Never speak harsh words, for once spoken they may return to you. Angry words are painful and there may be blows for blows." (133)*

*"But although a person may wear fine clothing, if one lives peacefully; and is good, self-possessed, has faith and is pure; and if one does not hurt any living thing, one is a holy Brahmin, a hermit of seclusion, a monk called a Bhikku." (142)*

*"Empty the boat of your life, O man; when empty it will sail swiftly. When empty of passions and harmful desires you are bound for the land of Nirvana." (369)*

**Bultmann, Rudolf** (1884-1976) - a German theologian who offered an important revision of Jesus as an historical figure and subsequent theological implications for eschatology.

In *The History of the Synoptic Tradition*, 1921, Bultmann complained (in "form criticism") that the real life of Jesus was buried under several oral traditions detectable in the Gospels of Mark, Matthew, and Luke. Bultmann was particularly effective in demonstrating the Greek or Hellenistic influence on the development of Christianity, that influence being a specific communal existence with its own myths and culture.

Additionally, Bultmann was disturbed by the Protestant habit of speaking of God in the past tense, limiting revelation to a particular epoch. Bultmann insisted that a coherent theology include the view of God as an eternal power, capable of revelation in the present.

As for modern educated Christians, Bultmann criticized their dependence on a set of worldly objects: their biological essence, their commitment to a career, and their over-involvement in the secular institutions of the state. It seemed to him a betrayal of the theological meaning of eschatology. Inherently, this side of Bultmann's theology also exhibited his *commitment to existentialism* as a tool to express solutions to many human problems.

Principal works include: *The History of the Synoptic Tradition*, 1921, *Jesus and the Word*, 1934, *Theology of the New Testament*, 1951, *Primitive Christianity*, 1957, *Faith and Understanding*, 1969.

> *"Every human being knows or can know about its limitedness, for - consciously or unconsciously - it is driven to an fro by its limitedness, as long as it exists. . . . . . Mankind has no power over the temporal and the eternal. The power which has power over the temporal and eternal is God."*

> *"Many a life is poor in friendship and in love, many another rich, but even the rich life is aware of a final solitude into which it is driven. . . . The power which drives mankind into this final solitude is God."*
> *Rudolf Bultmann, Essays; Philosophical and Theological, 1952*

**bumptious** - adj. the quality of being excessively and unpleasantly self-assertive.

**bunkum** - n. speechmaking by a politician that is deceitful, calculated to impress constituents.

**burke** - v. to murder so as to leave no traces, as by smothering.

**Bushido** - n. in the Shinto religion of Japan, "the way of the warrior". Bushido reflected a code of ideal conduct incorporating eight dispositions of the superior warrior: honor, reserve, politeness, truthfulness, justice, loyalty, gratitude, and courage.

Text to Consult: *Tokugawa Religion*, Robert N. Bellah.

**cabal** - n.  a small group of persons engaged in secret plotting, as against a political body.

**cachexia** - n.  a condition of general poor health, accompanied by emaciation as the result of chronic disease.

**cacodemon** - n.  a spirit possessing evil character and influence.

**cachinate** - v.  to laugh without restraint;  to laugh noisily in an almost irritating manner.

**cacology** - n. the study of defective speech.

**cadastral** - adj.  of or relating to property lines, boundaries.

**cadre** - n.  a group of skilled people who train others, especially in an expanding organization.

**caducity** - n.  from the Latin 'caducus', meaning perishable;  also a reference to senility.

**cafard** - n.  a mood of sadness, melancholy or severe depression.

**caitiff** - n. or adj.  a person who is cowardly, despicable, worthy of contempt.

**calcify** - v. to become inflexible and changeless; to harden.

**calescent** - adj.  increasing in heat.

**callet** - n.  a frivolous person;  in Medieval times, a court fool;  also a reference to a prostitute.

**callow** - adj.  lacking in maturity.

**calumniate** - v.  to accuse without proof.

**cameral** - adj.  relating to a judicial chamber.

**campy** - adj. exaggerated in speech or gesture; implying homosexuality.

**Camus, Albert** (1913-1960) - a French philosopher of existentialism, Camus became famous through his literary work and his association with Jean-Paul Sartre in producing the underground periodical *Combat*. Through the experience of WWII and the general character of the 20th Century, Camus focused on the absurdity of the human condition, in particular the way being is not given any definitive rational support. The absence of clear definitive meaning in life is the experience of absurdity. The life of humanity is not guided and seems lost in infinite moral choice. He interpreted Nazism as an exaggerated and desperate reaction to nihilism but itself devoid of any authentic social solidarity. In his final years, Camus expressed the view that life is purely a case of moral heroism in which one tries to preserve one's innocence while combating evil.

Principal works include: *The Stranger*, 1946, *The Plague*, 1948, *The Rebel*, 1954, *The Fall*, 1957, and *The Myth of Sysiphus*, 1955.

-*"Obscenity is like a form of despair."*

-*"What a man thinks, that does he become."*

-*"Politics, and the fate of mankind, are shaped by men without ideals and without greatness. Men who have greatness don't go in for politics."*

-*"One can, with no romanticism, feel nostalgic for lost poverty. A certain number of years lived without money are enough to create a whole sensibility."*
        -*Albert Camus, Notebooks 1935-1942*

**canny** - adj. cautious, clever, shrewd.

**captious** - adj. characterized by a tendency to find fault; difficult to please.

**carking** - adj. anxious, worried, disturbed; also stingy or miserly.

**Carnap, Rudolf** (1891-1970) - a German philosopher of logic whose contributions rank among the most important in the 20th Century. Carnap was a member of the Vienna Circle, a group of philosophers committed to elevating the status and influence of philosophy through the improvement of methods in science and mathematics.

In 1935, Carnap moved to the United States because of Nazism's threats to free-thinking and began teaching at the University of Chicago. Later, after the death of Hans Reichenbach, Carnap assumed the chair of philosophy at UCLA. He was associated with UCLA until his own death in 1970.

Carnap's theoretical work was influenced by Ludwig Wittgenstein, especially his views on metaphysics. Carnap concluded that any real progress in the use of language would require the removal of metaphysical expressions. Instead language must be guided by scientific observation and methods of logic.

Principal works include: *The Logical Construction of the World*, 1928, *The Unity of Science*, 1932, *Foundations of Logic and Mathematics*, 1939, and *Introduction to Semantics*, 1942.

> *"Logical analysis . . . pronounces the verdict of meaninglessness on any alleged knowledge that pretends to reach above or behind experience. This verdict hits, in the first place any speculative metaphysics, any alleged knowledge by 'pure thinking' or by 'pure intuition' that pretends to be able to do without experience.*
>
> *"Perhaps we may assume that metaphysics originated from mythology. The child is angry at the "wicked table" which hurt him. Primitive man endeavors to conciliate the threatening demon of earthquakes, or he worships the deity of the fertile rains in gratitude. Here we confront personifications of natural phenomena, which are the quasi-poetic expression of man's emotional relationship to his environment. The heritage of mythology is bequeathed on the one hand to poetry, which produces and intensifies the effects of mythology on life in a deliberate way; on the other hand, it is handed down to theology, which develops mythology into a system."*
>
> *-Rudolf Carnap, <u>The Elimination of Metaphysics</u>*

**carp** - v.  to find fault unreasonably; to emphasize minor objections.

**carpe diem** - n.  Latin meaning 'to enjoy the day';  getting the most out of life in the present without serious regard for the future.

**Caso, Antonio** (1883-1946) - a Mexican philosopher whose teaching and writings have had a lasting influence on Latin American philosophy.

Initially a positivist, and also an avid researcher into German philosophy (Kant, Husserl, Scheler, Hartmann, Nietzsche, and Heidegger), Caso gradually adopted a type of process philosophy through the study of Henri Bergson.

Caso concluded that life is essentially dynamic and resistant to purely scientific and logical description. Consciousness is the projection of freely designed structures onto the empirically experienced world. Caso develops this assumption within a metaphysics of freedom and spirit. True life is experienced ethically and aesthetically. Ethically, the life of humanity is involved with two triads of choice, which Caso also calls "levels of being":

      1) things, individuals, and persons.
      2) economics, disinterest, and love.

Things are objects without specific real value, in spiritual terms. Their existence is ordered economically as elements of utility. Humanity is perpetually entangled in the demands of utility and things. The challenge of existence is to move beyond the purely economic view of life into a type of creative spiritual altruism. Disinterest in the world fosters a value for love and persons over things and impersonal society. Thus, in Caso one also witnesses an existentialism which adopts a Christian metaphysical outlook.

Principal works include: *The Philosophy of Intuition*, 1914, *Existence as Economy, Disinterest and Love*, 1919, *Principles of Aesthetics*, 1925, and *The Human Person and the Totalitarian State*, 1941.

*"The purely psychical nature of man is not sufficient for defining the concept of a person. Over and above the psychical is the spiritual. Man is not only a psychical being, he is also a spiritual being. He is a "creator of values", as Nietzsche says so well. . . .*

*"The error of (de-spiritualized) individualism and socialism are very much alike because in their extreme forms both . . . ignore the superior nature of the human being, they ignore the quality of his spiritual reality. . .*

*"The recognition of the personality of human beings obliges society to accept their real inequality rather than an impossible uniformity."*
         *-Antonio Caso, The Human Person and the Totalitarian State*

**cassation** - n. cancellation.

**castigate** - v. to punish, to chastise, to reprove severely.

**casualism** - n. a philosophical doctrine holding that events occur by chance.

**casuist** - n. one skilled in the application of general moral rules to specific cases; also meaning one who reasons dishonestly.

**casus belli** - n. Latin, meaning an event which justifies war or conflict.

**catalepsy** - n. a physical condition associated with mental disorder; characterized by complete loss of sensation.

**catamite** - n. a young boy kept for homosexual gratification; a boy used by a pederast.

**cataphasia** - n. a speech disorder wherein there is a constant repetition of a word or phrase; e.g., the excessive use of the same obscenity.

**Categorical Imperative** - n. in the philosophy of Immanuel Kant (1724-1804) a principle for decision theory. It is expressed in two ways:
    1) *Act as if the maxim of thy act were to become by thy will a universal law of nature.*
    2) *Treat every man as an end in himself, and never only as a means.*
    Text to Consult: *The Foundations of the Metaphysics of Morals*, Immanuel Kant, 1785.

**catena (plural, catenae)** - n. extracts from the writings of the early fathers of the Church.

**catenate** - v. to connect or link together in a series.

**caudal** - adj. situated near the tail; also referring to cowardliness.

**causerie** - n.  a non-formal discussion, casual conversation.

**caveat** - n.  a legal notice to temporarily halt proceedings.

**cavil** - v.  to raise unimportant or trivial objections; to quibble.

**celerity** - n.  speed; rapidity.

**cenacle** - n.  from Latin 'cenaculum', meaning retreat house or dining room;  also a reference to the room where Jesus held the Last Supper.

**cenobite** - n.  a member of a religious group living in a commune setting.

**cenogenesis** - n.  in the philosophy of evolution and biology, the introduction of characteristics not found in ancestors;  differentiation from earlier phylogeny in a race or breed.

**cenotaph** - n.  a tomb erected as a memorial to a person buried somewhere else;  a memorial.

**cephalic** - adj.  relating to the head.

**cerulean** - adj.  resembling the blue of the sky;  also dark blue.

**cervine** - adj.  resembling a deer;  relating to deer.

**cession** - n.  from Latin 'cessus', meaning to withdraw;  to yield to another.

**chagrin** - n.  disappointment.

**charily** - adv.  carefully;  from 'chary' meaning discretion.

**charismatic** - n.  in Christianity, a person who views the validation of faith by experiences of religious ecstacy.  Included in the view is the belief that special powers or healing flow from divine grace.

**chemokinesis** - n.  increased activity of an organism as the consequence of a chemical substance.

**chevy** - v.  to run after;  to be anxious;  to nag;  to harass.

**chiliasm** - n.  the view that Christ will return to earth to reign 1,000 years; connected to millenarianism.  Its principal justification lies with the Book of Revelation, Ch. 20: 1-5.

**choplogic** - n.  a crude way of reasoning;  excessively complicated reasoning;  specious thought.

**chortle** - v.  to laugh triumphantly or with great satisfaction.

**chouse** - v. to cheat or swindle; also to ride herd aggressively.

**Christianity** - n. among major religions of the Middle East, it takes it roots from Zoroastrianism and Judaism, being followed historically by Islam. It was influenced by Greek philosophical traditions and has become part of the Western outlook, including the notion of technical and scientific progress, the ethical ideals of meliorism, and the linear view of time. Its religious views are rooted in the Old and New Testaments, the New Testament being considered by Christians as the source of the new religious prototype for humanity. In both spiritual and psychological terms, Christianity represents the first major elevation of women and outcasts of society in the Western world. Moreover, it has had a major impact on the moral and legal codes of the Western world.

    The major spiritual problem for Christianity is the unification of humanity with God since the alienation of the Fall. Sinfulness stems from the ego or self-consciousness. As alienation, sin is cured by faith in the teaching of Christ through the Gospels. Grace, faith and the sacraments represent the theological means to receive salvation.

    In particular, Christianity regards love as the highest virtue from which all other virtues flow. The theological dynamic of love is represented in God as "three Persons", with the Son of God being sent to bear the suffering of this world as an act of Divine altruism.

> *"Christianity, which ordains that men should love each other, would, without doubt, have every nation blest with the best civil, the best political laws; because these, next to this religion, are the greatest good that men can give and receive."*
> *- Charles L. Montesquieu (1689-1755), <u>The Spirit of Laws</u>*

> *"In Christianity we discern a transition from the religion of the cult to the prophetic religion of pure morals, from the religion of law to the religion of love, from the religion of priests to the religion of individual prayer and inward life, from the national God to the universal God."*
> *- Sarvepalli Radhakrishnan (1888-1975), <u>The Philosophy of Radhakrishnan</u>, ed. Paul Schlipp*

**Christology** - n. in theology, the study of Jesus the Person of Christ. Christology works out the Christocentric implications of the New Testament, especially the Gospel accounts which point to Christ as both God and man. To the Apostles, Christ is at least an agent of revelation from God. Additionally, Christ is seen as the manifestation of Being in ultimate form. Christology takes into account the many perspectives on Jesus. This includes the view that he was a member of the human race. It also evaluates his historical presence, that he was perceived by some, say Romans and Jews, as a teacher and even a rebel. The polarities of interpretation are categorized as being either *high Christology*, emphasizing the Divinity of Christ Jesus, or *low Christology,* emphasizing the humanity of Christ. The deeply rational and positivistic approach to modern Christology that one finds in some theological work is connected to the research of the 19th century, where theologians tried to untangle Christ from the accumulated effects of almost 2,000 years of speculation and ritual. Adolf Harnack (1851-1930), *What is Christianity?*, 1901, was especially helpful in exposing the Hellenistic influences on Christian theology. David F.

Strauss (1808-1874), *Life of Jesus*, 1836, created a shock wave with the thesis that the supernatural elements were introduced between the death of Jesus and the appearance of the Gospels in written form. Ernest Renan (1823-1892), *Life of Jesus*, 1863, also discarded the supernatural character of Jesus. Renan pictured Christ as an effective and friendly Galilean minister, even downplaying the ethical impact of Christ. He was rewarded with a dismissal from his position as professor of Hebrew at the College of France. Later, Renan softened his theological views on Christ.

> *"The son of God is unique. To appear for a moment, to flash forth a sympathetic but piercing radiance, to die very young, that is the life of a God."*
> - *Ernest Renan, St. Paul, 1869*

The modern controversies over the nature and essence of Christ have their basis in the many heretical positions of the past, the most important of which include:

*1) Arianism* - the views of Arius (250-336 A.D.) were primarily preserved in songs called the Thaleia, as he wrote very little. His effectiveness as a priest and preacher popularized the idea that the Logos (word or reason) was an 'ex nihilo' product of God, with the implication that Christ is a separate non-eternal phenomena. Christ is the Son of God as all men are the sons of God through a spiritual adoption and because of his supreme righteousness. The Council of Nicaea (325 A.D.) was the site of the first fight over its theological correctness.
*2) Monarchianism* - (2nd century) was a reaction to the idea of the Trinity. Monarchians argued that there is no separateness in Christ, that God is a set of *modes* represented as Father, Son, and Holy Spirit. These theologians sought to preserve the unity or monotheism of God by rejecting the theological emphasis on three Persons in God.

**chutzpa** - n. insolence; extreme self-confidence.

**ciborium** - n. a vaulted canopy, especially over a high altar.

**cicisbeism** - n. the practice of keeping a cicisbeo (the lover of a married woman).

**cincture** - n. something which encircles, like a belt or girdle.

**circadian** - adj. relating to a 24-hour period or cycle.

**circumjacent** - adj. lying all around.

**circumvent** - v. to avoid; to evade; to outwit.

**civil death** - n. the legal status of a person, as in punishment, so as to be deprived of civil rights.

**civil disobedience** - n. in political philosophy, a means of protesting law(s) by non-violent refusal to obey the law(s), especially with regard to law(s) representing a violation of what is morally good.

**civil liberty** - n. in philosophy of law, a reference to the freedom of assembly, speech, thought, press, and religious belief.

**clamant** - adj. important, urgent; noisy.

**clastic** - adj. from Greek 'klastos', meaning broken; disintegrating into fragments.

**claudicant** - adj. lameness; having a limp.

**clavus** - n. a headache psycho-somatic in nature but with apparent intensity; found in some forms of hysteria, thus associated with the hysterical personality.

**clement** - adj. gentle; merciful; mild.

**cleptobiosis** - n. in biology, a mode of existence in which one species steals food from another.

**cleptomania** - n. the irrepressible need to steal things, often things of little value.

**clerisy** - n. the clergy; the intellectual class.

**clingquant** - adj. glittering with tinsel.

**clique** - n. a group with identical interests; a narrowly defined group, exclusive in nature.

**coadjutant** - n. an assistant; (adj. providing assistance).

**coaptation** - n. a fitting together of independent parts.

**codicil** - n. a legal supplement or appendix.

**coetaneous** - adj. being of the same age.

**coeval** - adj. at the same time; contemporary.

**Cogito ergo sum** - Latin meaning "thought therefore existence" or "I think, therefore I am." In Cartesian philosophy (the views of Rene Descartes), this is the foundational truth upon which other truths are to be built. It reasons that no matter how deceived one is about knowing truth, one has to exist even to be a completely ignorant or wrong-minded person. Thus, knowledge of one's existence is a truth no matter what else one thinks.
  Text to consult: *Meditations,* Rene Descartes, 1641.

**cognomen** - n. surname; family name; also, nickname.

**cognoscenti** - n. the wise; those who are well informed on a particular subject.

**cognoscitive** - adj. having the ability to know.

**cognoscible** - adj.  capable of being known.

**Coherence Theory of Truth** - n.  in philosophy, a theory of truth advocated by rationalist thinkers, e.g., G.W.F. Hegel, Benedict Spinoza, F.H. Bradley, Otto Neurath, and Carl Hempel.  A system of thought is said to be true on the basis that any judgments (statements) in the system logically imply other judgments (statements) in the same system, usually by various applications of the rules of inference.  Some definitions of the theory hold that any judgment in a system must imply any other judgment in the system, so that it becomes impossible to accommodate belief in judgments from other systems.  For instance, a scientific atheist cannot somehow also hold the belief that God exists.  The coherence theory tends to force admission of the prevailing rational interpretation of nature, i.e., reality, and the rejection of thought systems outside that model.
 Text to Consult: *Theories of Truth*, *Richard Kirkham*, 1995.

**collectanea** - n. pl.  collected writings;  a collection of literary works.

**colligate** - v.  to bind together;  gather under a general heading.

**collimate** - v.  to make parallel;  to bring into alignment.

**collocate** - v.  to arrange or set in order;  to emphasize a proper order.

**collocation** - n.  the correct placement of words in a sentence.

**colloquy** - n.  a serious conversation or dialogue;  a conference.

**collude** - v.  to cooperate by secret agreement for deceptive or dishonest ends; to plot;  to conspire.

**colophon** - n.  symbol or inscription at the end of a book, detailing the printer, author, publisher, and place of publication;  an identifying emblem.

**colporteur** - n.  one who peddles books, especially religious books.

**comity** - n.  a courteous manner of behavior;  a friendly quality;  social harmony.

**commensal** - adj.  taking meals together, especially as a regular routine.

**comminate** - v.  to threaten, especially with divine involvement;  vengeance through God; to denounce.

**comminute** - v.  to pulverize.

**commove** - v.  to agitate violently;  to cause intense feelings.

**commutation** - n.  an act of substitution or replacement.  In logic, an expression of logical equality.  It allows the re-arrangement of statement components in both disjunctive and conjunctive statements.

Text to Consult: *Introduction to Logic*, Copi & Cohen, 1994.

**compathy** - n.  the sharing of feelings with others.

**compeer** - n.  one having equal rank, position, or ability.

**compendious** - adj.  concise;  expressing in a brief form the basic substance of a topic.

**complex question** - n.  in logic, a fallacy in which a question is posed in such a way as to force the acceptance of a conclusion embedded within that question. E.g.*"Answer the following question with yes or no:   Have you stopped using drugs?"* Answering yes or no implies one's involvement in the use of drugs.

**complot** - n.  a conspiracy;  v.  to conspire.

**composition** - n.  in logic, a fallacy in which the characteristics of the part(s) of a respective whole are said to be the characteristics of the whole itself.  E.g. *"This brick is not very heavy, so the building from which it came must not be very heavy."*

**Comte, Auguste** (1798-1857) - a French philosopher who attempted to re-organize society around a positivist philosophy for a new elite.  The main goal was to develop the emerging influence of science and technology, re-orient the intellectual climate of his time, and then to extend the effects of the Scientific Revolution into social, political, moral, and religious spheres.
Through his work, he was recognized as the founder of a new field of study, sociology.
    Comte argued that thought moves through three stages in the quest for truth:
1) *the theological* - here phenomena are causally explained as the result of divine influence; included are superstitious beliefs and irrational prejudices.  2) *the metaphysical* - here phenomena are calculated to be extensions of impersonal, abstract forces;  included are claims devoid of any observable facticity.   3) *the positivistic* - here the natural world is viewed strictly through the lens of rational science and references to the previous stages are abandoned.  According to Comte, the last stage holds the greatest prospect for coordinating a peaceful society, because it establishes knowledge in a public or verifiable way, reducing the opportunity for arbitrary disagreement.  Comte was particularly optimistic about the influence of science on the moral development of humanity.
    Principal works included:  *The Positive Philosophy*, 6 vols., 1830-1842,  *A System of Political Positivism*, 4 vols., 1851-1854, and *Catechism of Positivism*, 1852.

> *". . . each branch of our knowledge passes successively  through three different theoretical conditions:  the Theological or fictitious; the Metaphysical, or abstract; and the Scientific, or positive."*
> —*Auguste Comte, The Positive Philosophy*

> *"In regard to morals, I think it is indisputable that the gradual development of humanity favors a growing preponderance of the noblest tendencies of our nature . . . The lower instincts continue to manifest themselves in modified action, but their less sustained and more repressed exercise must tend to*

*debititate them by degrees; and their increasing regulation certainly brings them into involuntary concurrence in the maintenance of a good social economy."*

*Auguste Comte, The Positive Philosophy*

**conatus** - n.  a natural impulse or striving.

**concatenate** - v.  to unite in a series;  to link in a chain.

**concinnity** - n.  harmony and elegance of design.

**concinnous** - adj.  harmonious;  fitting.

**concrescence** - n.  a growing together as in plants or cellular development.

**concupiscence** - n.  sexual desire;  the internal pressure to find sexual relief.

**condign** - adj.  appropriate;  well deserved.

**condolent** - adj.  showing sorrow.

**conduce** - v.  tending to produce a particular result.

**confabulation** - n.  an informal discussion or conversation.

**conflation** - n.  the combining of two texts into one.

**confluent** - adj.  uniting into one.

**Confucius** (551-479 B.C.) - a Chinese humanist philosopher whose moral views had a powerful influence on Chinese culture and character.

Confucius rejected metaphysical concerns in favor of social and political interests.  Social harmony was more important to him than discovering the foundations of reality, because Confucius was unimpressed with the fruit of such reflection.  So, he outlined the virtues necessary for the creation of a stable and prosperous nation.

*Li* refers to the sense of propriety and the external presentation of acceptable habits and manners toward others.  Filial respect is the beginning of social harmony, and *Li* is useful to the formation of character.  It is also a method of avoiding social disgrace, since it is often only by good habits that we avoid expressing our primitive feelings in stressful settings.

*Jen* refers to the inner qualities of a person: truthfulness, sincerity, respect, love, loyalty, generosity, mental excellence, and discipline.  *Jen* reveals the level to which a person has mastered the *Tao* or Way.  Along with *Li*, *Jen* provides the basis for strong families and thus, a strong nation.  Rulers and parents dictate the nature and future of society.

Huston Smith asks the question whether Confucianism is a religion or merely an ethic.  This is due primarily to the absence of metaphysical concerns  which are featured in all other religions.

Principal work: *The Analects.*

*"The great man is sparing in words and prodigal in deeds."*
             *- Confucius, <u>Analects</u>*

Texts to consult: <u>*The Wisdom of Confucius*</u>, Lin Yutang, 1938, and <u>*World's Religions*</u>, Huston Smith.

**conjugal** - adj. relating to marriage or the married state.

**connate** - adj. inborn, innate; associated in origin.

**connotation** - n. in logic, that part of the theory of definition which refers to the meaning conveyed by a word apart from the thing named or described. It stands in conjunction with denotation which refers to the set of things named by a word.

**consanguineous** - adj. descended from the same ancestor; related by blood.

**Consciousness** - n. (German, *Bewusstheit*; Spanish *el estar consciente*)
According to Freud, it is a transient property which identifies internal and external perceptions from other psychical events.

**congruous** - adj. showing harmony in character or make-up.

**Consistency Theory of Truth** - n. in epistemology, the view that truth of a statement is measured by its ability to stand together with other statements essential to a system of thought.
        Text to consult: <u>*Theories of Truth*</u>, Richard Kirkham, 1995.

**consternate** - v. to dismay; to terrify.

**conterminous** - adj. adjacent; enclosed within a common boundary; bordering.

**contexture** - n. framework; structure.

**contiguous** - adj. adjoining; being in actual contact; touching.

**contra distinguish** - v. to make distinct, especially by contrasting or different qualities.

**contraposition** - n. in logic, categorical propositions, a valid type of immediate inference. A contrapositive is formed when the subject term is replaced by the complement of the predicate term in a categorical proposition. The contrapositive of *"All Marxists are Hegelians"* is *"All non-Hegelians are non-Marxists."*

**contravene** - v. to oppose; to act against or contrary to.

**contrite** - adj. full of sorrow; moved by deep remorse.

**contumacious** - adj. strongly disobedient.

**contumely** - n. insulting or rude language; also insulting behavior by words or deeds.

**convenance** - n. propriety, suitability.

**conventual** - adj. appropriate to monastic life or convent life.

**convive** - n. a companion, especially at meals.

**convivial** - adj. relating to feasting, good times, eating and drinking joyfully.

**convoluted** - adj. distorted; twisted; complicated.

**copacetic** - adj. wonderful; excellent; very satisfactory.

**coprolagnia** - n. in psychology, sexual excitement induced by excrement.

**coprophagous** - adj. feeding on dung.

**coprophiliac** - n. literally one who finds excitement in fecal matter; a morbid pre-occupation with excrement.

**coprophobia** - n. excessive fear of feces.

**coquette** - n. a flirtatious woman, especially one lacking sincere affection; a woman who seeks advantage through feigned love.

**corpulence** - adj. fat; excessive stoutness.

**Correspondence Theory of Truth** - n. in philosophy, the view that beliefs must correspond to fact. The theory holds that there must be a relation between a system of thought and objective reality. There is an assumption that reality is external to mind, that sensory experience is the organization of data into a picture of reality. It is the mental picture, as a system of beliefs, that must be mated to external reality for truth to exist. Verification of the correspondence is achieved, in part, through the practice of one's ideas.

From a purely theoretical standpoint, the theory has gone through a long history of evaluation. There are Platonic-Aristotelian versions of the theory, Scholastic versions, the Realist versions, and the meta-linguistic versions expressed through the thoughts of G.E. Moore, Bertrand Russell, Ludwig Wittgenstein, and Alfred Tarski.

Text to Consult: _Theories of Truth,_ Richard L. Kirkham, 1995.

**corrigendum** - n. a note regarding an error in a printed book.

**corroborant** - adj. confirming.

**corybantic** - adj. wild; frenzied; out-of-control; from the Greek 'Korybas', meaning a priest of Cybele known for wild orgiastic processions and rituals.

**cosset** - n. a pet lamb; one who is a favorite; a spoiled, pampered individual.

**coterie** - n. an intimate and exclusive group.

**countervail** - v. to act in opposition with equivalent power and force.

**coup de grace** - from French, meaning 'a death blow'; mercy killing.

**courtesan** - n. a royal prostitute; a sex professional for the upper classes.

**cozen** - v. to cheat or to fool shrewdly; to beguile; to defraud.

**credendum** - n. that which must be believed; an article of faith.

**crepitate** - v. to make a rustling or crackling sound.

**crescine** - adj. increasing; growing.

**criminal** - n. one who lives against the values of society; one who commits errors in acting according to the social standards of the time.

> *"The criminal type is the type of strong human being under unfavourable conditions, a strong human being made sick. What he lacks is the wilderness, a certain freer and more perilous nature and form of existence in which all that is attack and defense in the instinct of the strong human being comes into its own. His 'virtues' have been excommunicated by society; the liveliest drives within him forwith blend with the depressive emotions, with suspicion, fear, dishonor. But this is the recipe for physiological degeneration. He who has to do in secret what he does best and most likes to do, with protracted tension, caution, slyness, becomes anemic; and because he has never harvested anything from his instincts but danger, persecution, disaster, his feelings too turn against these instincts . . . he feels them to be a fatality. It is society, . . . tame, mediocre, gelded society, in which a human being raised in nature, who comes from the mountains or from adventures of the sea, necessarily degenerates into a criminal."*
>
> *- Friedrich Nietzsche(1844-1900),* <u>*Twilight of the Idols*</u>

**Crisis theology** - n. a Neo-orthodox view often connected with the views of Karl Barth (1886-1968). Barth worked out a philosophical theology proving the utter transcendence of God which included the complete and infinite superiority of God, especially when compared to any human striving and creativity. All worldly achievements are rooted in egoism and represent the final worthlessness of reason. All human institutions are fractured by the inevitable contradictions of human reason, creating despair in the possibility of control. Thus, human existence without God is doomed to crisis and failure.

Crisis theology attempts to lead humanity away from the positivism of science toward the spiritual power of divine revelation, grace, and faith.

Text to consult: *The Theology of Karl Barth*, H. Hartwell, 1964.

**cumbrance** - n.  a source of trouble.

**Cybernetics** - n.  from Greek 'kybernetes' meaning 'steersman'.  The term 'cybernetics' was first coined by Norbert Wiener (1894-1964), a mathematician, *Cybernetics: Control and Communication in the Animal and the Machine*, 1948.  It is that theoretical field which studies feedback systems and self-regulatory systems.  Thus, the history of cybernetics dates back to the earliest devices used to produce self-regulating actions, such as automatic outflow systems on reservoirs (ca. 1000 B.C.).  Cybernetics is deeply connected to mechanical engineering, from wind-mills to steam-engines to modern industrial equipment.  There are roughly four categories or stages of cybernetic engineering:  1) *basic tools* - human action is augmented by a specific implement such as an ax.  Judgment remains with the human user.  2)*tools plus energy* - human effort is reduced but judgment is still required for the machine to operate successfully according to its designed task, such as a chain saw  3) *machine plus energy and control* - human judgment is deeply augmented by automatic machine functions, as in modern logging machines which are programmed to remove the tree, de-bark it, cut it for length, and stack it.  Immediate control is with the machine.  Human judgment controls the goal.  4) *machines plus energy plus control plus autonomy of judgment* - the machine is developed to the extent that its determines its own history.  Human judgment is virtually eliminated.  This is the stage we are working on today.  The machine construction/design achieves virtually full operational parity with humans.

**cynosure** - n.  a center of attention.

**daedal** - adj. having skill; cleverly invented.

**Dalai Lama** - n. in Tibetan Buddhism, *"the measureless and superior one"*, the official spiritual leader of that faith.

**dalliance** - n. amorous conduct; foreplay; spiritual preparation.

**daimon** - n. in ancient philosophy, a spirit inhabitant or inward mentor. Socrates claimed to be guied by such a spirit which he viewed as a source of inspiration and moral guidance.

**Damming up the Libido** - n. (German, *Libidostauung*; Spanish, *estancamiento do la libido*) in psychology, an *economic* process accounts for a person's fall into a neurotic or psychotic condition. In psychoanalysis, the process signals underlying collections of energy, believed to be of a sexual type, which are deprived of release.

**Dao** - n. (Tao) in Daoism, a reference to the eternal principle present in all things.

**darkle** - v. to become dark; to become gloomy; to become indistinct.

**Darsana** - n. in Hinduism, a reference to "seeing the truth." It includes the notion that people must do more than believe in religious and philosophical principles. They must also understand in order to realize the highest kind of life.

**Darwinism** - n. the views and theories of Charles Darwin (1809-1882), *The Origin of Species,* 1859, *The Descent of Man,* 1871. Darwinism holds that all living things come into being, change, and sometimes go extinct. Biological reproduction increases in any progeny such that if unchecked it would dominate the earth. Multiplication is checked by competition, both within and outside a species, creating a dynamic struggle in which the best survive. Variation exists in biological entities as to their quality and function. These are passed on to succeeding generations. Favorable variations are preserved and passed on and unfavorable ones are eliminated. These observations apply to the human species as well, which Darwin considered an advanced primate. In later years, Darwin began to take a greater assessment of the environment's impact on evolution.

*"When I view all beings not as special creations, but as the lineal descendants of some few beings which lived long before the first bed of the Cambrian system was deposited, they seem to me to become ennobled. Judging from the past, we may safely infer that not one living species will transmit its unaltered likeness to a distant futurity. And of the species now living very few will transmit progeny of any kind to a far distant futurity; for the manner is which all organic beings are grouped, shows that the greater number of species in each genus, and all the species in many genera, have left no descendants, but have become utterly extinct."*

*-Charles Darwin, <u>The Descent of Man</u>*

**deanthropomorphism** - n. a philosophical view emphasizing the removal of human characteristics or beliefs.

**debauchery** - n. excessive involvement in sexuality; orgiastic activity; a conversion from virtue to vice through actions which reduce inhibitions.

**deduction** - n. in logic, one of the two types of argument; the other is induction. A deductive argument contains evidence which, when correctly arranged, forms the basis for one conclusion, a necessary conclusion. If the arrangement of evidence is correct then the argument is said to be valid; if the arrangement is incorrect, it is invalid.

**Defense** - n. (German, *Abwehr*; Spanish, *defensa*) in psychology, an action of the ego designed to push back threats to its interests and fantasies. Responses designed to reduce or eliminate changes in the bio-psychological constitution of the individual. Instinct is believed to underly 'defenses' and account for their compulsive appearance.

**defloration** - n. the act of removing a young person's virginity.

**deicide** - n. the killing of a god.

**deictic** - adj. in logic, serving to prove directly.

**Deism** - n. in philosophy and theology, belief in a God who created this world but does not intervene in its functions. It does not support a belief in miracles or revelation.
Pierre Viret, a Calvinist, first used the term in 1564 to refer to believers who accepted God as creator but rejected belief in Christ. Historically, deism marked the rise of rationalism, secularism, and modern theology. Thus, it also advanced the ethics of tolerance, since it became less and less permissible to dogmatically attack differences of belief.

**deleterious** - adj. harmful, especially in an obscure or unexpected way.

**delict** - n. an offense; a violation of law.

**delphic** - adj. (relating to the Delphic Oracle) obscure; ambiguous.

**delitiscent** - adj. concealed; hidden from view.

**demimondaine** - n.  a woman who has a reputation for indiscreet behavior;  especially a woman who is acquainted with wealthy lovers.

**demirep** - n.  ('demi' from Latin, 'demidiare', meaning to halve)  a person with a reputation for hanging around reprobates.

**Democritus** (460-370 B.C.) - a Greek pre-Socratic philosopher famous for his defense of a primitive theory of atomism.  Democritus believed in a hard irreducible type of atomic matter which explained the existence of all things through various combinations and processes of formation and disintegration.  This assumption was extended into his understanding of family life, economics, politics, and every area of human activity.

> *"Violent desire for one thing blinds the soul to all others."*
> *-Democritus, Fragments*

> *"The old man has been young; but the young man cannot know if he will reach old age. Thus the perfected good is better than the uncertain future."*
> *-Democritus, Fragments*

**demos** - n.  the population, people, viewed as a political unit.

**demotic** - adj.  of the people.

**demur** - v.  to delay;  to hesitate;  to object or protest;  to take exception.

**demure** - adj.  shy, modest, reserved.

**denizen** - n.  a creature or inhabitant of a particular locale.

**denouement** - n.  the climax of a dramatic or literary plot;  the outcome of a complex sequence of events.

**Deontological ethics** - n. in ethical theory, views that focus on the importance of *duty*. Thus, some moral acts are considered obligatory due to relationship or nature of other acts or entities.  Goodness is said to reside in the act itself rather than some other reward or consequence, thus the *obligatory* nature of the act.
Text to Consult: *Ethics*, William Frankena, 1973.

**depone** - v.  to declare under oath;  also to put down critically;  to testify.

**depredate** - v.  to attack;  to plunder or lay waste to.

**depurate** - v.  to make pure.

**depute** - v.  to appoint as a representative or agent.

**deracinate** - v.  to rip out;  to eradicate.

**dereism** - n.  a tendency to see life through daydreams and unrealistic fantasy;  a viewpoint or condition where there is little regard for reality.

**Descartes, Rene** (1596-1650) - a French philosopher and tutor of Queen Christina of Sweden, often called the "father of modern philosophy."  Descartes is known for his great contributions to the school of Rationalism and completed most of his philosophical work in the Netherlands, where a climate of intellectual diversity was strongest.  For, although very creative, history shows that Descartes was intimidated by authority and feared retribution for ideas which trampled on popular religious notions (taking note of Copernicus).  Nonetheless, Descartes made important contributions in mathematics and developed a method of reflection which required an aggressive skepticism regarding the senses.  This led to the famous formulation: *"Cogito, ergo sum"* (Thought, therefore existence) or (I think therefore, I am).

Descartes demonstrated that even the most demanding skepticism will not refute the proposition "I think, therefore I am" because one must exist even to have the most erroneous thoughts.  Descartes tested this with his examinations of hallucinations, illusions, and the idea of God as an evil genius who deceives his subjects.

The general direction of Descartes' work produced the rational view that the best understandings are not acquired through sense perception, rather they are the result of innate ideas, ideas which are formed by logical principles, including the existence of God and the external world.

Principal works include: *Discourse on Method*, 1637,  *Meditations on First Philosophy*, 1641, *Principles of Philosophy*, 1644, and *The Passions of the Soul*, 1649.

> *"Rule I: We must occupy ourselves only with those objects that our intellectual powers appear competent to know certainly and indubitably.*
>
> *"Rule III: As regards any subject we propose to investigate, we must inquire not what other people have thought, or what we ourselves conjecture, but what we can clearly and manifestly perceive by intuition or deduce with certainty.  For there is no other way of acquiring knowledge.*
>
> *"Rule VIII: If in a series of subjects to be examined we come to a subject of which our intellect cannot gain a good enough intuition, we must stop there; and we must not examine the other matters that follow, but must refrain from futile toil."*
>
> *-Rene Descartes, <u>Rules for the Direction of the Mind</u>*

**desiccate** - v.  from Latin 'desiccare', meaning to dry up;  also meaning to exhaust emotional or intellectual strength;  to eliminate vitality.

**desiderate** - v.  to wish for;  to desire or want.

**desideratum** - n.  something regarded as essential.

**despond** - v.  to lose heart;  to lose courage.

**desultory** - adj.  casual, disconnected;  lacking method and order.

**detrital** - adj. made up of trash or debris; composed of 'detritus'.

**detrivorous** - adj. surviving or feeding on organic debris; trash-eating.

**detrude** - v. to force down or away.

**deus ex machina** - n. literally 'god out of the machine'; reference to a god who intervenes and sorts out solutions in otherwise irresolvable entanglements.

**deuterogamy** - n. a second marriage.

**devolution** - n. a condition of biological degeneration.

**Dewey, John** (1859-1952) - an American philosopher of pragmatism, Dewey was very influential in the philosophy of education. Like other pragmatists, Dewey argued that the consequences of ideas are very important to their value. His version of pragmatism became known as "instrumentalism". Dewey rejected the rationalist position that the rules of logic are 'a priori' principles, arguing that the truth of propositions is dependent upon consequences. In this sense Dewey was also a meliorist. He believed in the moral call to develop and improve the world, so this required a philosophy which emphasized the importance of action.

Principal works include: *How We Think*, 1910, *Human Nature and Conduct*, 1922, *Experience and Nature*, 1925, and *The Teacher and Society*, 1937.

> *"For ordinary purposes, that is for practical purposes, the truth and the realness of things are synonymous."*
> -John Dewey, *The Practical Character of Reality*

> *"Happiness is fundamental in morality only because happiness is not something to be sought after, but is something now attained, even in the midst of pain and trouble, whenever recognition of our ties with nature and with fellow men releases and informs our action."*
> -John Dewey, *Human Nature and Conduct*

**dextral** - adj. a reference to right handedness; right sidedness.

**Dharma** - n. in Buddhism: natural law, especially with regard to the world's essence; also a reference to the ideal qualities in one's own nature, conformity to which produces spiritual harmony. Thus, in terms of Buddhahood, that which is the best way to remove suffering. Posed as an ethical principle, Dharma involves recognition of the Four Noble Truths:

1) *Suffering* - All stages of life bring suffering. Birth is suffering. Aging is suffering. Death is suffering. Things we despise bring suffering. Things we long for and do not acquire bring suffering.
2) *The Cause of Suffering* - Suffering is caused by craving. The desires of the body bring the need for pleasure, a full existence, and the accumulation of wealth. This produces a 'thirst' for this world.

47

3) *The Cessation of Suffering* - Suffering can be stopped. The destruction of desire does away with suffering.

4) *The Eightfold Path* - By following the eight holy principles, the soul is liberated from the feeling of suffering:

> i) *Right Belief* - belief in the Four Noble Truths.
>
> ii) *Right Purpose* - the promise or vow to overcome a life of sensual desire.
>
> iii) *Right Speech* - well-defined talk that is not hurtful or false.
>
> iv) *Right Conduct* - well-defined actions that bring only harmony to this world.
>
> v) *Right Livelihood* - choosing a subsistence that is right for one's talents and is consistent with the teachings of the Buddha.
>
> vi) *Right Effort* - striving in a way that preserves spiritual awareness of that which is wise and that which is foolish.
>
> vii) *Right Mindedness* - establishing good habits of thought and good topics of thought.
>
> viii) *Right Meditation* - commitment to the advanced stage of enlightenment so that the soul is prepared for its passage to *Nirvana*, the extinction of re-birth.

*"In this world, aspirants may find enlightenment by two different paths. For the contemplative is the path of knowledge. For the active one is the path of selfless action."*

*-Bhagavad Gita*

**dharna** - n. (India) a type of fasting designed to exact justice from an offending party; fasting at the door of another who has offended one's self.

**dialectic** - n. in philosophy, a reference to the exchange of ideas. It includes the examination of logical conclusions, criticism of data, and the presentation of counter-argument. It is an integral feature of healthy skepticism and one of the main ingredients in the general testing of theories and ideas.

**dialogic** - adj. relating or pertaining to dialogue, verbal or written.

**dianetics** - n. the theory that one's personality can be understood in terms of an individual's experiences before birth.

**dianoetic** - adj. pertaining to discursive reasoning (reasoning which passes from one topic to another).

**dianoia** - n. faculty used in discursive reasoning; a capacity for logically ordered reflection.

**diarchy** - n. government by two leaders or authorities.

**diatribe** - n. a seemingly endless speech; writing or speech that is abusive, including criticism that is satirical.

**didactic** - adj. designed to teach; also, that which is entertaining and pleasurable as well as instructional.

**didymous** - adj. from the Greek 'didymos', meaning 'twin'; the quality of growing in pairs.

**diffidence** - n. a lack of self-confidence; a failure to be self-assertive; hesitance.

**diffluence** - n. a flowing away or apart.

**digamy** - n. marriage to two people.

**dilemma** - n. in logic, a complex argument form in which two conclusions are forced, both of which are usually undesireable. It is typically constructed of two modus ponens arguments, side by side, united by the logical functions of conjunction and disjunction:

> *If I announce my philosophical views, I will be attacked and if I remain silent, I will lose my self-respect. I will either announce my philosophical views or I will remain silent. So, I will either be attacked or I will lose my self-respect.*

**dimerous** - adj. having two parts.

**diplopia** - n. a condition of sight in which a single object appears as two.

**dipsomania** - n. an uncontrollable craving for drink, especially alcoholic liquors.

**discept** - v. to argue, debate, or dispute.

**dispiteous** - adj. mean-minded; cruel; vicious.

**disputatious** - adj. provoking controversy; quarrelsome.

**disquiet** - n. anxiety; disturbance.

**distrait** - adj. weak attention or absent-mindedness due to worries.

**ditheism** - n. belief in two gods.

**divagate** - v. to wander about aimlessly.

**Divine command theory** - n. in ethical theory, the view that all moral guidelines are to be modelled on the will of God. The theory includes the development of an understanding regarding God's communication of divine will, i.e. revelation.

**dormient** - adj. sleeping.

**Dostoevsky, Fyodor** (1821-1881) - a Russian writer-philosopher considered to be an important influence on existentialist thought. Dostoevsky focused on the problem of freedom. He noted the tremendous pressures of modern society with its expectations and confinements in moral terms. The social, economic, religious, and legal forces require the strength to resist their suffocating effects on the individual who desires to be free.

Dostoevsky's philosophy leads to certain terrifying conclusions, especially the specter of nihilism: there is no God and there are no pre-set values. If humanity is totally free, then there are no guidelines for life. This is the meaning of 'total freedom'. Truth as something reliable disappears in his philosophy of freedom. Yet, the supreme truth is that humanity is free, and only this freedom can distinguish and define humanity as its true nature.

Dostoevsky's novels portray characters, somewhat autobiographically, who are enmeshed in the anguish of choice, whose lives are pained by errors of decision. It comes down to finding freedom that lifts life to the heights of fulfillment or a freedom that leads to despair and suicide.

Principal works include: *Notes From Underground*, 1864, *Crime and Punishment*, 1866,
*The Idiot*, 1869, *The Possessed*, 1872, and *The Brothers Karamozov*, 1880.

> *"Grand Inquisitor: . . . The most painful secrets of their conscience, all, all they will bring to us, and we shall have an answer for all. And they will be glad to believe our answer, for it will save them from the great anxiety and terrible agony they endure at present in making a free decision for themselves. "*
> -Fyodor Dostoevsky, <u>The Brothers Karamazov</u>

**dotage** - n. weakness or lack of mental poise due to aging.

**dukkha** - n. in Buddhist philosophy, a reference to the *sorrow* present in the endless cycle of birth, growth, decay, and death. This sorrow stems from the impermanence *(anicca)* which characterizes everything and of which reason is acutely aware. The self *(anatta)* is unable to find peace in a life which requires perpetual effort and becoming.

**dulcify** - v. to appease; mollify; to make agreeable or sweet.

**dulcinea** - n. secret lover, especially a mistress.

**dulocracy** - n. a government by former slaves.

**Durkheim, Emile** (1858-1917) - a French philosopher of society, Durkheim worked almost exclusively on creating a science of society. As a professor and editor, he constructed views on ethics as science and a logically congruent philosophy of social policy. Among his more original ideas was the notion of a "collective conscience". Durkheim believed that group psychology was external to the individual and often has a "coercive" effect on the individual, e.g. lynch mobs.

In his theory of social types, Durkheim was influenced by Darwinian thought. Durkheim concluded that "normal" social types exhibit objective characteristics that are advantageous for the survival of human beings. Whereas, "pathological" social types work against the overall well-being of the human race. With a focus on organic solidarity *(sui generis)*, Durkheim believed that pathological behavior, such as suicide, could and should be offset by healthy influences pressed onto the life of the individual by his or her specific occupational group. Such things as marital divorce, he believed, demonstrated the pathological existence of "anomie". The existence of social crisis, as evidenced primarily through economic uncertainty and the elimination of wholistic intellectual development via specialization, becomes a destructive factor in the life of individuals. Anomie, or lawlessness, is related to the society's failure to affirm values and plans that enhance survival through solidarity. Without communal designs for life, the individual is more and more left to his or her own devices to establish a sense of order, thus lessening the possibility of moral harmony within the group.

For Durkheim, the social group's inner values constitute the "social milieu". This provides a ground upon which to build causal explanations for human conduct in individuals. Concerns of this sort led him naturally to questions regarding sociology and religion. Here Durkheim simply extends his thesis that the specific content of a religion is secondary to its social role: to produce solidarity within the group. In totemism, for example, Durkheim argues that the totem symbolizes a clan and a god, never just a god.

In his work on suicide, Durkheim shows there is a relationship between individualism, intellectual development and voluntary death. The attempt to be self-sufficient is ultimately doomed. Durkheim, however, points out that the movement beyond the visions of one's group is uni-directional. Belief systems which are ruined or "carried away by the current of affairs" can only be successfully transcended through reason. Reason must find new bases for solidarity in order to avoid anomie and suicidal reactions.

Principal works include: *The Division of Labor in Society*, 1893, *The Rules of Sociological Method*, 1895, *Suicide*, 1897, *The Elementary Forms of Religious Life*, 1912, and *Moral Education*, 1925.

> *"Man seeks to learn and man kills himself because of the loss of cohesion in his religious society; he does not kill himself because of his learning. It is certainly not the learning he acquires that disorganizes religion; but the desire for knowledge wakens because religion becomes disorganized. Knowledge is not sought as a means to destroy accepted opinions but because their destruction has commenced. To be sure, once knowledge exists, it may battle in its own name and in its own cause, and set up as an antagonist to traditional sentiments. But its attacks would be ineffective if these sentiments still possessed vitality; or rather, would not even take place. Faith is not uprooted by dialectical proof; it must already be deeply shaken by the causes to be unable to withstand the shock of argument."*
>
> *-Emile Durkheim, Suicide*

> *". . . if the Jew manages to be both well instructed and very disinclined to suicide, it is because of the special origin of his desire for knowledge. . . . religious minorities, in order to protect themselves better against the hate to which they are exposed or merely through a sort of emulation, try to surpass in knowledge the populations surrounding them. . . . The Jew, therefore, seeks to learn, not in order to replace his collective prejudices by reflective thought, but merely to be better armed for the struggle. For him it is a means of offsetting the unfavorable position imposed on him by opinion and sometimes by law. And since knowledge by itself has no influence upon a tradition in full vigor, he*

*superimposes this intellectual life upon his habitual routine with no effect of the former on the latter.  This is the reason for the complexity he presents. Primitive in certain respects, in others he is an intellectual and a man of culture. He thus combines the advantages of the severe discipline characteristic of small ancient groups with the benefits of the intense culture enjoyed by our great societies.  He has all the intelligence of modern man without sharing his despair."*

*-Emile Durkheim, <u>Suicide</u>*

**dysgnosia** - n.  in philosophy of psychology,  an impairment of intellectual capacity to acquire knowledge.

**dysgenic** - adj.  causing inferiority or degeneration in biological descendants.

**dyspareunia** - n.  coitus which causes pain.

**dyspeptic** - adj.  having a sour or bitter disposition.

**dysphoria** - n.  a mental condition of deep dissatisfaction;  anxiety;  excessive concern marked by unhappiness.

**dysteleology** - n.  a philosophical doctrine which refutes the possibility of a final or ultimate cause of existence.

**dysthemia** - n.  a condition of severe despondency or dejection.

**ebullience** - n.  the quality of energy and enthusiasm, especially in the expression of ideas.

**ecdemic** - adj.  originating outside of the place where found.

**ecdysiast** - n.  a creature that sheds its skin; one who changes outward identity.

**Eckhart, Johannes** (1260-1327) - a German philosopher and theologian of mystical religion, Eckhart is sometimes compared favorably to some Eastern thinkers, especially Sankara (788-820 A.D.).  His influence is evident in the views of Jan van Ruysbroek and Heinrich Suso.

Officially condemned by the Papacy, Eckhart worked out a kind of psychology of contemplation.  He seems to have four levels for the soul's operation:

1) the bodily existence: sensations
2) the emotional existence: anger, joy, desire, etc.
3) the rational existence: higher intellectual understanding of the world
4) the Divine existence: abstract knowledge of God.

Eckhart's theology emphasized the prospect for a special experience of enlightenment in which the subjective and objective states of consciousness become one.  In fact, he maintained that the goal of contemplative life is to transcend the notion of God and reach the Godhead itself.

Eckhart's conflict with orthodoxy was purely unintentional.  His views were simply ahead of their time.

Principal work: *Treatises and Sermons*.

> *"The life of work is necessary and the life of contemplation is good.  In service one gathers the harvest that has been sown in contemplation."*
> *Meister Eckhart, <u>Sermons</u>*

> *"The less theorizing one does about God, the more receptive one is to his inpouring."*
> *Meister Eckhart, <u>Sermons</u>*

**echolalia** - n.  the involuntary repetition of someone else's words immediately after they have been spoken.

**echopraxia** - n.  the abnormal copying of another person's actions.

**éclat** - n.  brilliant reputation.

**eclecticism** - n.  a philosophical position which advocates collecting what appears to be the best in various doctrines, methods, or techniques.

**ectad** - adj.  outward from the inside.

**ectal** - adj.  exterior; outside.

**ectogenous** - adj.  growing externally;  e.g. a parasite.

**ectomorphic** - adj.  having a thin muscular body, e.g. Jesus Christ.

**ectopic** - adj.  occurring in an unusual position.

**ectype** - n.  a copy, as contrasted with an original or prototype.

**edacious** - adj.  relating to voraciousness or appetite;  devouring.

**edacity** - n.  voraciousness.

**edaphic** - adj.  of or relating to soil conditions rather than climatic or weather conditions; referring to drainage and its effects on natural and manmade objects.

**edify** - v.  from the Latin 'aedificare', meaning to instruct spiritually;  thus to instruct or improve morally or spiritually.

**effable** - adj.  possible to express or communicate (reference to the adequacy of language in describing phenomena).

**efferent** - adj.  carrying outward or away from.

**effleurage** - n.  a gentle stroking.

**effrontery** - n.  boldness marked by lack of concern;  shamelessness;  insolence.

**effuse** - v.  to pour out.

**Egoism** - n.  in philosophy of mind and ethics, the view that the ego factors in to explaining the acts and intentions of the agent. *Psychological egoism* is the view that people will only act in their own self-interest on all occasions.  Even altruism is then seen as being self-gratifying, if only for its spiritual benefits. *Ethical egoism* is the prescriptive view that all people *ought*  to act in their own self-interest, making selfishness a normative ethic.

**egregious** - adj.  distinguished by being of poor or inferior quality.

**egress** - n.  an act of leaving.

**eidetic** - adj.  of or pertaining to complete visual experience;  strong visual recall;  accuracy; a concern with essences.

**eidolon** - n.  a visual illusion;  apparition.

**eidos** - n.  the essence of a culture; the basic philosophical assumptions a culture uses to interpret experience and relate to reality.

**Einstein, Albert** (1879-1955) - a German-American philosopher of physics, Einstein made the greatest contributions of any physicist to the understanding of physical reality in the 20th century, receiving a Nobel prize in 1921.  In a way, Einstein can be considered a supreme metaphysician, since his work did so much to tighten the relationship between an understanding of the foundations of reality and empiricism.

Summarily, Einstein worked on the assumption that there is a basic order and uniformity in nature.  His work in physics was devoted to demonstrating the 'discoverability' of this intrinsic order.  Moreover, his ethical philosophy reflected the influence of his perceptions of universal harmony.  Einstein was, thus, also a strong advocate of peace and the advancement of knowledge.

Principal work: *Relativity*, 1937, *Autobiographical Notes*, 1949, and *The Collected Papers of Albert Einstein*, 1987.

> *"A theory is the more impressive the greater the simplicity of its premises, the more different kinds of things it relates, and the more extended its area of applicability.  Therefore the deep impression which classical thermodynamics made upon me.  It is the only theory of universal content concerning which I am convinced that, within the framework of the applicability of its basic concepts, it will never be overthrown."*
>
> Albert Einstein, <u>Autobiographical Notes</u>

**eisegesis** - n.  a biased interpretation, especially of a written manuscript;  a reading into.

**ejecta** - n.  matter thrown out of.

**elan** - n.  a spirit of vitality;  vigorous enthusiasm; panache.

**elate** - v.  to make happy.

**eldritch** - adj.  weird; unusual; uncanny.

**Electra Complex** - n. (German, *Elektrakomplex*, Spanish, *complejo de Electra*) in the psychology of Carl Jung, the female equivalent of the Oedipus complex, wherein the girl expresses an attachment toward the father or father figure.

Text to Consult: <u>*The Theory of Psycho-Analysis*</u>, Carl Jung, 1913.

**elegiac** - adj.  suitable for use as a lamentation;  of or relating to an elegy.

**elegy** - n.  a poem or song expressing sorrow;  melancholy.

**elenchus** - n.  a logical refutation.

**elicit** - v.  to draw forth.

**ellipsis** - n.  an omission of a word or phrase from a sentence, especially one which makes the construction  logically incomplete.

**elliptical** - adj.  extreme economy of speech or writing;  obscure.

**elocution** - n.  voice control;  effective public speaking.

**eloign** - v.  to conceal;  to move away to an obscure location;  to keep at a distance.

**Eleusinians** - n.  devotees of Demeter and Persephone; a mystery religion of Ancient Greece modeling its philosophy of personal growth and rebirth on the succession of seasons, especially spring.

**elutriate** - v.  to purify by rinsing in water, especially in a current.

**eluviate** - v.  to move through soil by the action of water, especially relating to matter.

**embosk** - v.  to conceal, especially with or in foliage.

**embower** - v.  to cover or hide in foliage.

**embrangle** - v.  to cause confusion or perplexity.

**embrocate** - v.  to apply an ointment or lotion, especially a part of the body;  to moisten.

**emend** - v.  to edit or censure;  to remove mistakes.

**emesis** - n.  an instance of vomiting;  the unexpected purging of foreign substances.

**emetic** - adj.  conducive to vomiting or purging.

**emiction** - n.  the passing of urine; the elimination of waste.

**emollient** - adj.  ability to soften the skin; that which makes a roughness soft.

**emolument** - n.  payment for a service;  salary.

**empathize** - v.  to communicate;  to participate in another's feelings.

**empathy** - n.  identification with the feelings of another self.

**Empedocles** (ca. 490-430 B.C.) - a Greek pre-Socratic philosopher, known primarily for his theory that matter is composed of four basic elements: earth, air, fire, and water. Change is explained as the outcome of dynamic properties within these elements, which foster separation and combination. This view of physics and cosmology dominated the Western view up to the Renaissance period.

Empedocles was considered to have supernatural powers by the people of his day, and many sought out his advice and healing powers. By his own egotistical estimate, he proclaimed himself a "deathless god".

Principal works: *On the Nature of Things* and *Purifications*.


*"The intelligence of Man grows toward the material that is present."*
*-Empedocles, On Nature*


**empyreal** - adj. belonging to the highest heaven in ancient cosmology.

**emperean** - n. the most exalted heavenly state.

**Empiricism** - n. in philosophy, an important theory of knowledge developed principally by John Locke (1632-1704), George Berkeley (1685-1753), and David Hume (1711-1776). The emphasis of empiricism is the claim that all knowledge originates in sense experience. Reason, in contrast, operates as an organizing mental property. Of course, the theory has ancient roots in Aristotle, whose epistemology was inductive, concentrating on the observation of cases in nature. Moreover, other thinkers such as Copernicus (1473-1543), Kepler (1571-1630), and Galileo (1564-1642), had established the importance of sense data.

One of the most important features of empiricism was it aggressive examination of sensory powers. This was, in a way, a kind of skepticism which produced a positive result. By noting the nature and content of sensation, concerns about the limits of sensation produced a technology of extended and refined sensation, e.g. telescopes and microscopes. In this sense, it is surprising that Spinoza, a lens maker, was not more enamored of the potential of sensation to yield knowledge. The push for empirical knowledge is the parent of other extensions of sensation such as radar, infra-red vision, X-ray vision, auditory detection devices, tactile instrumentation, CAT scan, electron microscopes, linear accelerators, etc.

In the philosophy of pragmatism, empiricism became an important model of truth. Thus, empiricism is the philosophical willingness to limit and control the role of abstract reasoning. This emphasis, in pragmatism, is the empirical concern with the consequences of actions. The utility of knowledge is implicit in the attempts to improve life.

In the 20th Century, empiricism even influenced the logical positivist movement. Truth of statements is contingent on empirical verification. Empirical observation, which is the principle tool of scientists, motivated philosophers to consider the importance of the correspondence theory of truth.

**emulous** - adj. having the desire or wish to equal or imitate.

**enchiridion** - n. handbook.

**enclave** - n. usually an outlying district, especially of a country almost entirely surrounded by another country.

**encomiast** - n. one who praises; eulogist.

**endemic** adj. restricted to a certain locale; native.

**endogamy** - n. marriage within a social group.

**endomorphic** - adj. having a heavy, round, and soft body build, especially with tendency to become and remain fat; massiveness, especially of digestive viscera.

**endophasia** - n. speech that is internalized and inaudible.

**endosmosis** - n. the movement of a substance from an area of lesser concentration to an area of greater concentration.

**endothermic** - adj. warm-blooded; involving the absorption of heat..

**energumen** - n. someone possessed by an evil spirit, especially a fanatic.

**enervate** - v. to make weak, especially in the sense of mental or moral strength; to reduce vigor.

**Engels, Friedrich** (1820-1895) - a German socialist philosopher and poet, Engels was the life-long co-worker and supporter of Karl Marx.

Raised in a wealthy family, Engels acquired a Protestant view of work and society. He rejected both his faith and the capitalist affections of Protestantism due to the influence of Hegelianism and his personal observation of starving textile workers. Engels developed the social view, close to Marx of course, that economics determines social form. Yet, social forms are not without effect on economics. This was an implication of Hegelian dialectics.

Principal works: *Economic and Philosophic Manuscripts of 1844*, 1844, *Anti-Duhring*, 1878, *Socialism: Utopian and Scientific*, 1883, *The Origin of the Family, Private Property, and the State*, 1884, *Ludwig Feuerbach and the Outcome of Classical German Philosophy*, 1888, *Principles of Communism*, 1919, and *The Dialectics of Nature*, 1925.

> *"The proletarian is . . . in law and in fact, the slave of the bourgeoisie, which can decree his life or death. It offers him the means of living, but only for an "equivalent" for his work. It even lets him have the appearance of acting from a free choice, of making a contract with free unconstrained consent, as a responsible agent who has attained his majority.*
> *"Fine freedom, where the proletarian has no other choice than that of either accepting the conditions which the bourgeoisie offers him, or of starving, of freezing to death, of sleeping naked among the beasts of the forests! A fine "equivalent" valued at pleasure by the bourgeoisie. And if one proletarian is such a fool as to starve rather than to agree to the equitable propositions of the*

**engender** - v. to cause to exist or develop; to bring about.

**englut** - v. to swallow; to gulp down.

**engorge** - v. to swallow at great speed.

**enigma** - n. something which cannot be explained.

**enjoin** - v. to command or proscribe; to direct by authoritative request; also, to prohibit.

**enmity**- n. typically mutual hatred or ill-will, especially active hatred.

**ennui** - n. boredom, especially as in weariness or dissatisfaction.

**enology** - n. the study of wine-making.

**enosis** - n. union, especially political.

**enounce** - v. to declare or enunciate.

**ensanguine** - v. to stain with blood.

**ensconce** - v. to settle in; to shelter; to conceal or make safe.

**ensorcell** - v. to put under a spell.

**entelechy** - n. an actualization by form-giving cause; a manifestation; contrasted with mere potentiality.

**entente** - n. an agreement between nations outlining a common course of action.

**enthetic** - adj. brought in from the outside.

**entourage** - n. one's surroundings, especially including one's servants.

**entre nous** - adj. French, meaning 'just between the two of us'; secretly.

**entropy** - n. the decline of matter and energy in the universe until a uniform level is reached.

**enucleate** - v. to remove the center or nucleus.

**eonism** - n. the adoption of female attitudes and habits by a male.

**epeiric** - adj.  reaching toward the interior, especially with regard to land.

**ephemera** - n.  something lasting only a short time;  transience.

**epicene** - adj.  reflecting male and female characteristics;  inter-sexual;  effeminate;  also weak or  feeble.

**epicrisis** - n.  a minor disturbance following on a major one.

**epicritic** - adj.  the ability to respond to small differences in sensation, including temperature.

**Epictetus** (50-130 A.D.) - the slave-philosopher and most important member of the Stoic school of thought.  Perhaps from personal experience, Epictetus exhibited an enormous ability to absorb suffering and misery.  This attitude is at the center of Stoicism, which adopts a fatalistic view of many of life's events.  In *Roman Stoicism* (1958), E.V. Arnold depicts Epictetus as a very kind human being, very fond of children and loved by many people, especially his disciples.
    Principal works: *Enchiridion* and *Discourses*.

*"Once a child is born, it is no longer in our power not to love it."*
                              -Epictetus, <u>Discourses</u>

*"Remember that you are an actor in a play, which is as the playwright (God) wants it to be: short if he wants it short, long if he wants is long.  If he wants you to play a beggar, play even this part skillfully, or a cripple, or a public official, or a private citizen.  What is yours is to play the assigned part well.  But to choose it belongs to someone else."*
                              -Epictetus, <u>Enchiridion</u>

*"Let death and exile and everything terrible appear before your eyes everyday, especially death; and you will never have anything contemptible in your thoughts or crave anything excessively."*
                              -Epictetus, <u>Enchiridion</u>

**Epicureanism** - n.  the philosophy of Epicurus (341-270 B.C.) *Letter to Menoeceus*, and *Principal Doctrines*.  He argued that the goal of life is happiness.  He accepted the physics of Democritus, that reality is composed of atoms.  This contributed to his observation that fear, which is a cause of human misery, is often unfounded.  Fear of God is irrational, since God does not control the events of this world.  Everything is explained as the result of atomic action.  Fear of death is also irrational, since death is the cessation of all feeling.  One can have a painful life, but one cannot have a painful death.  Epicurus advocated a balanced hedonism, realizing the psychic misery connected to sensual abandon.  Ultimately,  happiness is understood as *ataraxia* (intellectual tranquillity or peace).  Moreover, he had little confidence in the production of social happiness, complaining that the life of the average person is a complex tangle of needs and problems which tend to have negative social effects.  The best life is to be found by cultivating a few good friendships which can provide simple physical and intellectual satisfaction.

*"Death is nothing to us: for that which is dissolved is without sensation; and that which lacks sensation is nothing to us." (II, <u>Principal Doctrines</u>)*

*"No pleasure is a bad thing in itself: but the means which produce some pleasures bring with them disturbances many times greater than the pleasures." (VII)*

*"The most unalloyed source of protection from men, which is secured to some extent by a certain force of expulsion, is in fact the immunity which results from a quiet life and retirement from the world." (XIV)*

*"The wealth demanded by nature is both limited and easily procured; that demanded by idle imaginings stretches on to infinity." (XV)*

*"Of desires, all that do not lead to a sense of pain, if they are not satisfied, are not necessary, but involve a craving which is easily dispelled, when the object is hard to procure or they seem likely to produce harm." (XXVI)*

*"Of all the things which wisdom acquires to produce the blessedness of a complete life, far the greatest is the possession of friendship." (XXVII)*

**epigamic** - adj.  attractive to the opposite sex during mating season.

**epigeal** - adj.  living near the ground (as with insects).

**epigone** - n.  an imitator, especially of a famous writer;  an inferior follower.

**epigram** - n.  a witty, cryptic, or pointed remark;  a paradoxical saying, especially one which reveals a surprising turn of insight.

**epigraph** - n.  a quotation at the beginning of a written work.

**Epiphenomenalism** - n.  in philosophy,  the view that spiritual characteristics are the effect of more foundational substances, i.e., matter.  It is a proposed solution to the mind-body problem, a problem in philosophy of mind and biology regarding the relationship between the dis-similar entities of mind and body.  Mind is merely the effect of complex bio-chemical arrangements.

**epiphylaxis** - n.  a boost in the body's defense of disease.

**Epistemology** - n.  in philosophy, the study of the sources, nature, and validity of knowledge.  Theories of knowledge fall into two general categories, 1) empiricism: reliance on sense data, 2) rationalism: reliance on principles of reason.

  Empiricism is generally associated with the views of John Locke (1632-1704), *Essay Concerning Human Understanding,* 1690.  Locke argued that the mind is a 'tabula rasa' or blank slate and that all our ideas derive from experience.  Locke's philosophy is powerfully augmented by the work of David Hume (1711-1776),*An Inquiry Concerning Human Understanding,* 1748. Hume argued that one does not understand beyond one's experience. His radical advocacy of empiricism proposed that causality itself is not strictly defensible, since 'causality' is simply a prediction based on past experience. There can be no strict predictions of anything which will take place in the future. All statements of 'fact' are contingent upon careful observation, and observation, no matter how careful, cannot capture every detail.

Rationalism is generally associated with the views of Rene Descartes (1596-1650), *Discourse on Method,* 1637, and *Meditations,* 1641. Descartes called for a scrapping of all past ideas and insisted on a fresh deployment of skepticism to discover rational principles which stand *a priori,* of necessity. The foundation of his viewpoint is self-consciousness, 'Cogito, ergo sum' (I think therefore I am), for no matter what sort of deception or errors exist, the awareness of self cannot be a deception. In order to be deceived one must nevertheless exist. Thus, self-consciousness is beyond any type of skepticism. From here Descartes moves to the existence of God as the first 'clear and distinct' idea and the veracity of other ideas through the existence and goodness of God.

> *"My question is, what can we hope to achieve with reason, when all the material and assistance of experience are taken away?"*
> *Immanuel Kant (1724-1804), <u>The Critique of Pure Reason</u>*

**epistolary** - n. a series of letters (as in correspondence).

**epithet** - n. a word or words ascribing an attribute to someone or something.

**epitome** - n. a summary.

**epitomize** - v. to show what is typical.

**eponym** - n. a person, real or not, whose name is adopted as the description of something.

**epuration** - n. a cleansing or purge; elimination.

**equable** - adj. unvarying, uniform; marked by a lack of extreme difference.

**equanimity** - n. a state of composure; serenity.

**equinox** - n. the solar time when night and day are of equal length everywhere; occurring about March 21 and September 22.

**equipose** - n. balance; equality of force.

**Erasmus, Desiderius** (1467-1536) - a Dutch philosopher and theologian, Erasmus advocated a theological humanism and opposed the evangelistic efforts of Martin Luther. Both Luther and Erasmus were ordained priests but with very different solutions to the problems of the Reformation Period. Erasmus advocated internal moral renewal, claiming that establishment of other Christian churches outside the mainstream of Catholicism would permanently damage the unity of Christendom.

Principal works: *The Contempt of the World*, 1490, *In Praise of Folly*, 1509, and *The Epicurean*, 1533.

> *"Formerly monasteries were nothing other than retreats where good men betook themselves when they were weary of pleasure and vice, or feared the moral contamination when pagans lived with Christians; or else they dreaded the cruel persecutions then raging, and betook themselves to the neighboring mountains, where they lived . . . in prayer and meditation. After laboring with their hands and living on the coarsest food, they spent the rest of their time reciting the psalms, or in pious reading or conversation, in prayer or works of charity, such as helping the sick and needy. . . . To be a monk in those days was simply to be a Christian . . . Control over others was conspicuous by its absence, since all were only too eager to advance towards perfection, and there was more need of the bit than the spur. . . . Now, alas, many monasteries are tinged with the follies of the world. . . . In these there is such a lack of discipline that they are nothing but schools of impiety, in which no one can be pure or good; and their title to the name of religious serves them only to do with impunity what they desire."*
>
> Erasmus, <u>Contempt of the World</u>

**erethism** - n. excessive stimulation of an organ or tissue, involving abnormal irritation.

**ergomania** - n. ceaseless toil, especially by a psychotic individual.

**ergophobia** - n. unnatural aversion to work; excessive fear of effort.

**eristic** - adj. controversial; characterized by disputatious or questionable reasoning.

**Eros** - n. in Greek philosophy, the god of physical love; though correctly interpreted to mean sexual love, the term also includes a general love of the physical life.

**erotogenesis** - n. stimulation of sexual impulses.

**erotomania** - n. abnormal sexual desire, including pathological physical affection for another person.

**ersatz** - adj. being a superficial or inferior substitute.

**eruct** - v. to belch; to throw forth violently.

**erudition** - n. extensive knowledge acquired primarily from books and lacking a basis in experience.

**erumpent** - adj. the quality of bursting out.

**escalade** - n. the act of climbing up by means of ladders, especially of walls or fortifications.

**escalate** - v.  to increase.

**escarpment** - n.  a ridge of high land.

**escharotic** - adj.  caustic.

**Eschatology** - n.  in theology, the study of the end of the world;  the doctrine of the last things.  It speculates on the nature and meaning of immortality, the resurrection, death, the Second Coming of Christ, and the notion of a last judgment.  Thus, it has a meaning on two levels.  One is the reference to the personal destiny of each person after their death.  The other is the reference to the purpose *(telos)* of society in history.

**eschew** - v.  to avoid or shun.

**esculent** - adj.  edible.

**esne** - n.  laborer.

**esperance** - n.  hope;  expectation.

**espial** - n.  act of observing or spying.

**estivate** - v.  to pass the summer as in a certain place.

**esurient** - adj.  greedy or voracious.

**Eternal Return, Theory of** - n.  in philosophy, the belief that all events will happen again in their exact and specific details over and over again.  A finite universe in an infinite expanse of time logically implies the recurrence of any configurations now present.  This cyclical view of time and reality is present in Ancient and Modern philosophy:  Pythagoras, Plato, Aristotle, and Nietzsche.  The theory depends on viewing matter as a constant, i.e. atoms of the classical type.  The theory is generally rejected by philosophers who emphasize the notions of becoming, novelty, and immortal past-time.

**ethereal** - adj.  delicate, tenuous;  also spiritual.

**Ethical relativism** - n.  in ethical theory, the view that values are subjective.  Thus, each person or each culture makes its own values.  As a theory, it is antagonistic toward absolutism and objectivism.

**Ethics** - n.  from the Greek 'ethos' meaning character.  Ethics is the study of action and theories of action, especially in individuals but also in groups.  The concern with practical action is aimed at uncovering 'right' (good) and 'wrong' (bad) decisions.  Decisions to act are theoretically connected to the acquisition of social and individual happiness.  Subsequently, 'effectiveness' of the agent in producing happiness socially and individually ranks the person or society in its formation of 'values'.

The study of ethics is principally represented by the following theories:

1) *Theocentric Ethics or Divine Command Theory* - the view that rules and principles of judgment derive from God. Thus, ethical values are linked to metaphysical and religious concerns about the nature and will of God.

2) *Utilitarianism* - the view that the good is decided by considering the "greatest good for the greatest number". Though evident in the philosophies of Thomas Hobbes and David Hume, this theory was popularized by John Stuart Mill (1806-1873), *Utilitarianism,* 1863. Mill's view did outline pleasure as a source of happiness but avoided raw hedonism: *"Better to be a Socrates dissatisfied than a pig satisfied."* He argued that rational beings discern the quality of their experiences as well as the quantity.

3) *Deontology* - the study of duty or obligation. It includes the observation that duty may override personal happiness or that happiness is secondary to a true understanding of 'the Good'. Doing 'good' for rewards may be an inferior motive compared to doing good for the sake of a better world. Immanuel Kant (1724-1804) did the most to advance this approach to decision theory.

*"The majesty of duty has nothing to do with the enjoyment of life."*
— I. Kant, <u>Critique of Practical Reason</u>

*"Nothing can possibly be conceived in the world, or even out of it, which can be called good, without qualification, except a good will."*
— I. Kant, <u>Critique of Practical Reason</u>

*"There is therefore but one categorical imperative, namely this: act only on that maxim whereby thou canst at the same time will that it should become a universal law."*
I. Kant, <u>The Metaphysics of Morals</u>

4) *Aretaic Ethics* - concerns itself with the creation of 'excellence'. It is sometimes called 'virtue-based ethics'. It emphasizes the importance of character-traits over rules and principles of judgment.

5) *Hedonism* - the view that the best life is found through the pursuit of pleasure.

*"The scent of flowers does not travel against the wind, nor that of sandalwood . . . but the fragrance of good people travels even against wind; a good person influences every place."*
— <u>The Dhammapada</u>, 500 B.C.

*"I have found little that is 'good' about human beings on the whole. In my experience most of them are trash, no matter whether they subscribe to this or that ethical doctrine or to none at all."*
—Sigmund Freud, <u>Psychoanalysis and Faith</u>

*"Goodness is a product of the ethical and spiritual artistry of individuals; it cannot be mass-produced."*
—Aldous Huxley (1894-1963), <u>Grey Eminence</u>

**ethnocentrism** - n.  the view that one's group or race is superior to any other.

**ethnogeny** - n.  the ordering of distinctive groups or races.

**ethnology** - n.  the study of the origin of races.

**ethos** - n.  the distinguishing character of a person or group, especially its moral nature.

**etiology** - n.  a branch of epistemology (knowledge) dealing with causes;  in medicine, the study of the causes of disease.

**eudaemonia** - n.  happiness.

**Eudaemonism** - n.  the study of happiness or spiritual well-being, especially as a consequence of the life committed to reason.  Aristotle (384-322 B.C.) was the first strong advocate of this view.  He believed in a connection between reason and self-fulfillment. Reason guides us to the most beneficial pleasures which are an added touch to the balanced contemplative life.

> *"True happiness flows from the possession of wisdom and virtue and not from the possession of external goods."*
>
> *-Aristotle, Politics*

In the philosophy of Plato, happiness is not equated with pleasure, as pleasure is a consequence of *eputhemia* (desire).  Desire is perceived as a natural element of the soul and its fulfillment is to be guided by reason.  Unhappiness stems from the reversal of this hierarchy.  As desire grows, the need for satisfaction grows.  Going beyond natural limits introduces various kinds of evil, since desire as justification is not always consistent with good judgment.

The problematic expansion of choices due to increased desire can be analyzed in the experience of hunger.  As the desire for food grows, so does the range of choices. What was once outside the individual's diet becomes a means of satisfying the craving for food, e.g. cannibalism.  This example reveals the basis for containing desire in its various manifestations.  Desire, when allowed or encouraged to grow, produces a willingness to participate in acts that are more extreme and perhaps dangerous.  Moreover, 'excess' desire produces a narrowing of experience and thus, a narrowing of life.  From the standpoint of eudaemonism, which includes the perception that happiness is a 'flourishing', it is important to flourish through reason.  According to Plato, a rational or creative life is essentially more fulfilling than a pleasurable life.  The former involves the life of the mind and the body, and the latter involves the life of the body alone.

> *"Happiness is gained by a use, and right use, of the things of life, and the right use of them, and good fortune in the use of them is given by knowledge."*
>
> *-Plato (428-348 B.C.), Euthydemus*

**eugonic** - adj.  the quality of living on artificial foodstuffs.

**eulogize** - v.  to provide high praise.

**eunomy** - n. good social order due to just government and laws.

**eunuchoid** - n. a sexually deficient individual.

**eupepsia** - n. satisfactory digestion.

**eupeptic** - adj. relating to good digestion; cheerful, happy, optimistic.

**euphonize** - v. to make pleasant to the ear.

**eupotamic** - adj. inhabiting fresh water.

**eurytopic** - adj. able to take wide variations in climate.

**eustacy** - n. a change in the sea level around the world.

**euthenics** - n. the philosophy or science of improving the human condition by improving human surroundings.

**evanesce** - v. to fade slowly.

**eversible** - adj. having the ability to be turned inside out.

**evert** - v. to turn to the outside.

**evitable** - adj. avoidable.

**evulsion** - n. the act of pulling out.

**exacerbate** - v. to intensify irritation.

**excerpta** - n. an extract; parts taken out.

**excide** - v. to cut out.

**excogitate** - v. to think out.

**excoriate** - v. to censure without mercy.

**excruciation** - n. the act of providing great pain or anguish.

**excursive** - adj. to be digressive in speech and thought.

**execrable** - adj. detestable; horrible.

**execrate** - v. to hate.

**ex facie** - adj. from the face of; apparently; presumable (as in a legal document).

**exigent** - adj. demanding or urgent..

**exiguous** - adj. small, scanty, meager, or inadequate.

**eximious** - adj. outstanding, excellent; eminent.

**Existentialism** - n. in philosophy, the concern with the individual person and his or her freedom. Existentialism is tied to phenomenology in its investigative technique, especially with regard to the presence or absence of meaning in the individual. It is also concerned with the nature of Being. Thus, existentialism is committed to ontological observations, including the analysis of life in a mass culture.

Karl Jaspers (1883-1969), *General Psychopathology*, 1913, *Existence Philosophy*, 1938, *The Way to Wisdom*, 1950, a key figure in the development of existential thought, used existentialism to criticize deterministic scientific psychology. According to Jaspers, who was also a trained psychiatrist, it is wrong to treat actual outcomes in a person's life as the necessary outcomes. Freedom of choice is not revealed by examining the past. Freedom and the true self are only observable in "boundary situations" (*Grenzsituationen*). These are situations in which real awareness of self is also an awareness of suffering, struggle, despair, urgency, guilt, anxiety, and even death. These mental situations are circumstances for recognizing pure responsibility and freedom.

The deepest property of being human is to be creative. Creativity is an inner choice to produce meaning in thought and action. This is accomplished by the development of authentic personal interests. This development, this fulfillment of personal curiosity, is perpetually in danger of being lost in the bureaucratic and mechanistic organization of modern life. The point of all existentialism is to attack this tendency through preserving the natural existence of freedom, cultivating an awareness of dynamic choice over the corrupting influence of life in a mass-culture. Though existentialists are about evenly divided into theistic, atheistic, and agnostic polarities, the issue of God is technically a separate philosophical consideration from the true interests of existentialism.

Key figures include: Jean-Paul Sartre (1905-1980), Soren Kierkegaard (1813-1855), Friedrich Nietzsche (1844-1900), Martin Buber (1878-1965), Paul Tillich (1886-1965), Gabriel Marcel (1889-1973), Martin Heidegger (1884-1976), Albert Camus (1913-1960), Rudolf Bultmann (1884-1976) and Maurice Merleau-Ponty (1908-1961).

**ex officio** - adj. in the capacity of official position.

**exogamy** - n. marriage outside a specific group.

**exogenous** - adj. with an external origin.

**exopathic** - adj. (medicine) externally caused.

**exorable** - adj. persuadable.

**exoteric** - adj. appropriate for general distribution (public use).

**exothermic** - adj.  giving off heat.

**ex parte** - adj.  from one side only, as in a dispute.

**expatiate** - v.  to enlarge upon;  to move about freely.

**expiate** - v.  to make amends;  to atone.

**expletive** - n.  an exclamatory word or phrase, especially one that is obscene;  words without real meaning but placed for emphasis.

**ex post facto** - adj.  Latin for "after the fact".

**expugnable** - adj.  defeatable; vulnerable to elimination.

**exscind** - v.  to cut out;  to remove;  to tear off.

**exsert** - v.  to thrust out.

**exsiccate** - v.  to remove moisture from;  to dry out.

**extenuate** - v.  to show an offense less serious;  to lessen the strength or effect of;  to mitigate.

**extirpate** - v.  to destroy totally;  to uproot;  to exterminate.

**extrapolate** - v.  to deduce from a known;  to project from given fact.

**extrinsic** - adj.  from the outside.

**extrusile** - adj.  to be able to be pushed or forced out.

**eyre** - n.  a periodic journey made in a circuit.

**fabulist** - n.  a liar.

**facetious**  - adj.  amusing but somewhat inappropriate.

**facile** - adj.  easily accomplished;  dexterous;  fluent.

**facinorous** - adj.  excessively wicked.

**factitious** - adj.  artificial;  produced by human rather than natural forces.

**facture** - n.  the act of making something.

**facultative** - adj.  granting a special privilege;  having permission or authority.

**fainague** - v.  to cheat or deceive.

**faineant** - adj.  idle or lazy.

**Faith** - n.  from the Latin *fidere* "to trust".  In theology, faith is the first of three cardinal virtues, faith, hope, and charity.  Theologically, faith is the response to the Divine truth, measured in the words of Jesus as the 'childlike acceptance' of life and the Kingdom of God.  Moreover, faith is described theologically as God's action in the soul.  This action is considered impossible without the existential entry into Christian life, wherein the individual also comes to a full acceptance of the self as whole and sufficient in spiritual terms.  Faith then is also an ontological measurement of being and Being.  It is the elimination of self-estrangement.

> *"Faith is the acceptance of the 'kerygma' (Christ's teaching) not as mere*
> *cognizance of it and agreement with it but as genuine obedience to it which*
> *includes a new understanding of one's self."*
> *-Rudolf Bultmann (1884-1976), Theology of the New Testament*

*"Faith means being grasped by a power that is greater than we are, a power that shakes us and turns us, and transforms and heals us. Surrender to this power is faith."*
— Paul Tillich (1886-1965), <u>The New Being</u>

*"The faith of a Christian . . . is trust in God, in a good God who created a good world, though the world is not now good; in a good God, powerful and good enough finally to destroy the evil that humanity does and redeem them of their sins."*
— Reinhold Niebuhr (1892-1971), <u>Beyond Tragedy</u>

*"Faith is a gift of God; do not believe that we said it was a gift of reasoning."*
— Blaise Pascal (1623-1662), <u>Pensees</u>


**Fallacy** - n. an error in reasoning. Fallacies are divided into two general categories, formal and informal. Formal fallacies break accepted structural arrangement or form in deductive argumentation. Informal fallacies are rational errors or deceptions in the linguistic presentation of an argument. Common fallacies used in everyday thinking include:

1) *Accent* - by placing emphasis on a word or phrase, it is possible to create extra meanings which confuse the issue or introduce unwarranted conclusions. Advertising strategies often employ this tactic to attract people: "Free" followed by an asterik, the asterik footnoting a requirement that must be met before something is received "free".

2) *Argumentum ad hominem* - attacking some person or institution in an abusive manner in order to discredit them, thus failing to address the issue at hand.

3) *Syntactical Ambiguity* - errors in the use of grammar, thus introducing multiple meanings: "All the cars Jack owns are worth at least $25,000 dollars." The careless use of 'all' makes it difficult to know whether they are $25k each or $25k total.

4) *Semantical Ambiguity* - confusion introduced through words which carry multiple meanings. "Few of us ever test our powers of deduction, except when filling out our income tax forms."

5) *Apriorism* - refusal to consider evidence which counts against one's own thinking. E.g. "I don't care what studies show, pornographic material does not have an effect on the thoughts of mature adults."

6) *Fallacy of the Continuum* - arguing that small differences are not real or important differences, thus ignoring the need for standardization of limits. "What's the big deal, so the average temperature of the earth rose 2 degrees in five years. It's only 2 degrees. The temperature around here in the Mojave Desert changes up to 50 or 60 degrees in a single day." or "If you buy this car on payments, it will only cost you $5 per day." This kind of reasoning allows further incremental changes to be accepted without concern for the real and cumulative effect.

7) *Hypothesis Contrary to Fact* - reasoning how things might have turned out if certain steps were taken in the past. Also called "Monday morning

quarterbacking".  Reasoning of this sort is pointless, because the changes cannot be produced.

*8) Distinction without a Difference* - using language to rename or re-describe an event or entity without any real difference being involved.  "I'm not a bad driver, I'm a practical driver.  I get more done if I write or read while driving."

*9) Appeal to Computer Error* - (the computer in business and finance).  An evasive fallacy in which the individual sheds responsibility for a mistake by claiming it is the fault of a machine.  Judgment always lies with the operator of a specific technology.  Technological errors are human errors.

*10) Fallacy of Fake Precision* - using mathematical claims that cannot be proven.  Statistical facts are often asserted in such a way that they distort the truth.  "73 percent of the American population believes in the moral correctness of capital punishment."  It is impossible to document the opinions of every person in the United States regarding capital punishment.

*11) Gambler's Fallacy* - occurs when one believes that the probability of winning is influenced by the number of times one participates in a game situation.  If a betting arrangement produces a 25 to 1 probability of losing,  that ratio holds in every betting act.
It does not change to 5 to 1 because one has lost in 20 betting acts.

*12) Appeal to Humor* - is sometimes used to avoid a logical defense, especially if the evidence in a defense is weak or unavailable.  Humor tends to sidetrack poorly trained minds.  Humor is an evasive tactic.

*13) Inference from a Label* - assuming that the name brand or title of something provides sufficient information to form solid conclusions about product service or institutional integrity.  "World's finest chocolate" does not guarantee that it is indeed the best chocolate in the world.  "Department of Defense" does not guarantee that the activities and experiments of the Defense Department are in fact good for or protecting the best interests of civilians and soldiers.

*14) Complex Question* - a question designed to direct the individual to a specific choice or conclusion.  "Have you stopped beating your spouse?" presupposes that the beating is or has taken place.   To answer yes or no would imply responsibility.

*15) Appeal to Novelty* - arguing that something is better because it is 'new'.

*16) Rationalization* - coming up with plausible but false justification for a position that one is unwilling to defend on another and less acceptable basis.

**famacide** - n.  a slanderer;  the death of a reputation.

**famulus** - n.  an assistant, especially of a scholar and, at one time, a medieval sorcerer.

**fanfaron** - n.  a boaster;  empty bragger.

**fanfaronade** - n.  boastful talk.

**Faraday, Michael** (1791-1867) - a British philosopher of science, whose work in chemistry and physics is generally regarded as one of the greatest achievements in the history of experimental science.  His personal circumstances make his achievements even more astounding.  Coming from a very poor family and having no formal training beyond the elementary level, Faraday possessed an intense natural curiosity which he focused on chemistry and electricity. In 1831, Faraday discovered the secrets of electromagnetic induction, with which, in later experiments, he identified the role of friction in the creation of electric power. Part of his success is due, strangely enough, to the fact that he was not trained in the mathematics of his day. This allowed (forced) him to find alternate paths of theoretical explanation with regards to the way electricity works. His chemical experiments, equally representative of strong natural curiosity at work, yielded the discovery of the liquefaction of chlorine gas.

*"I am persuaded that all persons may find in natural things an admirable school for self-instruction, and a field for the necessary mental exercise; that they may easily apply their habits of thought, thus formed, to a social use; and that they ought to do this, as a duty to themselves and their generation."*
*-Michael Faraday, Observations on Mental Education*

**farraginous** - adj. made of mixed materials.

**fastidious** - adj. having high and sometimes capricious standards; difficult to please.

**fastuous** - adj. overbearing, haughty, arrogant.

**fatidic** - adj. relating to prophecy or divination.

**fatuitous** - adj. foolish; possessing poor judgment.

**fatuity** - n. stupidity; marked inability to honor fact.

**faute de mieux** - from the French, meaning "for lack of anything better".

**faze** - v. to frighten; to cause to feel disconcerted; to cause discomposure.

**fealty** - n. loyalty.

**fecit** - from the Latin, meaning "made by".

**fecund** - adj. fruitful, abundant, prolific.

**felicity** - n. happiness.

**ferial** - adj. pertaining to a holiday.

**ferine** - adj. from 'feral', meaning wild or untamed.

**ferity** - n. from the Latin 'feritas', meaning "the condition of being wild".

**fervent** - adj. having warm or deep feeling; passionate; hot.

**Festschrift** - n. from the German 'fest', meaning festival plus 'schrift', meaning writing;

thus, a collection of articles contributed and published in honor of a writer or scholar.

**fetid** - adj. stinking; rotten.

**fetor** - n. a strong and disgusting odor; stench.

**fiasco** - n. a complete failure.

**Fichte, Johann Gottlieb** (1762-1814) - a German philosopher, influenced by Kant and recognized as the founder of German Idealism, Fichte pushed for the priority of practical reason over theoretical reason. Fichte argued this because he believed moral will to be the basis of idealism.

Fichte explained, prior to Hegel, that thinking is started on assumptions, realizes counterpoints, and synthesizes the conflict of ideas to achieve a new basis. Thus, the progress of thought is dialectical and formulated as: *Thesis + Antithesis = Synthesis*.

Fichte also adjusted Kant's view of *things-in-themselves*. Kant had argued that things exist but are ultimately unknowable. Fichte argued that knowledge of existence is a knowledge of things and that one could move from there. Moreover, it is more correct to say, "one thinks one sees an object" than to say, "one sees an object." Awareness is an awareness of self and the world. The self and the world are assumptions upon which we work teleologically and dialectically. This dialectical pursuit of knowledge has a moral objective: *to increase our virtue through successful interaction with the world.*

The moral focus of Fichte's epistemology characterizes his idealism. The human *vocation* is to exercise our duties in preserving freedom and protecting the rights of every person. This moral order is then identified with God as the *logos* in the world.

Principal works: *The Basis of All Theory of Science*, 1794, *The Foundation of Natural Rights*, 1796, *A System of Ethics*, 1798, *The Vocation of Man*, 1800, and *Way to a Blessed Life*, 1806.

> *"There is nothing real, lasting, imperishable in me, but these two elements: the voice of conscience and my free obedience."*
>
> J.G. Fichte, *The Vocation of Man*

**filicide** - n. the killing of a son or daughter; the act of.

**firmament** - n. the arch or vault of the sky.

**flaccid** - adj. lacking firmness; without vigor.

**flagitious** - adj. heinous; terrible.

**flaneur** - n. a person without aims or goals; an intellectual fake.

**fling** - n. a period of time devoted to self-indulgence; a momentary participation in dangerous forms of pleasure.

**fluvial** - adj. relating to a river or stream.

**foible** - n. a weakness of will.

**foison** -n. abundant harvest; plenty.

**foist** - v. to force another to accept by deceptive means.

**foment** - v. to instigate; rouse.

**foozle** - v. to bungle or botch.

**fop** - n. one devoted to vanity, especially about appearances; a foolish person.

**forensic** - adj. suitable to public discussion or debate.

**forfend** - v. to protect.

**forte** - n. strength or skill.

**fortitudinous** - adj. marked by strength.

**fortuity** - n. chance; luck.

**fractious** - adj. irritable.

**frangible** - adj. breakable.

**fratricide** - n. the act of killing a brother.

**Frege, Gottlob** (1848-1925) - a German philosopher of logic and mathematics, Frege is universally recognized as the founder of modern mathematical logic. He was successful in showing that all mathematical work owes its structural order to the principles of logic. Moreover, Frege placed logic at the front of all philosophical investigations by showing that all branches of philosophy must progress with the tools of logic. Without a correct understanding of logic, all subsequent efforts to construct knowledge must be flawed. Frege had a direct influence on the work of Edmund Husserl, Bertrand Russell, and Ludwig Wittgenstein. The modern use of variables and the notion of quantifiers (to handle the problem of generality) are stock elements in symbolic logic.

Frege was particularly successful in overturning the views of psychologism: the theory that the meanings of words must be accounted for in terms of mental processes which supposedly hold the true sense of a word.

Principal works: *Begriffschrift*, 1879, *Die Grundlagen der Arithmetik (The Foundations of Arithmetic)*, 1884, *Function and Concept*, 1891, and *Grundgesetze der Arithmetik (The Basic Laws of Arithmetic)*, 1903.

> *"A definition of a concept must be complete; it must unambiguously determine, as regards any object, whether or not it falls under the concept. Thus there must not be any object as regards which the definition leaves in doubt whether it falls*

*under the concept; though for us men, with our defective knowledge, the*
*question may not always be decidable."*

*-Gottlob Frege, Grundgesetze der Arithmetik*

**Freud, Sigmund** (1856-1939) - an Austrian philosopher of psychology, Freud developed the general architecture of modern psychoanalysis. Through the influence of Jean Martin Charcot (1825-1893) and Joseph Breuer (1842-1925), Freud discovered the basis of psychoanalytic practices. Freud became interested in the role of fantasies and the method of catharsis developed by Breuer. He also made use of Breuer's hypnotic techniques which developed into the theory of free association. Charcot, likewise, gave Freud important lessons in the use of hypnosis. Freud moved beyond simple hypnosis on the suspicion that neurosis included clever defenses, *repression,* which prevented the analysis of causal factors. Increasingly, he proposed that sexuality played an important role in the development of the self. It was especially important, in Freud's view, to note the interaction between children and their parents in understanding the psychosexual self.

In *Three Contributions to the Theory of Sex,* 1906, Freud presented ideas which had a strong influence on modern theories of personality development. And, during a period of self-analysis, Freud developed notions on the importance of dreams and their role in understanding the subconscious self. This led to one of his most durable books, *The Interpretation of Dreams,* 1900.

Principal works include: *The Psychopathology of Everyday Life,* 1904, *Wit and Its Relation to the Unconscious,* 1905, *Lectures on Psychoanalysis,* 1922, *Beyond the Pleasure Principle,* 1922, *The Ego and the Id,* 1923, *New Lectures on Psychoanalysis,* 1933, and *Inhibitions,Symptoms, and Anxiety,* 1936.

*"In psychoanalytic treatment nothing happens but an exchange of words between the patient and the physician. . . . Words and magic were in the beginning one and the same thing, and even today words retain much of their magical power. By words each of us can give to another the greatest happiness or bring about utter despair; by words the teacher imparts knowledge to the student; by words the orator sweeps his audience with him and determines its judgments and decisions. Words call forth emotions and are universally the means by which we influence our fellow creatures."*

*- Sigmund Freud, Introduction to Psychoanalysis*

**fugacious** - adj. fleeting, temporary.

**fulgent** - adj. very bright; dazzling.

**fuliginous** - adj. obscured by smoke; sooty; full of smoke.

**fulminate** - v. to explode; to utter with denunciation; to put down in rank.

**funest** - adj. sinister; fatal.

76

**furibund** - adj.  being furious or frenzied.

**fustigate** - v. to beat with a stick;  to criticize mercilessly.

**gaffe** - n.  a careless remark;  a social blunder.

**galvanize** - v. to coat with zinc;  to make resistant to wear;  also, to excite or motivate.

**gam** - n.  a visit and conversation among whalers;  a school of whales.

**Gandhi, Mohandas** (1869-1948) - n.  Indian philosopher and social reformer, Gandhi exhibited the ideological and spiritual influences of Hinduism and Christianity, particularly the Sermon on the Mount in the Gospel of Matthew.  He was assassinated in 1948 by a fanatical Hindu.
    Gandhi's work centers on the advancement of pacifism and social non-violence. His philosophy emphasizes the use of *"passive resistance"* to counter-act false institutional forms of justice.  The title *"mahatma" (great souled)* was bestowed on him by the millions of Hindus who perceived him as a saint and holy man.  He was singularly responsible for the expulsion of British rule in India.
    Principal work: *Indian Home Rule*, 1919.

> *"Passive resistance is a method of securing rights by personal suffering; it is the reverse of resistance by arms.  When I refuse to do a thing that is repugnant to my conscience, I use soul-force.  For instance, the government of the day has passed a law which is applicable to me.  I do not like it.  If, by using violence, I force the government to repeal the law, I am employing what may be termed body-force.  If I do not obey the law, and accept the penalty for its breach, I use soul-force.  It involves sacrifice of self."*
> Gandhi, <u>Indian Home Rule</u>

**gantry** - n.  a structure or platform designed to span over something, having only end support, as in gallows.

**garrote** - v. to strangle;  originally execution by use of an iron collar.

**garrulous** - adj.  pointlessly talkative;  excessive chatter;  loquacious or wordy.

**gauche** - adj.  tactless;  crude;  lacking social skill or grace.

78

**gelid** - adj. extremely cold; frozen.

**geomancy** - n. divination by throwing a handful of earth at random; also by drawing lines in the dirt.

**germane** - adj. relevant; logically connected.

**gerontocracy** - n. government by the old.

**gerontology** - n. the study of old age; its mental, spiritual, and physical attributes.

**Gestalt** - n. from German meaning 'a unified whole' that cannot be derived from the sum of its parts; *Gestalt* has particular importance as a philosophy of being. In psychotherapy it has modified the philosophy of treatment for inner crisis to emphasize a balanced awareness of mind and body. Moreover, in emphasizing the person as a whole it recommends a strong recognition of personal responsibility while resisting the interpretive or intrusive techniques of traditional psychoanalysis.

The development of *Gestalt* therapy was undertaken by several philosophers of mind, including Max Wertheimer (1880-1943), Wolfgang Kohler (1887-1967), and Kurt Koffka (1886-1941). Their work laid the foundation for the dynamic influence of Fritz Perls (1893-1970). Perls, more than anyone perhaps, used his extraordinary talents as a thinker to promote and prove the value of *Gestalt* therapy. The holistic approach works on the individual's awareness, especially of his or her self in relation to the external world. Perls called *Gestalt* therapy a "psychology of the obvious", training people to see what was happening in the present, similar to the way Zen trains the mind to focus on the now. Moreover, achieving wholeness demands a certain independence from authority models and the often damaging effects of the superego. Balancing this objective with certain virtues like discipline has presented challenges to the theory. Removing obstacles to successful development does not eliminate the need for desirable character traits which can often help the individual move right through obstacles. One of the greatest differences between *Gestalt* therapy and traditional psychoanalytic work is the greater autonomy of the patient. Whereas psychoanalysis may encourage greater passivity and alienation from one's own rational power, *Gestalt* therapy creates a continual self-reference to thoughts and perceptions with the therapist offering limited forms of guidance.

> *"Fortunately men believe in their will, and even if they are philosophically convinced of determinism, they will not make use of it in actual situations."*
> *-Max Wertheimer, Freedom: Its Meaning, ed. Ruth Nanda Anshen, 1940*

**gesticulate** - v. communicating with the use of gestures, in addition to words.

**glabrous** - adj. smooth; bald.

**glosseme** - n. the smallest meaningful signal in language, composed of a morpheme and a tagmeme; a word stem or grammatical unit.

**gnathonic** - adj. obsequious; servile.

**gnome** - n. aphorism; a short but very meaningful saying.

**gnomist** - n. writer of maxims.

**gnomology** - n. the study of maxims; also the collecting of.

**Gnosticism**- n. from the term *gnosis* meaning knowledge. Gnosticism was a Christian sect of the 2nd Century, claiming to have a mystical understanding and the only genuine knowledge of the meaning of Christ.

It was lead by Valentine and Saturninus, who held that Judaism was a corruption of religion and that the Old Testament was an invalid document revealed by an inferior spirituality. Jesus was a human whose body was used by a heavenly Christ. This Christ had a stature beneath God and angels.

**God** - n. in philosophy and theology, a metaphysical object of the highest rank. In philosophy God as an object of inquiry remains open to definition. In theology, God is a presupposition for further reflection on the meaning of life. Philosophy is strictly committed to the use of reason in the investigation of God. Theology on the other hand counts on the validity of 'faith' in addition to reason. This faith is an intuitive recognition of God and an affirmation of God's personal nature. Included, then, is the idea of worship as an aspect of one's faith. In the Judeo-Christian model of God, reason harkens back to the story of the Fall, sometimes called 'the Fall upward' since it represents an alienation from God through reason; in theological terms 'a corrupted transcendence of being'. In the myth of the Fall, humanity is estranged from God through reason's egotistical nature. The relationship with God is compromised by eating the 'forbidden fruit' (*knowledge/reason*). Reason acquires the reputation of atheism. The struggle to agree on a theology is the history of religion in the West, extending through Islam, the Reformation, and the subsequent splintering of views on God in the modern world.

In philosophy, the efforts of reason are focused on proofs for the existence of God:

> 1) *Cosmological Argument* - employed by both philosophers and theologians, the logic of this proof is variously presented with the following sorts of claims:
>> i) Every thing has a cause.
>> ii) No thing is the cause of itself.
>> iii) The universe is a thing.
>> iv) The universe is not the cause of itself.
>
> The conclusion that God is the cause of the universe works on the qualification that God is independent of causality, is even the source of causality. In Aristotle's (384-322 B.C.) presentation of the argument, God is called the "Unmoved Mover." It is important here to accept the operational differences between metaphysical causation and physical causation.
>
> 2) *Teleological Argument* - employs the concept of 'design' (*telos* meaning design or purpose). Nature reveals designs and patterns of almost i       nfinite complexity, especially with regard to life forms. These designs and       patterns

80

reveal a type of logical architecture which is too much to explain under the idea of chance. The chance that there is a Designer is infinitely greater than that there is not. William Paley (1745-1805) advanced this logic as the "Watchmaker Argument". If one finds a watch on a deserted island, the inductive conclusion that there is or was a human presence is very strong. Moreover, the watch implies a watchmaker. In the case of God, even if God no longer has a relationship to Creation (deism), God's history is tied up with the existence of a world.

3) *Ontological Argument* - thought of by St. Anselm of Canterbury (1033-1109), it plays on the observation that God is a being of the highest rank. A being of the highest rank cannot be lacking in a basic feature, meaning existence. St. Anselm avoided the problems of further definition in the formulation: "God is that being greater than which nothing can be thought of."

4) *Moral Argument* - employed by Immanuel Kant (1724-1804), this argument proposes the existence of moral consciousness as *a priori* (necessary). The source of this moral consciousness is God, the highest moral consciousness. Moreover, the possibility of true justice does not lie with humanity. Ultimate justice is defined by the metaphysical properties of the soul and immortality. Only a universe were there is a God can be a morally sensible universe. Without God, the soul, and immortality, good and evil are equally nullified or emptied in death.

**Good, the** - n. a primary philosophical target of ethical theory, 'good' has been variously defined. Aristotle says that honor, friendship, wisdom, and pleasure are good, but their independent essences make 'good' seem different in each instance. In some instances, it is seen mainly as approval or disapproval of some feature of life.

In the notion of *eudaemonia,* happiness, spiritual well-being, and flourishing represent the good. Thus, good is identified as something to be sought for its own sake.

On other accounts, the good is equated with certain virtues and seen as necessary for the individual, social, and political needs of life.

**Gorgias** (483-380 B.C.) - n. the main character in Plato's dialogue *Gorgias.* He is classified as a Sophist who maintained the impossiblity of knowledge. Gorgias was a complete skeptic who summed up his position in three claims: (1) Nothing exists; (2) even if something exists, we cannot know it due to the difference between thoughts and things; (3) even if things exist and we could know them, we could not really communicate knowledge due to the apparent gap between any two minds.

According to Guthrie, Gorgias taught his students to tailor their words to the audience and the situation. Gorgias himself garnered large fees for his talents as a teacher and public speaker.

Principal work: *On Nature or the Non-existent.*

Text to Consult: *A History of Greek Philosophy*, vol. 3, W.K.C. Guthrie.

**gorgonize** - v. to hypnotize.

**Grace** - n. from Latin 'gratus' meaning 'beloved'. In theology, grace is a reference to God's presence in a life. It also refers to the assistance God may grant to a rational being with the aim of advancing that being's sanctification. The interpretation of how God provides this assistance has been a matter of discussion since the early formation of Christianity. In the theology of St. Paul of Tarsus, grace refers to the favor God shows toward those who may appear undeserving or ungrateful but needful of God's redemptive presence. According to St. Paul, faith is connected to the reception of grace (Rom. 4:13-16, Eph. 2:5-8). In the theology of St. Augustine (354-430 A.D.), grace is strictly connected to salvation and purely necessary due to the Fall. Later, grace was attached to participation in the sacraments, i.e., sacramental grace. Sacramental grace became the outward appearance of inner grace. The theological difficulties of providing a conclusive definition of grace have produced three distinctions:

1) *Sanctifying grace* - the presence of God which enables persons to perform noble acts. This grace arrives through authentic participation in the Sacraments.

2) *Actual grace* - the general presence of God in persons, even the un-Baptized, for the production of some specific act of goodness.

3) *Prevenient grace* - the spiritual influence which inspires a movement toward the soul's sanctification without involvement in the Sacraments. This grace is said to be gratuitous and unmerited.

Text to Consult: *Early Christian Doctrines*, J.N.D. Kelly.

**gramary** - n. the lore of sorcery.

**gray eminence** - n. power behind the throne or political position; a person who holds power but wields it through another.

**grimalkin** - an old female cat; an old and unpleasant female personality.

**grum** - adj. appearing glum and unhappy.

**gulosity** - n. excessive appetite; also, greed.

**guttle** -v. to eat or devour greedily.

**gynarchy** - n. government by women.

**gyrovague** - n. itinerant monk, especially one who travels between monasteries.

**habitude** - n. usual state of mind; disposition.

**haecceity** - n. the quality that gives something its individuality.

**hagiocracy** - n. government by those deemed holy or spiritually enlightened.

**hagiolatry** - n. the worship of saints.

**hajj** - n. annual pilgrimage to Mecca.

**halcyon** - adj. bearing calmness, peace, happiness, prosperity.

**hapax legomenon** - n. Gr. meaning a word or group of words of which there is only one recorded use.

**haplography** - n. a copying error by which a letter(s) which should be repeated are omitted, e.g., 'repition' for 'repetition'.

**Harnack, Adolf von** (1851-1930) - a German theologian and the main advocate of liberal theology in the 19th century, Harnack taught both Karl Barth and Dietrich Bonhoeffer. For Harnack, liberal theology meant a complete commitment to both reason and faith. It meant that theology had to become more than moral philosophy defended on Divine authority. Harnack defended "doubt" as the essence of intellectual honesty, a kind of sequel to Cartesianism necessary for good theology.
    Principal works include: *What is Christianity*, 1901, *History of Dogma*, 1897, *Essays on the Social Gospel*, 1907 and *Christianity and History*, 1896.

**harridan** - n. an old woman, particularly a hag.

**hebephrenia** - n. a type of split personality disorder, allied to puberty; characterized by childish emotionality.

**hebetate** - v. to make dull or inert.

**hebetude** - n. the state of being dull or lethargic.

**hedonics** - n. the study of pleasurable and non-pleasurable states of mind.

**Hedonism** - n. the philosophy of pleasure, hedonism is studied under the related concerns of ethics and psychology. Ethical hedonism argues that we 'ought' always to pursue life in a manner that provides the greatest amount of pleasure. Psychological hedonism argues that we must, as a type of nature instinct, always act from a motive to derive pleasure from life. The later view incorporates behavioristic assumptions about human life and diminishes the role of free choice.

**Hegel, George Wilhelm Friedrich** (1770-1831) - a German idealist philosopher, Hegel influenced Karl Marx and, thus helped to shape the philosophy of dialectical materialism (Communism). Hegel viewed life as an organic process infused with a spiritual Absolute. He attempted to stay between materialism and pantheism, arguing that while there is unity in reality, it is a complex arrangement.

The hallmark of Hegel's philosophy is the special definition he provides for 'dialectic'. Becoming is a consequence or result of triadic movement explained as *thesis + antithesis = synthesis*. Each synthetic conclusion in turn becomes or acts as a new thesis. Included in this understanding is the assumption that all of reality is rationality or thought. Absolute Spirit or Thought acts as a kind polarity which draws forth the organic process.

Hegel's views are influenced by the work of Kant and Fichte.

Principal works: *The Phenomenology of Mind*, 1807, *Philosophy of Right*, 1821, and *Philosophy of History*, 1837.

> *"The history of the world begins with its general aim, the realization of the idea of spirit, only in an <u>implicit</u> form, that is, as nature; a hidden, most profoundly hidden, unconscious instinct; and the whole process of history is directed toward rendering this unconscious impulse a conscious one."*
> G.W.F. Hegel, <u>Philosophy of History</u>

**hegira** - n. a journey undertaken to escape from a dangerous or undesirable life.

**Heidegger, Martin** (1884-1976) - a German philosopher and one of the main representatives of existentialism, Heidegger is also famous for his strange supportive remarks of Hitler, probably the consequence of a naive anticipation of Nietzsche's views in German politics. This circumstantial *ad hominem* notwithstanding, Heidegger's penetrating analysis of human existence also exhibits the influence of Edmund Husserl, his teacher. And, by 1935 he had turned critical of the Nazi misuse of Nietzschean thought.

Favorite themes in Heidegger's thought include the notions of *Angst* (anxiety), *Dasein* (Being), and *Sorge* (concern). Anxiety includes a recognition of one's finitude and thus, the issue of one's death or non-Being. *Dasein* issues in the notion of authentic existence, which is linked to *Sorge*. The individual who lacks authentic concern regarding Being is unable to discover one's self, unable to produce originality of thought, and is submissive to the crowd. In reflection, one becomes aware of Nothingness or Non-Being and, thus, also Being. Heidegger tries to uncover the relationship between Being and Nothingness. The work of reflection must also, then, comprehend the role of Time in existence.

*Dasein* involves three aspects:

   1) 'understanding' - seeing the purpose and inter-connectedness of things.

   2) 'mood' - describes our attitude toward Being. It will lie somewhere between the attitude of joyfulness and exuberance on the one hand and despair on the other hand. It reflects the way in which the world appears and exists for us.

   3) 'discourse' - the formulation of a language to express what it is that we understand and experience.

In Heidegger's thought there is a powerful push into ontological reflection. His works offer a nearly inexhaustible resource for speculation and can be seen as a serious extension of the phenomenology of Husserl.

Principal works: *Being and Time*, 1927, *The Basic Problems of Phenomenology*, 1928, *What is Metaphysics?*, 1929, *What is Thinking?*, 1954, and *Phenomenology and Theology*, 1970.

**heliolatry** - n. worship of the sun.

**helot** - n. a Spartan class of serf or slave.

**helotry** - n. a state of slavery.

**hemal** - adj. pertaining to blood.

**henotheism** - n. recognizing several gods but the worship of one.

**heortology** - n. the study of religious festivals.

**Heraclitus** (540-475 B.C.) - a Greek pre-Socratic philosopher, Heraclitus was often called "the dark philosopher", as he was somewhat pessimistic especially toward religion and democratic politics.

As an ancient forerunner to process philosophy, Heraclitus focused on the problem of *change*. His observation that everything changes led him to suppose that the underlying reality is fire (logos). In fire one finds constant transformation or 'flux'. Furthermore, the changes one witnesses in nature are not random, so there must be some ordering and universal *logos* (God). This universal logos or fire, in turn, implies that everything is one in a pantheistic sense.

Heraclitus viewed the various types of strife as part of the full definition of reality. Change or flux requires a constant conflict of opposites. Good and evil, war and peace, are simply extensions of reality which should be viewed as normal features and not as calamities that can be prevented. What appears to be chaotic is actually part of a larger order and harmony.

Principal work: *Fragments of Heraclitus*

*"War is both king of all and father of all, and it has revealed some as gods, others as men; some it has made slaves, others free."*

*"To God, all things are beautiful, good and just; but men have assumed some things to be unjust, others just."*

*"It is hard to fight against impulse; whatever it wishes, it buys at the expense of the soul."*

*"Men who love wisdom must be inquirers into very many things indeed."*
                                        *-Heraclitus, Fragments*

**heresiology** - n.  the study of heresies (deviations from religious doctrine).

**hermaphrodite** - n.  one having male and female sex organs;  a homosexual; a person possessing or exhibiting male and female qualities.

**Hermeneutics** - n.  the science of interpretation;  methods of interpretation, especially with regard to religious manuscripts such as the Bible.  From the Greek 'hermeneutikos' meaning 'interpretation':
　　　　1) In philosophy, hermeneutics advances research by systematic evaluation and observation of phenomena, the interpretation of what exists.  Martin Heidegger's (1884-1976) work in phenomenology employed some of the techniques recommended by Friedrich Schleiermacher (1768-1834) on miracles and the hermeneutical work in theology.  Edward Spranger (1882-1963) also depended upon hermeneutical technique to explore ideal human types, *Forms of Life: A Sketch,* 1914, and *Problems of Cultural Morphology,* 1936.
　　　　2) In theology, hermeneutics is embedded within the aims of Scriptural exegesis. Exegesis is the work of explaining textual meaning.  Hermeneutics is the construction of procedures for validating interpretations.  For one thing, it works on the awareness of ambiguity in sacred texts.  This concern is an outcome of the many theological disagreements which arise from the study of sacred texts.  The work of Wilhelm Dilthey (1833-1911), *Types of World View,* 1911, *Studies on the Foundations of the Spirit,* 1905, helped to show the limitations of historical analysis of reality through hermeneutical sensitivity, believing history and philosophy to be relative to specific times.  The pure meaningfulness of each age is essentially lost in history-keeping.  According to Dilthey, this limits the interpretational power of both cultural and spiritual sciences (*Geisteswissenschaften)* to make clear the real nature of spiritual life in the past.

**Hesperian** - adj.  from the Greek 'hesperos', meaning 'evening' (thus Western from western setting of the sun); western.

**Hesperus** - n.  evening star;  Venus.

**hetaera** - n.  a highly cultured courtesan in Ancient Greece;  demimondaine; female companion.

**hetaerism** - n.  a social system wherein women are common property.

**heuristic** - adj.  exploratory.

86

**hiatus** - n. a gap or break, especially in a sequence.

**hiemal** - adj. pertaining to winter.

**hieratic** - adj. pertaining to sacred things.

**hierocracy** - n. government by priests.

**Hinduism** - n. the original religion of India, 'Hindu' simply means one who lives in India. As a religious philosophy, it contains a wide range of ideas ranging from determinism to existentialism. Hindu beliefs are contained in two primary sources, *The Upanishads* (containing the philosophical principles of the faith) and the *Bhagavadgita* (containing advice on daily practices).

A central belief is that reality is changing but never changing. This logic is subsumed under the term 'Brahman'. Only Brahman is reality. Everything else, including souls and things, is a manifestation of Brahman.

'Atman' is the Hindu concept of soul or self. The atman, as the true self, is connected with Brahman. The empirical world is a set of appearances or illusions, depending on Brahman. The self or atman is Brahman appearing in limited form.

Hinduism recognizes four primary values, *Artha, Kama, Dharma,* and *Moksha.* Artha is the lowest value and means wealth. Kama represents pleasure. Dharma is higher and represents law and the duty towards its enactment. And, Moksha is enlightenment and the highest value. These values correspond roughly to stages of life, with Moksha generally occurring with age.

The law of *karma* provides for the salvation and damnation of souls, though no soul in Hinduism is eternally lost because of an inferior moral life. Karma is the belief in strict cause and effect within the framework of moral life. The existence one experiences is an outcome of moral choices which influence the spiritual well-being of the individual. The philosophy of karma is the source of the caste system.

The stages of life which correspond roughly to the four values are called *ashramas.* These stages point the individual to spiritual liberation. First, from 0-25 yrs. the person is a student of life. Second, from about 25-50 yrs. the person is expected to marry and become a parent. Third, from 55-70 yrs., roughly, is a period of reflection and meditation. And, in the fourth ashrama the person seeks full union with Brahman by means of a strict self-control in order to succeed in acquiring full peace and harmony.

*Yoga* is a special type of physical and spiritual training which seeks to unify atman and Brahman. Traditional yoga is practiced under a master or *guru.* Training is closely supervised and demands the elimination of all material distractions. In folk yoga, training is not as rigorous and is carried out in a group. Folk yoga is more ritualistic with its use of such aids as incense and animal sacrifice. Both forms of yoga claim to strive toward enlightenment and liberation.

Text to consult: *The Indian Way*, John M. Koller, 1982.

**hircine** - adj. lustful, lecherous; also, goatlike.

**histogenesis** - n. the production and differentiation of tissues.

**histopathology** - n. the study of diseased tissue.

**historicism** - n.  the theory that events are pre-determined;  history as a standard of value; events are unaffected by human action and thought.

**histrionics** - n.  exaggerated, insincere speech or conduct.

**Hobbes, Thomas** (1588-1679) - a British political philosopher, best known for the phrase, "Man is a wolf to his fellow man."  Impressed early on by the quality of mathematical thought, Hobbes hoped to create similar quality in the construction of political, psychological, and social theory.

Historically, Hobbes is often called the father of totalitarianism, primarily because of the way he describes the relationship between rulers and their subjects. Hobbes worked out a pessimistic model of man in nature, subsequently he believed that the only way to tame the vicious character of the race was through the establishment of a strict "social contract".

In nature, there is a "right of all to all".  There is a type of brutal equality wherein one takes what one can and does what one can to pursue one's own self interest. Hobbes believed that in nature the pervading mood is fear, especially fear of a violent death.  His primitive psychological behaviorism explained human action under a set of "aversions" and "appetites".

The social contract was a way out of the natural condition of anarchy: "I authorize and give up my right of governing myself, to this man, or to this assembly of men, on this condition, that thou give up thy right to him, and authorize all his actions in like manner."  One of the provisions of this contract, according to Hobbes, is that there can be no "unjust law".  This is because justice and law begin with a sovereign.  Justice, for Hobbes, is simply a matter of universal application of law and universal obedience to that law.

Principal works: *The Citizen*, 1642, *Concerning Body*, 1655, *Concerning Man*, 1658, and *Leviathan*, 1651.

> *"If the essential rights of sovereignty . . . be taken away, the Commonwealth is thereby dissolved, and everyman returneth into the condition and calamity of a war with every other man, which is the greatest evil that can happen in this life."*
> *-Thomas Hobbes, Leviathan*

**holism** - n.  a philosophical theory that natural phenomena are entities, more than the sum of different parts.

**holophrasis** - n.  the use of a single word to express ideas contained in a whole sentence or phrase.

**holozoic** - adj.  feeding in the manner of most animals on solid nutrients.

**homocentric** - adj.  having the same center.

**homo-eroticism** - n.  homosexuality.

**homological** - adj.  having the same relative structure or condition.

**homomorphism** - n. likeness in form.

**homothetic** - adj. similarly positioned.

**homunculus** - n. midget; small person.

**hormic** - adj. purposeful; teleological.

**hortatory** - adj. the characteristic of urging or exhorting.

**hot spur** - n. a rash person; impetuous individual.

**hoyden** - n. a girl or woman who is carefree, boisterous, and rude.

**Human condition** - n. in philosophy, the object of study for purposes of defining the nature and destiny of humanity. It is a concern with the awareness of the finitude of life in the context of the infinite. It is also a study of the constants which exist in every life.

> *"Nothing can be meaner than the anxiety to live on, to live on anyhow and in any shape; a spirit with any honor is not willing to live except in its own way."*
> *- George Santayana (1863-1952), Winds of Doctrine*

> *"Human life must be some kind of mistake."*
> *- Arthur Schopenhauer (1788-1860), Vanity of Existence*

> *"To have contemplated human life for forty years is the same as to have contemplated it for ten thousand years."*
> *- Marcus Aurelius (121-180 A.D.), Meditations*

> *"Let us imagine a number of men in chains and all condemned to death, where some are killed each day in the sight of the others, and those who remain see their own fate in that of their fellows and wait their turn, looking at each other sorrowfully and without hope. It is an image of the condition of humanity."*
> *- Blaise Pascal (1623-1662), Pensees*

> *"My wish for myself and for those whom I love is to be successful now, and now to meet with a check; thus passing through life amid alternate good and ill, rather than with perpetual good fortune. For never yet did I hear of anyone succeeding in all his undertakings, who did not meet with calamity at last, and come to utter ruin."*
> *- Herodotus (ca. 500 B.C.), History*

**Hume, David** (1711-1776) - a Scottish philosopher, known primarily for his contributions to epistemology. Hume concluded that all knowledge is the result of sensory impressions. Inward impressions are the emotions, e.g. love, hate, anger, patience. Outward impressions are the experiences of the senses themselves, e.g. color, taste, sound, tactility, and auditory experiences. These experiences are the basis of all ideas. The ideas themselves hang together in a type of order called "association of ideas".

Association is made possible by principles such as resemblance between experiences, contiguity in time, and observation of cause and effect.

Hume's analysis of causality reveals an inductive process of reasoning. A cause *x* does not necessarily entail an effect *y*. Causal relationships are contingent relationships. Contingency varies from one phenomena to the next. Thus, there is always a 'probability factor' in causal explanations. Custom, repetition of experience, or habit incline us to expect certain effects, but there is no logical necessity which permits us to predict with certainty what will occur among events. The anticipation of certain effects is merely a psychological anticipation based on prior experience.

Ultimately, Hume is pessimistic about knowledge which is outside the domain of experience. Ideas about God and cosmology are never really justified in any logical sense, since these represent notions beyond the ground warranted by experience. But, it is natural for the human mind to seek out higher and higher explanations of design and order, so the notion of God and a cosmology are too tempting for most people to discard in the absence of other explanations.

Principal works: *Treatise on Human Nature*, 1739, *An Inquiry Concerning Human Understanding*, 1748, and *Dialogues Concerning Natural Religion*, 1779.

> *". . . while the body is confined to one planet, along which it creeps with pain and difficulty, the thought can in an instant transport us into the most distant regions of the universe; or even beyond the universe, into the unbounded chaos, where nature is supposed to lie in total confusion. What never was seen, or heard off, may yet be conceived; nor is anything beyond the power of thought, except what implies an absolute contradiction.*
>
> *But though our thought seems to possess this unbounded liberty, we shall find, upon a nearer examination, that it is really confined within very narrow limits, and that all this creative power of the mind amounts to no more than the faculty of compounding, transposing, augmenting, or diminishing the materials afforded us by the senses and experience. . . . all the materials of thinking are derived either from outward or inward sentiment: the mixture and composition of these belongs alone to the mind and will. Or, to express myself in philosophical language, all our ideas or more feeble perceptions are copies of our impressions or more lively ones."*
>
> -David Hume, *An Inquiry Concerning Human Understanding*

**Husserl, Edmund** (1859-1938) - a German philosopher, educated at the University of Vienna and the acknowledged founder of phenomenology.

A phenomena is any appearance of basic reality; it is the subject's confrontation with an experience. Phenomenology, for Husserl, is the science of description of subjective processes. Thus, it takes a Cartesian approach in analyzing the ego and its presentations. Moreover, phenomenology is prior to psychology because it asserts the importance of logic in its methodology. Rational inquiry is a type of analysis of relational factors in one's experience of phenomena. Psychology over-steps the necessary establishment of logical principles in its analysis of the mind, since it is primarily an empirical science. Phenomenology is defined by the requirements of logic. Logic, like mathematics, is the study of necessary truths rather than contingent truths. Consciousness is seen as a collection or stream of intentional awareness, wherein mental objects point to other mental objects. Consciousness is always consciousness of some phenomenon.

Logic is necessary to evaluate the coherence of relationships between ideas (mental objects) of phenomena.

Principal works: *Logical Investigations, 2 vols.*, 1900, *Ideas on a Pure Phenomenology and Phenomenological Philosophy*, 1913, and *The Crisis of European Science and Transcendental Phenomenology*, 1936.

> *"If . . . we disregard any metaphysical purpose of the critique of cognition and confine ourselves purely to the task of clarifying the essence of cognition and of being an object of cognition, then this will be phenomenology of cognition and of being an object of cognition and will be the first and principal part of phenomenology as a whole."*
> -Edmund Husserl, <u>The Idea of Phenomenology</u>

**hyaline** - adj.  glassy; transparent.

**hydrophobia** - n.  morbid fear of water, e.g., rabies.

**hydromancy** - n.  divination by means of water, e.g. baptism, holy water.

**Hygeia** - n.  goddess of health in Greek mythology; thus, 'hygiene'.

**hylomorphic** - adj.  made up of corporeal and spiritual matter.

**hylomorphism** - n.  the view that real existence occurs only in material forms.

**hylotheism** - n.  the view that gods and matter are intimately related.

**hylozoism** - n.  the view that all matter is animated;  a doctrine held by early Greek philosophers to account for 'change'.

**hyperacusis** - n.  unusually acute hearing.

**hyperalgesia** - n.  heightened sensitivity or reaction to pain.

**hyperaphia** - n.  abnormal sensitivity to touch.

**hyperbole** - n.  deliberate exaggeration.

**hyperborean** - adj.  pertaining to the extreme north.

**hypercryalgesia** - n.  unusual sensitivity to cold.

**hyperdulia** - n.  worship of the Virgin Mary above all other divine references.

**hyperosmia** - n.  unusually acute sense of smell.

**hyperphagia** - n.  excessive hunger.

**hyperprosexia** - n.  excessive attention to relatively unimportant sense data.

**hypersomnia** - n.  abnormally long sleep.

**hypnology** - n.  the study of sleeping.

**hypocorism** - n.  the use of pet names.

**hypognathous** - adj.  having a long protruding lower jaw.

**hypophonia** - n.  abnormally weak voice due to deficiency in the vocal chords; whispering.

**hypopraxia** - n.  the absence of action;  listlessness.

**hypostasis** - n.  in science, the condition of settling to the bottom, especially by a substance in a fluid.  In theology, a reference to the fundamental divine substance of God as trinity.  Thus, in metaphysical terms, an essential transcendent entity: also, logos, world soul, or nous (mind).

**hypothecate** - v.  to pledge something as security without giving up title or possession.

**hysterogenic** - adj.  producing hysteria or uncontrolled emotional expression.

**hysteron proteron** - n.  a reversal of a rational or causal order;  a logical fallacy in which the premise holds what is yet to be proved.

**iatric** - adj.  relating to medicine.

**ictus** - n.  a sudden stroke or seizure, especially accompanied by convulsions.

**Id** - n.  in psychoanalysis, the source of primitive instinctual urges and drives;  the directive force toward amoral, immediate gratifications.  In the philosophy of Freud, the id represents the unconscious.  As such it holds, in Freud's view, the dynamic and often illogical properties of the psychosexual self.  In theory, the id often influences human choice without regard for the external realities of life.  The destructive potential of the unrestricted action of the id, through the pleasure principle, explains much of the suffering of humanity.

**Idealism** - n.  any system of thought which organizes itself and reality around the Greek term 'idea', meaning 'vision' or 'contemplation'.  Idealism denies the material primacy of reality.  Thus, if the world is not principally matter, idealism is also suspicious of knowledge built exclusively on the observation of matter.  Laws of thought are more important to idealists than empirical data.  Logical-spiritual approaches to reality are the key to discerning order and harmony.  Idealism implies that views of the universe are dependent upon mind.  Still, commitment to idealism varies from thinker to thinker:

1) *Subjective idealism* - holds that ideas alone exist.  What appear to be objects are only perceptions.  Perceptions are the only material to work with in the view of subjective idealism. The philosophy of George Berkeley (1685-1753), referred to as *immaterialism,* maintained that nothing ever exists without its being perceived.  "To be is to be perceived" (Esse est percipi).  In subjective idealism the knower, the subject mind, is seen as the center of the issue.  There is nothing to say or think about so-called 'things' if they are not perceived.  Thus, it is argued that matter is a creation of mind.  As a system of thought, subjective idealism is easily attacked due to its skepticism regarding the external world.

2) *Objective idealism* - does not deny the existence of an objective reality. Instead objective idealists maximize the existence of order and designs within nature to produce a philosophical mirror of that order and design.  Objective idealism frequently works toward the identification of some Absolute Source and remains committed to developing theory about the foundations of being.  However, it does not allow self or subjectivity to override the dynamic flow of its logic, which involves an honoring of external reality.  William Ernest Hocking (1873-1966) developed a type of objective

idealism in *The Meaning of God in Human Experience,* 1912. Hocking believed in the real, the pragmatic, and the ideal. He blended these assumptions into a powerful analysis of human life and the relationship to God.

**idioglossia** - n. speech invented for private communication; also, speech that is unintelligible, a consequence of mental pathology.

**igneous** - adj. produced by intense heat.

**illation** - n. a deduction; a conclusion inferred.

**imbrangle** - v. to perplex.

**imbricate** - v. to overlap methodically; roofing (imbrication).

**imbrute** - v. to degrade to the level of a primitive animal.

**immerge** - v. to plunge into a liquid, e.g., blacksmithing.

**immolate** - v. to kill or destroy by sacrificial practice.

**immotile** - adj. incapable of motion.

**immure** - v. to enclose within; to wall in; imprison.

**impanation** - n. the doctrine that Christ is physically present in bread after consecration.

**impeccant** - adj. without faults; perfect.

**impedimenta** - n. objects which hinder progress.

**impercipient** - adj. not perceiving.

**impetrate** - v. to obtain by request.

**impignorate** - v. to pawn.

**impolitical** - adj. unwise; foolish.

**importune** - v. to demand urgently; to solicit persistently to the point of being troublesome.

**imprecate** - v. to curse; to invoke evil upon.

**improbity** - n. lack of principle.

**impudicity** - n. lack of shame.

**impugn** - v. to attack or assault by argument.

**impuissant** - adj. feeble; powerless.

**imputrescible** - adj. incorruptible.

**in absentia** - from Latin, meaning "in the absence of".

**incalescent** - adj. increasing in warmth.

**incept** - v. to take in, as of an organism.

**inchoate** - adj. incomplete; having just begun.

**incondite** - adj. unpolished; ill-composed.

**incursion** - n. a hostile entry into another's territory.

**incuse** - v. to form by hammering or stamping, e.g., coins, blacksmithing.

**indite** - v. to compose; to put into words.

**indigent** - adj. poor; needy; without self-sufficiency.

**indurate** - v. to harden; to make resistant.

**in flagrante delicto** - Latin, meaning "the very act of committing an offense", especially a sexual one.

**infra dignitatem** - Latin, meaning "beneath one's dignity".

**ingeminate** - v. to repeat, reiterate.

**innocuous** - adj. harmless.

**insalubrious** - adj. unhealthy.

**insentient** - adj. without feeling or sensation.

**insidious** - adj. seductively harmful; having a slow effect.

**insipid** - adj. lacking in qualities that stimulate; also, tasteless.

**insouciance** - n. light-hearted indifference.

**Instinct** - n. (German, *Instinkt*; Spanish, *instinto*) in psychology, a behavior that is peculiar and common to a species. It signifies a behavior that occurs on a timeline that seems similar in all members of the species. Moreover, it is resistant to change or elimination and seems to be part of a design within the creature.

**intellection** - n. the process of understanding.

**interdict** - v. prohibit; prevent.

**interlocutory** - adj. intermediate; not decisive.

**internecine** - adj. mutually destructive; characterized by slaughter.

**interstice** - n. a small opening between things or their parts.

**intransigent** - adj. unyielding; immovable; not to be influenced.

**intumesce** - v. to swell; to inflate; enlarge.

**intussuscept** - v. to draw in from without; invaginate.

**inure** - v. to condition the acceptance of something undesirable.

**inutile** - adj. useless.

**invective** - n. an abusive denunciation.

**inveigh** - v. to attack verbally.

**invidious** - adj. causing dislike.

**involuted** - adj. complex.

**iracund** - adj. angry; passionate.

**irascible** - adj. easily angered.

**irrecusable** - adj. not to be refused or turned down.

**irrefragable** - adj. not to be denied; impossible to refute.

**irrefrangible** - adj. not to be broken; not capable of being refracted, e.g., radiation.

**irremeable** - adj. offering no possibility of return; irreversible, e.g., a life history.

**irrupt** - v. to force in violently.

**Islam** - n. a Middle-Eastern religion, *Islam* is translated as 'peace'. *Muslim* is translated to mean 'one who submits.' Islam was founded by Mohammed (570-629 A.D.) (the last in a line of prophets including Jesus) a man known for his honesty, generosity, spirituality, and ability to reconcile conflicts. Upon his marriage to a widow named Khadija, he began a process of meditation and received Divine revelations which are recorded in the Koran.

Mohammed's concern for the poor and the politically weak became the basis of his social work. After much persecution, he established a successful community in Medina. This community became the nucleus for the eventual spread of Islam throughout the world.

Koran means 'recitation'. It is the word of Allah, eternal and unchangeable in Arabic. Moreover, no translations are considered valid. Muslims seek to memorize the full text in Arabic. It offers guidelines for daily existence, especially individual and social morality. It recommends prayer five times each day, almsgiving, and fasting during the month of Ramadan and the holy pilgrimage to Mecca. Prior religious manuscripts of Zoroastrianism, Judaism, and Christianity are considered corrupt and theologically useless for a correct understanding of the will of God.

Three principal sects exist in Sunnites, Shiites, and Sufis. Sunna means 'way' and Sunnites follow the way of Mohammed without the possibility of further interpretations or revelations. Shiites (from *Shia* meaning 'party') believe in valid successors of Mohammed, called *imams*. Sufis (*sufi* meaning 'wool clad') emphasize the inward path to salvation through meditation and asceticism.

Texts to Consult: *Islam*, Fazlur Rahman, 1979, and *What is Sufism?*, Martin Lings, 1981.

**Islamic philosophy** - n. the views and thought of the Arab world. Islamic philosophy holds an interesting place in the transmission of Greek philosophy. Greece was a major influence on the Arab world. As Greece declined, the Arab world provided the main advances in science, mathematics, medicine, literature, and philosophy. Greek-based Islamic thought played a major role in maintaining the momentum of discovery. Her principal philosophers included Al-Farabi (ca. 875-950 A.D.), Al-Ghazzali (1058-1111), Averroes (1126-1198), and Avicenna (980-1037). Through their work the preservation of Aristotelian and Platonic writings and ideas at Alexandria became the basis for educating Europe in the 12th and 13th centuries.

**isochronal** - adj. happening in an equal amount of time.

**isocracy** - n. government in which all people have an equal amount of power.

**isodose** - adj. relating to all points in a region or area having equal radioactive contamination or exposure.

**isodynamic** - adj. characterized by equality or uniformity of force.

**isogonal** - adj. having equal angles.

**isomorphism** - n. equal form; similarity of structure. Two groups of entities can be said to be isomorphic when a one-to-one correspondence can be established between members of one group and the members of another group.

**isotimic** - adj. possessing an equal quantitative value at a given time.

**jactation** - n.  excessive self-congratulation;  boasting.

**Jainism** - n.  in philosophy of religion, an Indian philosophy which teaches a type of pluralistic realism.  Embracing the notion of karma, Jainism teaches that the soul is enmeshed in a body as a result of physical attachments.  Liberation is dependent upon the three jewels (*triratna*):  1) right belief or faith (*samyag-darsana*) in Jainist teachings,  2) right knowledge (*samyag-jnana*) of nature as it is found, and 3) right conduct (*samyag-caritra*) by the values of truthfulness, detachment from things, chastity, and non-violence. Jainism is atheistic but reserves a kind of divine status for liberated souls, who are then both immortal and omniscient.  The central document of Jainism is the *Yagur Veda*. Mahavira (598-527 B.C.) was the last great teacher of Jainism.  Jainism survives today in isolated portions of India.
> Text to consult: <u>*The Jaina Path of Purification*</u>, Padmanabh Jaini, 1979.

> *"I renounce all killing of living beings, whether movable or immovable.  Nor shall I myself kill living beings not cause others to do it, nor consent to it.  As long as I live I confess, and blame, and exempt myself of these sins, in mind, speech, and body."*
> *"I renounce all vices of lying speech arising from anger or greed or fear or mirth."*
> *"I renounce all taking of anything not given, either in a village or a town or wood, either a little or much, of great or small, of living or lifeless."*
> *"I renounce all sexual pleasure.  I shall not give way to sensuality, nor cause others to do so, nor consent to their doing so."*
> *-Mahavira (attributed)*

**James, William** (1842-1910) - an American philosopher of pragmatism, James was known for his emphasis on the average person's use of philosophy.  Thus, in James one sees a strong melioristic bent.  Knowledge is for the sake of life.  Why one would want to know anything is to improve one's own existence.  James accepted this as a valid pre-supposition to thinking.

James was also a physician.  Subsequently, his views reveal the functional and biological concerns of a man of medicine.  His pragmatism emphasized truth or falsity of statements according to their ability to fulfill and satisfy our biological and emotional needs. True propositions lead to success and false propositions lead to failure. Expedience and practicality distinguish the thinking of James. As with the Greek term *pragmatikos*, James saw 'acts' or 'deeds' as the focal point of human understanding. True ideas are corroborated in actions. Verification of the merit of ideas comes from their practical application. They should be socially and individually effective.

In the occurrence of novelty, James saw proof for a pluralistic universe. Successful problem solving recognizes the existence of variety and multiplicity of choice. A universe that is monistic, absolutist, and undifferentiated would paralyze the will. Freedom to live intelligently requires options of thought and action.

Reason itself is secondary to experience. Reality is experience. Reason supplements this reality experience. Life is presented in pure sensual form, in a type of uncorrupted encounter before reason occurs. It is always somewhat beyond our rational comprehension for this reason.

Theologically, James advocates a type of theism. He perceives God as a companion, both morally and spiritually. As such, God is also limited in influence. God as finite cannot be a guarantor of a purely good world. God requires the assistance of humanity to produce good in this world.

Principal works: *Psychology, 2 vols.*, 1890, *The Will to Believe*, 1897, *Varieties of Religious Experience*, 1902, *Pragmatism*, 1907, and *The Meaning of Truth*, 1909.

*"The whole function of philosophy ought to be to find out what definite difference it will make to you and me, at definite instants of our life, if this world formula or that world formula be the true one."*
                    William James, <u>Pragmatism</u>

*"My experience is what I agree to attend to. Only those items which I 'notice' shape my mind - without selective interest, experience is an utter chaos. Interest alone gives accent and emphasis, light and shade, background and foreground - intelligible perspective, in a word. It varies in every creature, but without it the consciousness of every creature would be a gray chaotic indiscriminateness, impossible for us even to conceive."*
                    William James, <u>Psychology</u>

*"Outside of their own business, the ideas gained by men before they are twenty-five are practically the only ideas they shall have in their lives. They cannot get anything new. Disinterested curiosity is past, the mental grooves and channels set, the power of assimilation gone. If by chance we ever do learn anything about some entirely new topic we are afflicted with a strange sense of insecurity, and we fear to advance a resolute opinion. But with things learned in the plastic days of instinctive curiosity we never lose entirely our sense of being at home. There remains a kinship, a sentiment of intimate acquaintance, which, even when we know we have failed to keep abreast of the subject, flatters us with a sense of power over it, and makes us feel not altogether out of the pale."*
                    William James, <u>Psychology</u>

**jejune** - adj. uninteresting; lacking significance.

**jihad** - n.  Moslem holy war; originally signifying the inner struggle or war of the soul within the individual disciple of Islam, *jihad* gradually became a reference to political militance as well.

**jinn** - n.  Islamic spirit or angel.

**jocose** - adj.  inclined to joking; wittiness.

**john** - n.  a prostitute's client.

**Judaism** - n. a Middle-Eastern religion, whose detectable origins go back to about 1,800 B.C.  It represents the first religion to clearly affirm a theology of monotheism.

Judaism emphasizes God's creation of the world out of nothing, the selective preference for "the Chosen People of God", the finitude of humanity and its dependence on God, the linear nature of time in which God is seen as a supernatural influence, and a theology of hope: that God will re-establish His "Covenant" through the coming of a Messiah.

Judaism relies heavily on its traditions and rituals to separate itself from the Gentile world, which it views as a consequence of the alienation from God.  Moreover, the survival of Judaism has been spiritually master-minded through the metaphysics of suffering, wherein suffering is seen as a natural feature of this world and a type of crisis turned to advantage in the assumption that Divine justice will prevail.

Traditional social divisions include: (1) Sadducees - those who saw Judaism primarily through its written traditions, particularly the *Torah* (the Old Testament and Jewish theology in general), (2) Pharisees - a rabbinic element who saw the oral traditions as equally important with written law, and (3) Essenes - a monastic element, which emphasized spirituality and ascetic practices to be the true core of Judaism. These divisions have played an important role in the subsequent theology of Judaism.

Texts to consult: *Old Testament Theology*, 2 vols., Gerhard von Rad, *The History of Israel,* Martin Noth, and *Prophetic Faith,* Martin Buber.

> *"As long as Judaism continues, nobody will be able to say that the soul of man has allowed itself to be subjugated."*
> *- Leo Baeck, The Essence of Judaism*

> *"The emancipation of the Jews in its last significance is the emancipation of mankind from Judaism."*
> *- Karl Marx, On the Jewish Question*

**Juliana of Norwich** (1342-1413) - n.  an English philosopher and mystic, she used her religious experiences as the basis of spiritual meditations on the meaning  and nature of life.   Influenced by Neoplatonism and St. John of the Cross, she reasoned that faith, prayer, and the love of God are central influences on the correct formation of the personality.   She claimed that the absence of Divine reality and presence of evil is cured by the spiritual effects of Divine Love.

Principal work: *The Sixteen Revelations of Divine Love*, 1385.

**Jung, Carl Gustav** (1875-1961) - a Swiss psychologist and a temporary supporter of Freudian theories, Jung moved into more metaphysical concerns regarding the nature of the self. In particular, Jung developed important views on the extrovert and introvert personality types, the notion of archetypes and their relation to the unconscious, and the way in which archetypes are found in the religions, myths, and art of human beings.

Jung's views were tangled up with his own religious and moral searching. He never resolved the issue of God's existence, though he made faint progress in a book entitled *Answer to Job*, 1952. And, during a part of his life he used painting to explore the meaning of symbols and was attracted to the Eastern use of *mandalas*, symbols having four parts to represent self-unity. Jung interpreted the *mandalas* to be connected with the struggle of the conscious and unconscious, as well as discordant parts of the personality, especially as a means of avoiding personal disintegration. Within its archetypal symbolism, God the Father is a projection of the self in its most idealistic form.

Jung also developed an alternate view of Freud's death wish. For Jung, an archetype he called the Shadow, represented the hidden tendency to self-destruct. The Shadow archetype was used to explain the often disastrous choices people make, bringing misfortune on themselves.

Principal works include: *Psychological Types*, 1921, *In Search of a Soul*, 1933, *The Structure and Dynamics of the Psyche*, 1940, *Archetypes and the Collective Unconscious*, 1950, *The Practice of Psychotherapy*, and *The Development of Personality*.

> *"Freud has unfortunately overlooked the fact that man has never been able single-handedly to hold his own against the powers of darkness, that is, of the unconscious. Man has always stood in need of the spiritual help which each individual's own religion held out to him. It is religion which lifts him out of his distress."*
>
> - Carl Jung, <u>In Search of a Soul</u>

Text to consult: <u>The Portable Jung</u>, ed. Joseph Campbell.

**junta** - n. group rule established by revolutionary seizure of power.

**juration** - n. the administration of an oath.

**juvenescence** - n. the state of being young or growing young.

**kainophobia** - n. intense fear of that which is new.

**kakistocracy** - n. government by the worst people in a society.

**Kant, Immanuel** (1724-1804) - a German philosopher, whose work exercised a vast influence on modern philosophy. Kant was able to form a reconciliation of empiricism and rationalism, arguing that knowledge is derived from experience but it is organized according to innate *a priori* rational principles. This distinction in turn divides judgments into a) analytic and b) synthetic.

Analytic judgments are logically complete. These are judgments (statements) which possess a type of necessary connection between the nouns they contain, e.g. "All carpenters are craftsmen." Whereas, synthetic judgments are logically contingent. These are judgments (statements) which lack a necessary connection between the nouns they contain, e.g. "All carpenters have ten fingers." Analytic judgments are *a priori* (necessary), while synthetic judgments are *a posteriori* (probable). From this, Kant derives a sentential hybrid called a *synthetic a priori*. The synthetic a priori is a judgment (statement) necessarily true but whose nouns are separately incapable of producing the inherent necessity of truth that the synthetic judgment asserts, e.g. "7 plus 5 give us 12". Separately, 7 or 5 do not automatically imply 12.

Kant agreed with Hume that experience brings something to the mind, but Kant also argued that the mind, as an active rational agent, does something with experiences. Mind organizes experience. This is referred to as "Kant's Copernican Revolution".

Kant's concern with the "moral law within" produced a duty-based moral theory, deontological ethics. Good is defined as a good will, a will guided by what one "ought" to do. Kant's "categorical imperative" emphasizes the role of duty toward the good; good for its own sake.

Principal works: *Critique of Pure Reason*, 1781, *Foundations of the Metaphysics of Morals*, 1785, *Critique of Practical Reason*, 1788, and *Critique of Judgment*.

> *"A good will is good not because of what it performs or effects, not by its aptness for the attainment of some proposed end, but simply by virtue of the volition; That is, it is good in itself, and considered by itself is to be esteemed*

*much higher than all that can be brought about by it in favour of any inclination."*

*Immanuel Kant, Foundations of the Metaphysics of Morals*

*"There is . . . but one categorical imperative, namely this: Act only on that maxim whereby thou canst at the same time will that it should become a universal law."*

*Immanuel Kant, Foundations of the Metaphysics of Morals*

*"Reason never has an immediate relation to an object; it relates immediately to the understanding alone. It is only through the understanding that it can be employed in the field of experience. It does not form conceptions of objects, it merely arranges them and gives them that unity which they are capable of possessing when the sphere of their application has been extended as widely as possible."*

*Immanuel Kant, Critique of Pure Reason*

**katabasis** - n.  a military retreat.

**Kathenotheism** - n.  in the philosophy of religion, Vedic monotheism. The spectrum of gods is structured so that one God is honored at a time, without entailing non-belief of the other gods who are, in a way, regarded as dormant.  The term 'kathenotheism' was coined by Friedrich Max Muller (1823-1900).  One of the most learned individuals of his day, Muller was a comparative philologist at Oxford with a special interest in Eastern religions.  His work included: *History of Ancient Sanskrit Literature*, 1859, *The Sacred Books of the East*, 1875, *The Origin and Growth of Religion*, 1878.

**katzen jammer** - n.  a hangover;  distress, moral or physical.

**Keynes, John Maynard** (1883-1946) - an English logician and economist, Keynes was at home in a number of fields: journalism, business, and philosophy.  Keynes revolutionized economic philosophy after 1930.  Economic theorists prior to Keynes argued for the quantity theory of money (Say's Law) and the flexibility of wages, holding that unemployment can be countered by lower wages with the same quantity of money in circulation.  In Keynesian theory, full employment is the exception in a normal economy. So, governmental stimulation of jobs is necessary to a degree.  Moreover, Keynes argued for policies which control inflationary pressure.

Keynes did not approve of Marxist theory and viewed it as a threat to individualism.  He sought adjustments in capitalism to insure full employment and create price stability, but he did not have confidence in strong forms of socialism, due primarily to the psychological features of human existence.  Human interrelationships are impossible to control and predict beyond certain general principles.  The egoism that is often manifested in primitive capitalism is just as real in advanced forms of socialism and can only be countered by a rational-legal model of competition.

Principal works: *A Treatise on Probability*, 1921, and *General Theory of Employment, Interest, and Money*, 1936.

*"Money . . . serves two principal purposes. By acting as a money of account, it facilitates exchanges without its being necessary that it should ever itself come into the picture as a*
*substantive object. In this respect it is a convenience which is devoid of significance or real influence. In the second place, it is a store of wealth. So we are told, without a smile on the face. But in the world of classical economy, what an insane use to which to put it! For it is a recognized characteristic of money as a store of wealth that it is barren; whereas practically every other form of storing wealth yields some interest or profit. Why should anyone outside a lunatic asylum wish to use money as a store of wealth?"*

*"The owner of wealth, who has been induced not to hold his wealth in the shape of hoarded money, still has two alternatives between which to choose. He can lend his money at the current rate of money-interest or he can purchase some kind of capital- asset. Clearly in equilibrium these two alternatives must offer an equal advantage to the marginal investor in each of them. This is brought about by shifts in the money-prices of capital-assets relative to the price of money loans. The prices of capital-assets move until, having regard to their prospective yields and account being taken of all those elements of doubt and uncertainty, interested and disinterested advice, fashion, convention, and what else you will, which affect the mind of the investor, they offer an equal apparent advantage to the marginal investor who is wavering between one kind of investment and another."*

*John Keynes, <u>General Theory</u>*

**Kierkegaard, Soren** (1813-1855) - a Danish philosopher of existentialism, Kierkegaard reacted against the systematic idealism of G.W.F. Hegel emphasizing the subjective nature of truth. Truth is particular to each person's mental construction. What is universal alone is the necessity of choice. Each person is confronted with choosing a life, a commitment, that is objectively uncertain. In this special irrationalist stance, Kierkegaard argues that reason does not offer us the kinds of security we seek. People who are well educated (rational) may still be quite unhappy and very unsuccessful.

Kierkegaard believed in three stages of being: the *aesthetic*, the *ethical*, and the *religious*. The *aesthetic* stage is a life of impulse and emotion; the individual has no specific moral or religious beliefs and exercises no limits over questions of sensual life. The aesthetic stage denies spirit, eventually producing a feeling of despair and anxiety. The individual is then confronted with a continuation of this emptiness or a choice is made to go beyond it to the *ethical* stage ("either/or" is the term Kierkegaard uses to describe this crisis of choice). In abandoning the sensual life, the individual accepts moral and legal limits to action. Acts like marriage exhibit the essence of this stage. There is a commitment to moral direction and completeness. But moral self-sufficiency, too, has limited meaning. In fact, living up to moral self-sufficiency is too difficult and ushers in feelings of guilt, which Kierkegaard sees as the onset of another crisis of meaning. The individual is again confronted by a feeling of emptiness which can only be transcended by entering the *religious* stage, which is a personal encounter with God. In the personal, subjective, encounter with God the individual encounters true self-fulfillment.

Principal works: *The Concept of Irony*, 1841, *Either/Or*, 1843, *Fear and Trembling*, 1843, *Philosophical Fragments*, 1844, *The Present Age*, 1847, *Works of Love*, 1848, and *Sickness Unto Death*, 1849.

> *"Faith is the highest passion in a man. There are perhaps many in every generation who do not even reach it, but no one gets further."*
> Soren Kierkegaard, *Fear and Trembling*

**kinesiology** - n. the study of human muscles, including musculature and movement.

**kinetosis** - n. motion sickness.

**kinetic** - adj. dynamic; active; having to do with the energy and motion of material bodies.

**King, Martin Luther** (1929-1968) - n. an American philosopher of social ethics and reform, who was the principal leader of the civil rights movement in the United States from 1960-1968. He received the Nobel Prize for Peace in 1964 for his social effectiveness. His philosophy garnered opposition from both Blacks and Whites, and he was assassinated in 1968.

His thinking was deeply influenced by Gandhi, especially his commitment to *ahimsa* (non-violence) and the views of Christ, especially the Sermon on the Mount. King spent time during his doctoral research investigating the theology of Alfred North Whitehead and came to accept the importance of process philosophy.

Principal works: *Stride Toward Freedom*, 1958, *Why We Can't Wait*, 1964, and *Where Do We Go From Here: Chaos or Community?*, 1967.

> *"Power properly understood is the ability to achieve purpose. It is the strength required to bring about social, political, or economic changes. In this sense power is not only desireable but necessary to implement the demands of love and justice. One of the greatest problems of history is that the concepts of love and power are usually contrasted as polar opposites. Love is identified with a resignation of power and power with a denial of love. It was this misinterpretation that caused Nietzsche, the philosopher of the "will to power", to reject the Christian concept of love. It was the same misinterpretation which induced Christian theologians to reject Nietzsche's philosophy of the "will to power" in the name of the Christian idea of love. What is needed is a realization that power without love is reckless and abusive and that love without power is sentimental and anemic. Power at its best is love implementing the demands of justice. Justice at its best is love correcting everything that stands against love."*
>
> Martin Luther King, Jr., *Where Do We Go From Here: Chaos or Community?*

**kiosk** - n. an open summerhouse; pavilion.

**kitsch** - n. writing of shallow, popular appeal.

**kleptomania** - n. compulsive stealing, often of objects which have no real intrinsic worth.

**koan** - n. a Zen Buddhist puzzle designed to reduce attachment to reason and bring about intuitive enlightenment.

> *"What was the appearance of your face before your ancestors were born?"*
> *- Zen koan*

**koniology** - n. the study of impurities in the air.

**krummholz** - n. a forest of stunted timberline trees; alpine boundary.

**kshatriya** - n. in Hinduism, an individual of an upper caste, especially one in government or military leadership.

**kudo** - n. award, honor, praise.

**Kyudo** - n. in Japanese philosophy, the practice of archery as a means of physical, spiritual, and moral development. In *kyudo* it is believed that three elements guide the soul: truth, goodness, and beauty. Truth is modeled in *kyudo* as right-mindedness. The archer must have the correct mental outlook *(seishahichu)* as well as great skill *(noshahichu)* in handling his or her equipment. A perfect shot lying in the center of the target, *tekichu*, must be achieved in the correct way.

Goodness is the second element of *kyudo*. The arrow's flight is spoiled by destructive emotions. The sound made by the bowstring *(tsurune)* reveals the level of tension in the body of the archer. The good archer is a person whose emotions are balanced; the mind is calm and well-disciplined. This state of being is called *heijoshin*, ordinary mind. Moreover, the archer's relation to other archers is marked by courtesy and compassion.

Beauty is the third element of *kyudo*. Without the first two elements *kyudo* cannot be beautiful, but beauty is also extended to the appearance of the bow, the arrows themselves, and the attire of the archer. The actions of the archer are marked by correct etiquette and the archery range *(kyudojo)* is maintained with attention to the general themes of grace, dignity, and tranquility.

The origins of *kyudo* go back to about 7,000 B.C. in the hunting life of the earliest known inhabitants of the Japanese islands, the *Jomon* people. Through time it came under the influence of tribal warfare, advanced military use, and most of all Zen. Zen emphasized the importance of balanced effort, the working of the spirit, and the discovery of ultimate reality.

Text to consult: *Kyudo: The Essence and Practice of Japanese Archery,* Dan and Jackie Deprospero, with Hideharu Onuma, 1993.

**labefaction** - n. weakening, downfall.

**labile** - adj. readily open to change; unstable.

**labyrinth** - n. a place full of intricate passageways and blind alleys.

**laconic** - adj. brief, concise in speech.

**lacrimation** - n. excessive secretion of tears.

**lacuna** - n. a gap; a missing portion.

**lacustrine** - adj. relating to a lake.

**lagan** - n. debris or objects thrown into the sea with a buoy attached so as to be found.

**Lakota, Oglala** - n. in the study of religion, the spiritual traditions of the Sioux. Among the principal features of Lakota philosophy is the *circle* and its *center*. The cirlce represents the cosmos and thus the camp is laid in the fashion of *the sacred hoop,* with its entrance facing the east. The Lakota home, *tipi,* also embodies the spirituality of the circle and its center. Inherent within its meaning is the principal of unity, tribally, individually, and ecologically.

Among other elements, the sacred pipe or *chanunpa wakan,* is the most valued holy object of the Lakota. Its use promotes the spiritual union of the Lakota people with the surrounding universe. As sacred smoke rises and drifts, it is part of a praying for and with everything.

*Hanblecheya* or "crying for a vision", is a ritual of catharsis. The person seeks purification through fasting for 3-4 days. During this ascetic practice, the individual awaits a vision. The vision resembles the advice of sacred animals or thunder spirits, bestowing holiness and spiritual wisdom.

Upon the death of a Lakota, the soul may be kept, *wanagi yuhapi,* for a period to mark the spiritual significance of death. The deceased's hair is cut and placed with a sacred pipe in a deerskin sleeve, the rolled into a bundle and kept in its own *tipi.* This ritual is concluded by a great feast to mark the release of the soul, with possessions being given away to honor the spiritual nature of the nomadic life.

*Inikagapi* is the practice of the sweat lodge, symbolizing "renewed life. A construction of willow branches and buffalo skins create a dome representing the universe. Participants in this purification process leave behind their impure habits and meditate on who they really, emptying their egotistical tendencies in favor of humility toward the Mother Earth.

Texts to Consult: *Black Elk: the Sacred Ways of a Lakota* , Wallace Black Elk and William Lyon, 1990. *Lame Deer, Seeker of Visions*, John Lame Deer, 1972. *How to Take Part in Lakota Ceremonies*, William Stolzman, S.J., 1986.

**lallation** - n. infantile babbling; the repetition of sounds without logical structure.

**lalophobia** - n. excessive fear of speaking.

**lam** - n. sudden or hurried flight, especially from the law.

**lama** - n. in Tibetan Buddhism, "superior one"; a reference to a spiritual preceptor or monk.

**lambent** - adj. a surface effect; having soft radiance; dealing softly and expertly with a topic.

**lamia** - n. a female demon; vampire; a woman of a particularly vicious character.

**lampoon** - n. light ridicule.

**lancinate** - v. to pierce.

**languid** - adj. weak, sluggish, listless.

**languor** - n. weakness, especially of body and mind; weariness.

**Lao Tzu** (ca. 500 B.C.) - a Chinese philosopher and the founder of Taoism, Lao Tzu had obvious concern for the deplorable social conditions of his time. While Confucius attempted to heal the problems of China with an emphasis upon human goodness, Lao Tzu emphasized a spiritual union with the natural world.

*Tao* is the reference to a spiritual path. Humans must use their consciousness to discern the workings of the *Tao* in their life. Within this logic is the assumption that things work toward perfection naturally, and the problems of human existence stem from a resistance to the natural flow of reality. In laying out his remedy to the puzzle of existence, Lao Tzu taught the following points:

1. Desire seems to rule the life of humanity. It is the motive behind most human action.
2. The strife of society is caused by competing for the things which desire seeks.
3. Morality is a tool to promote harmony in society and put checks on desire.
4. Morality is useless, since the guidelines of moral philosophies do not prevent the evil from working the world to their own satisfaction. Plus, the principles of morality seem to change with the passage of time.

5. It is necessary to go beyond morality in order to find true harmony and happiness.

6. Going beyond morality can only be achieved by abandoning the desires which necessitate the creation of moral philosophies.

7. Transcending desire requires an acceptance of the *Tao*.

8. The creation of a better society rests upon the education of the people in the way of the *Tao*.

Principal work: *Tao-Te Ching (The Way and Its Virtue).*

> *"Who is rich in character is like a child.*
> *No poisonous insects sting him,*
> *No wild beasts attack him,*
> *And no birds of prey pounce upon him.*
> *His bones are soft, his sinews tender, yet his grip is strong.*
> *Not knowing the union of male and female, yet his organs are complete, which means his vigor is unspoiled.*
> *Crying the whole day, yet his voice never runs hoarse, which means his natural harmony is perfect.*
> *To know harmony is to be in accord with the eternal, and to know eternity is called discerning. But to improve upon life is called an ill-omen; to let go the emotions through impulse is called assertiveness. For things age after reaching their prime; that assertiveness would be against Tao. He who is against Tao perishes young."*
>
> *-Lao Tzu, Tao-Te Ching*

**lapactic** - adj. aperient; causing a purge.

**lapidate** - v. to stone to death.

**largess** - n. ample giving of money or gifts; innate generosity of mind and spirit; sometimes ostentatious giving as if to an inferior.

**lascivious** - adj. wanton; lustful.

**latent** - adj. existing but not yet manifest.

**latitudinarian** - n. one who is liberal and open in religious belief and conduct.

**lavation** - n. the act of washing.

**Law, William** (1686-1761) - an English theologian and mystical philosopher who defined knowledge as a communion between the one who knows and that which is known. His ideas were conveyed in the example of divine self-communication as love. Thus, his philosophical and theological work was devoted to establishing the importance of the Christian life and maintaining the validity of faith as opposed to strict rationalism. Law insisted that God and reality are more complex than rationalism allows and that spiritual intuitive knowledge is necessary for a real understanding of life.

Principal works: *Christian Perfection*, 1726, *A Serious Call to a Devout and Holy Life*, 1728, and *The Spirit of Prayer*, 1749.

*"The Spirit of Prayer is a pressing forth of the soul out of this earthly life. It is a stretching with all its desire after the life of God."*

William Law, <u>The Spirit of Prayer</u>

*"The one who has learned to pray has learned the greatest secret of a holy and happy life.*

William Law, <u>Christian Perfection</u>

**Laws of thought** - n. in traditional logic, three foundational principles regarded as a basis to all logical reasoning: 1) Law of Identity - "whatever is, is" or "A is A", 2) Law of Non-contradiction - "Contradictories cannot both be true" or "A is not not-A", 3) Law of the Excluded Middle - "Contradictories cannot both be false" or "Everything is either A or not A". In modern logic these traditional suppositions are regarded as tautologies.

Text to Consult: <u>Introduction to Logic,</u> Irving Copi & Carl Cohen.

**Lebensraum** - n. German, meaning the space necessary for life, growth and self-sufficiency.

**Leibniz, Gottfried Wilhelm** (1646-1716) - a German philosopher of the rationalist school, Leibniz presented a theory of matter similar to 20th Century notions in physics. According to Leibniz, the universe is composed of 'monads', which he described as a type of eternal energy without shape or size. Each monad is an independent entity with its own created purpose. Leibniz intended monads to operate as metaphysical elements or the foundation of empirical reality.

Leibniz encountered problems with the notion of freedom and found it difficult to rid his system of deterministic features. The idea of built-in or created purposes was partly countered with the idea of self-development, which was described as change that is free of forces applied from without.

The problem of evil, for Leibniz, is handled as the absence of perfection. God created the best possible world, not the best world. Creation is made of limited objects, thus the existence of imperfection is a necessary consequence of such objects. Evil or imperfection is not incompatible with a loving God. Moreover, it is necessary for the moral requirements of a universe that evil exist.

God is a perfect monad and represents the source of general harmony throughout the universe. Humanity, being limited and imperfect, suffers from limited understandings. God, however, as the perfect highest being transcends all monads.

Leibniz's view of knowledge argues that universal and necessary truth is based solely on logical principles and cannot be derived from experience. The universe is primarily built on a logical-mathematical model.

Principal works: *Meditations on Knowledge, Truth, and Ideas*, 1664, *Discourse on Metaphysics*, 1686, *On the Origin of Things*, 1696, and *Monadology*, 1714.

There are two kinds of truth: *"those of reasoning and those of fact. Truths of reasoning are necessary and their opposite is impossible: truths of fact are contingent and their opposite is possible. When a truth is necessary, its reason can be found by analysis, resolving it into more simple ideas and truths, until we come to those which are primary."*
*G.W. Leibniz, <u>Monadology</u>*

**leitmotiv** - n.  a dominant or recurring theme.

**lemma** - n.  the starting point in a proof;  a statement allowed as 'true' to begin argumentation.

**Lenin, Vladimir Ilyich** (1870-1924) - a Russian Marxist philosopher and political leader whose real name was V.I. Ulyanov.  As early as 1887 Lenin began to establish a reputation for strong-willed resistance to authority, perhaps as the direct result of the arrest and hanging of his brother, Aleksandr, who was convicted of plotting against the Czar.  A steady philosophical development produced a loyalty and devotion to the ideas of Karl Marx and Friedrich Engels. The Marxist ideology fit well with his upbringing, which emphasized deep concern for the welfare of others.  He led the Bolsheviks from 1903, and after the revolution of 1917, he headed the Soviet Union until his death.

Lenin's influence on modern Communism produced the label "Marxism-Leninism".  Ideologically, Lenin was a Hegelian who, like Marx, saw no difficulty in using the idea of 'dialectic' along with a materialist position.  In fact, Lenin believed there was no difference between dialectic, logic and epistemology.

Lenin went beyond the principles and tactics of Marx's theory of social reconstruction, especially in his cry to establish a "dictatorship of the proletariat."  This entailed the destruction of the bourgeois state machinery.  This conclusion was derived from the 'oppositional' nature of dialectical thought, which for Lenin meant the destruction of the thesis by the anti-thesis.   Lenin's emphasis was "from each according to his ability, and to each according to his need."  In constructing his strongest version of Marxism, Lenin pictured a withering away of the state and the pure classless society outlined by Marx.

Principal work: *State and Revolution.*

*"The teaching of Marx and Engels regarding the inevitability of a violent revolution refers to the bourgeois state.  It cannot be replaced by the proletarian state through "withering away", but as a general rule, only through a violent revolution . . .  The replacement of the bourgeois by the proletariat state is impossible without a violent revolution.  The abolition of the proletarian state, i.e. of all states, is only possible through "withering away".*
*Lenin, <u>State and Revolution</u>*

**lentic** - adj.  living in still water, e.g., swamps, ponds.

**lestobiosis** - n.  a form of living characterized by furtive or secret stealing;  as one of the ways a society is ordered, e.g., ant communities.

111

**levity** - n.  lack of seriousness; frivolity.

**lexiphonic** - adj.  pretentious, showy, bombastic, especially with speech and words.

**lex talionis** - from Latin, meaning law of retaliation.

**li** - n.  in Confucianism, a reference to propriety and etiquette;  external forms of order and ceremony which serve to cover the possible roughness of inner tendencies.

**libertine** - n.  one who is unrestrained by conventions and morality; one who lives a dissolute existence.

**Libido** - n.  in psychoanalysis, the unconscious energy through which life instincts (often the sexual instinct or drive) perform their function;  for Jung, life energy or psychic energy.  For Freud, the libido represents energy stemming from the sexual instinct;  manifested in three areas of behavior, (1) displacement of cathexes (object of sexual craving), (2) sublimation (non-sexual behavior used to soften the pressure of sexual craving), and (3) the erotic parts of the body (the somatic evidence of stimulation, attended by a mental awareness of erotogenic zones).
    Texts to Consult: _Three Essays on the Theory of Sexuality_ and _Group Psychology and the Analysis of the Ego._ Sigmund Freud.

**libidinous** - adj.  lustful;  referrring to "pressure" to act out sexual desires.

**licentious** - adj.  lacking legal or moral restraint, especially sexual;  marked disregard for rules and correctness.

**ligature** - n.  a binding up.

**liparous** - adj.  having an obese physique.

**litany** - n.  a prayer consisting of invocations and supplications by the leader with responses by the congregation;  also, a long monotonous narration.

**lithe** - adj.  characterized by grace and flexibility.

**loath** - adj.  unwilling;  disinclined to act against one's interests.

**loathe** - v.  to show disgust;  to detest.

**Locke, John** (1632-1704) - an English philosopher of empiricism and political thought, Locke is best known for the view that mind is a _tabula rasa_ or blank slate.  Locke rejects the rationalist view that ideas are innate, since reflection only follows sensation.  All ideas stem from experience.  If there were innate ideas such as "God" or "numbers", Locke argued, it would not be necessary to introduce these ideas to children.
    Locke's epistemology divides ideas into simple and complex  types.  Basically, simple ideas are those received passively through the senses or originating with

elementary reflection on experience. Complex ideas are those actively synthesized by analysis. An extension of this distinction moved on to the identification of primary and secondary qualities. Basically, a primary quality of an object is (reality) one inherent in the object, such as shape and size. Secondary qualities are (appearance) sensory qualities, such as color, taste, and sound.

Locke's political thought starts with observations on the state of nature, arguing somewhat optimistically that peace and self-restraint are natural boundaries of action, since violating the welfare of others leads to open conflict and thus, self-harm. Still, the crude conditions of a natural state require some refinement, made possible by civil government. The state acts as guarantor of life, freedom, and property. If governments should be dissolved through revolution, it would be with the aim of perfecting or improving upon the quality of sovereignty.

Locke was religiously inclined toward Christianity and accepted the divinity of Christ, the principal virtues of faith, charity, and love, as well as the concept of God as a father. He believed in the theological validity of the New Testament and argued that it was consonant with human rationality.

Principal works: *On Toleration*, 1689, *Two Treatises on Government*, 1689, *Essay Concerning Human Understanding*, 1690, and *Thoughts on Education*, 1693.

> ". . . suppose the mind to be, as we say, white paper, void of all characters, without any ideas: How comes it to be furnished? Whence comes it by that vast store which the busy and boundless fancy of man has painted on it with almost endless variety? . . . To this I answer, in one word, 'experience'. In that all knowledge is founded; and from that it ultimately derives itself. Our observation employed either, about external sensible objects, or about the internal operations of our minds perceived and reflected on by ourselves, is that which supplies our understanding with all the materials of thinking."
>
> John Locke, Essay Concerning Human Understanding

> "The great skill of a teacher is to get and keep the attention of his scholar; whilst he has that, he is sure to advance as fast as the learner's abilities will carry him; and without that, all his bustle and pother will be to little or no purpose. To attain this, he should make the child comprehend, as much as may be, the usefulness of what he teaches him, and let him see, by what he has learned, that he can do something which he could not do before; something which gives him some power and real advantage above others who are ignorant of it. To this he should add sweetness in all his instructions, and by a certain tenderness in his whole carriage make the child sensible that he loves and designs nothing but his good, the only way to beget love in the child, which will make him hearken to his lessons . . . "
>
> John Locke, Concerning Education

**Logic** - n. a branch of philosophy which characterizes the difference between correct and incorrect reasoning. It recognizes two kinds of argumentation, a) *deduction* - which is the use of sentential arrangements or forms that force the acceptance of their conclusions, and

b) *induction* - which is the use of case examples to provide partial support for conclusions. Deductive arguments are judged 'valid' or 'invalid', while inductive arguments are judged somewhere between 'strong' and 'weak'. Arguments are not judged 'true' or 'false'. These values are applied only to statements. Thus, it is technically wrong to regard arguments as true or false; this usually indicates the absence of training in critical thinking.

An example of a valid deductive argument:

> *Terrorists are a danger to society.*
> *John is a terrorist.*
> *So, John is a danger to society.*

An example of a moderately strong inductive argument:

> *5,000 rats on a diet of aspartame (NutraSweet) showed no ill-effects over a 5-year period. So, aspartame is safe for human consumption.*

Philosophers agree that logic is the most important branch of philosophy to understand since all other theories in all other fields are dependent upon its principles and methods of analysis to test their value as forms of knowledge. Logic includes the study of definition, language, conflict resolution, rules of inference, axiomatic reasoning, probability, quantification theory, predicate calculus, metalogic, modal logic, Greek logic, scientific hypothesis, and general proof theory.

Text to Consult: *Introduction to Logic,* Irving Copi & Carl Cohen.

**logion** - n. proverb, adage; also, a saying of Christ.

**logomachy** - n. a dispute over words; controversy marked by verbal entanglement.

**logorrhea** - n. unnecessary and incoherent chatter; excessive talkativeness.

**lollygag** - v. to waste time; dawdle.

**longanimity** - n. patience.

**loquacious** - adj. talkative; garrulous; inability to remain silent.

**lorica** - n. a defensive covering, especially of bones, scales, or plates, e.g., fish.

**losel** - n. a useless person.

**lothario** - n. a man whose life revolves around seducing and deceiving women; a rake.

**lotic** - adj. living in moving water, e.g., rivers, streams.

**lout** - n. an awkward person; a clown.

**lucent** - adj.  glowing, especially with light; marked by clarity.

**lucid** - adj.  being easily understood.

**lucubration** - n.  night study, night work;  laborious involvement.

**luculent** - adj.  convincing thought or expression; clear.

**lues** - n.  disease, plague, syphilis.

**luetic** - adj.  being diseased; morally decadent.

**lugubrious** - adj.  morbid, gloomy;  seemingly permanent state of mourning.

**lumen** - n.  a measurement of the rate of transmission of light.

**luminescence** - n.  the cold transmission of light.

**luminous** - adj.  enlightened, intelligent.

**lurch** - v.  to move about secretly;  loiter;  steal.

**lurdane** - n.  a dull ignorant fool.

**lurid** - adj.  invoking terror;  gruesome;  causing horror.

**Luther, Martin** (1483-1546) - a Christian monk and theologian who led the Protestant Reformation, Luther was theologically influenced by William of Ockham and St. Augustine.  It was especially through Augustine that Luther received extra inspiration to attack reason and philosophy as "the Devil's whore".  Luther's judgment in general was completely affected by his personal struggle to correct the unprecendented decay in the ecclesiastical structure of the Church, manifested in his literary style.  (He also struggled all his life with the nightmares of his childhood, brought on by the vicious and bloody attacks by his father and mother, who believed that all children are born as demons requiring frequent whippings.) Nonetheless, he was known as a powerful orator with a strong command of language, whose pessimism about this world led straight to the condemnation of human efforts to succeed without God.

Luther's personal quest for a relationship with God led to the doctrine of salvation by faith alone *(sola fide)*.  According to Luther, without a Christo-centric orientation humanity is completely influenced by evil and utterly lost in vanity and hopelessness.  Somewhat logically, the theology of Luther was decidedly Pauline.

Luther's reformation theology emphasized the *"priesthood of all believers"*. This in itself pleased many who had a pure contempt for the Vatican.  Now each person could be a ministerial follower of Christ.

Principal work: *Luthers Werke - Kritische Gesamtausgabe*, 1883.

*"The world is a drunken peasant. If you lift him into the saddle on one side, he will fall off on the other side. One can't help him no matter how one tries. He wants to be the devil's."*
  Martin Luther, *Table Talk*

*"To him that believeth not in Christ, not only all his sins are damnable, but even his good works are also his sins."*
  Martin Luther, *Commentary on Galatians*

**lycanthrope** - n.  a werewolf.

**lycanthropy** - n.  a state of insanity in which the individual believes one's self to be a wolf.

**lyssophobia** - n.  fear of going insane.

**macerate** - v.  to reduce or waste away, especially by fasting.

**Machiavelli, Niccolo** (1469-1527) - an Italian political philosopher, famous for the phrase, "The end justifies the means".  Machiavelli argued a type of political egoism on the assumption that every successful political leader develops a double-standard of operation in order to acquire power: one for rulers and one for the ruled.  Rulers should give people the impression that they are sincere, religious, moral, and concerned about the interests of the population.  Then, they should enact another agenda for personal control, one that is built upon craftiness and the calculated deployment of power.  It is important to notice that pagans rule the world because they are fierce, unlike Christians, who are meek and humble and, thus, unsuccessful.

Machiavelli believed people are not loyal to one master and change loyalties with their own best interests.  Rulers should know this.  Rulers should also watch carefully those closest to them, for they are often the source of treachery, being interested in their own advancement at the expense of others.  While a ruler should feign virtue, ruthlessness must sometimes be used, for it is better to be feared than loved.  Public executions are useful to ensure security of the state, for it is important for people to see the consequences of disloyalty and helps them take the ruler seriously.  Moreover, the ruler must maintain a powerful, well-disciplined military force to preserve independence.

Principal works:  *The Prince*, 1513, *The Art of War*, 1520, *Mandragola*, 1524, and *Discourses*, 1532.

> *"A prince need not actually have all the qualities I have enumerated, but it is absolutely necessary that he seem to have them.  Indeed, I shall even venture to assert that there is a danger in having those qualities and always respecting them.  It is useful to seem, and actually to be, compassionate, faithful, humane, frank, and pious.  Yet a prince's mind should be so enlightened that when you do not need to have these qualities, you have the knowledge and the ability to become the opposite."*
>
> N. Machiavelli, <u>The Prince</u>

**machismo** - n.  excessive masculinity;  the opposite of homosexual femininity.

**macro** -  adj. Greek prefix meaning "large".

117

**macula** - n.  spot or blemish; imperfection.

**maelstrom** - n.  a powerful streaming force, capable of sucking in objects coming near it; reference to any destructive turbulence.

**maenad** - n.  a female participant in Dionysian rituals;  an unnaturally frenzied or lustful woman.

**magnanimity** - n.  the quality of being generous, understanding, especially in the way of sacrifices and bearing trouble patiently.

**magnum** - n.  a large bottle of wine, about 50 ounces or more.

**maieutics** - n.  the Socratic method of instruction;  drawing ideas from ideas; stemming from the Greek 'maia' (midwife).

**malediction** - n.  a curse.

**malefaction** - n.  an evil act.

**maleficence** - n.  harm.

**malevolence** - n.  the desire to harm.

**Malthus, Thomas Robert** (1776-1834) - an English moral philosopher and economist, whose work had an influence on John M. Keynes.  Malthus was concerned about population growth in the absence of natural checks.  The progress of science threatened natural population leveling which would eventually intensify survival requirements.

Darwin articulated his views with Malthusian considerations, as it was Malthus who coined the term "struggle for existence".  Though many viewed his theories as overly pessimistic, others like Keynes described his outlook as "prosaic sanity".

Malthus posed a moral question in asking what checks "ought" to be active in a population: *Positive checks* are natural causes of premature death.  *Preventive checks* are natural  limits on the birthrate.  *Moral checks* are limits voluntarily enacted to control population.

Principal works: *An Essay on the Principle of Population*, 1798, and *The Second Essay on Principle of Population*, 1803.

> *"A laborer who marries without being able to support a family may in some respects be considered as an enemy to all his fellow laborers."*
> Thomas Malthus, *An Essay on the Principle of Population*

**Manichaeism** - n.  in philosophy, the views of Mani (215-276 A.D.); executed for his ideas.  A highly moralistic religion, it claimed God was present in prior ages with Buddha and Zoroaster.  Moreover, after primal man, humanity is the tool of Satan, to limit the light of God.  Christ is the messenger of warning, especially with regard to the dangers of sensual life.

**manifest** - adj. easily perceived by the senses.

**Manifest Content** - n. (German - *manifester Inhalt*; Spanish, *contenido manifesto*) in the philosophy of psychoanalysis, a reference to the psychological material to be studied and interpreted. It assumes the role of phenomenology in the interpretational work. Freud coined the term in *The Interpretation of Dreams*. There it has to do with the subject of a dream before it receives analytic consideration. Freud considered the possibility that there is more than one content to a dream.
   Text to consult: <u>*Interpretation of Dreams*</u>, Sigmund Freud.

**manism** - n. ancestor worship.

**mansuetude** - n. gentleness.

**Mantra** - n. Sanskrit for "tool of meditation". The sound *'om'* is regarded as the perfect sound for meditating on the harmony of the universe, especially in *mantra yoga*. In both Hinduism and Buddhism, devotional and ritualistic use of sounds are important to producing contact with the architecture of ultimate reality. The use of mantras involves correct body position, correct setting, and correct mental focus. In the *Vedas*, mantras are part of the prayers and poetry of enlightenment.

**manumission** - n. liberation, especially from slavery.

**Marcel, Gabriel** (1889-1973) - a French existentialist philosopher who worked out a theistic model of existentialism, largely in opposition to Jean-Paul Sartre's atheistic existentialism. He labeled mankind *Homo Viator* (Man the Wanderer) to highlight the spiritual homelessness of life in mass society.
   In his epistemology, Marcel distinguished two kinds of reflection: *primary reflection* and *secondary reflection*. *Primary reflection* is thought organized around criteria of the objective, the verifiable, and the analytic. This kind of reflection deals with the problematic and pragmatic issues of life. Furthermore, it entails specific solutions to its difficulties, which tend to center on scientific and technological topics. Whereas, *secondary reflection* is concerned with ontology and the mystery of Being. This kind of reflection deals with the spiritual issues of life, including the presence of God, the development of virtue, and the notion of personhood as it relates to transcendence and spiritual availability.
   Marcel coined the term "broken world" to describe the impersonal nature of modern society. He noted the absence of fellowship and love. He also noted the relationship between absurdity and a world that is spiritually impoverished. Thus, Marcel was also quite pessimistic about the prospect of technological salvation over moral requirements of social excellence.
   Marcel took seriously the warnings of Friedrich Nietzsche regarding nihilism. He emphasized an existentialism in which the individual chooses to go beyond egocentricity toward an appreciation of other selves in determining the quality of one's life. For Marcel, the essence of life is *"to be in a situation"*, specifically a situation of choice.

Principal works: *Metaphysical Journal*, 1927, *Being and Having*, 1935, *Creative Fidelity*, 1940, *The Mystery of Being*, 1950, *Men Against Humanity*, 1951, and *The Existential Background of Human Dignity*, 1963.

> *"Egocentrism . . . is possible only in a being which has not properly mastered its own experience, which has not really assimilated it. It is worth devoting our attention to this for a few moments, for it has an important bearing on the rest of our inquiry.*
>
> *Insofar as I am obsessed by an ego-centric preoccupation, that preoccupation acts as a barrier between me and others; and by others must be understood in this connection the life and experience of others. But let us suppose this barrier has been overthrown. The paradox is that at the same time it is also my own personal experience that I rediscover in some way, for in reality my experience is in a real communion with other experiences."*
>
> Gabriel Marcel, <u>Mystery of Being</u>, vol. 2

**Marcus Aurelius** (121-180) - a Roman philosopher-king, Marcus Aurelius acted as Emperor from 161-180 A.D. In advancing the views of the Stoics, Aurelius lived by the principles of his philosophy even endowing the major schools of philosophy at Athens with financial support.

Aurelius was very fond of his warriors and revealed tremendous concern for their safety and well-being in battle. He often advocated the importance of each person's social duties in bringing about a good life.

Principal work: *Meditations*.

> *"Receive wealth or prosperity without arrogance; and be prepared to let it go."*
>
> Marcus Aurelius, <u>Meditations</u>

**martinet** - n. a very strict disciplinarian; one who insists on rigid adherence to details and rules.

**Marx, Karl** (1818-1883) - a German economist and philosopher, having had the widest social impact of any modern philosopher, Marx's views blend the dialectical theory of G.W.F. Hegel (1770-1831) with the atheistic materialism of Ludwig Feuerbach (1804-1872) in what is called "dialectical materialism".

Marx collaborated throughout his life with Friedrich Engels (1820-1895) whose literary skills gave expression to Marx's economic and political theory. In *Das Kapital*, Marx argues that the wealth of the capitalist class is produced through the exploitation of the proletariat or working class. The concept of *surplus value* (value that does not go to the worker) is used to show how capitalists acquire wealth and power over workers and smaller competition.

Marx argued that the central problem of society is class-struggle, outlined through five major historical epochs - 1) primitive communalism 2) slave society 3) feudal society 4) capitalist society, and 5) communist-socialist society. Moreover, class-struggle is exhibited in religious, philosophic, and ethical ideals, which are often used to control the lower classes, supplementing the economic plans of the capitalist class. Along these lines, Marx a pragmatist as well, preferred the validity of action over the theoretical claims of philosophy.

Principal works: *Economic and Philosophic Manuscripts of 1844*, *The German Ideology*, 1846, *The Communist Manifesto*, 1848, and *Das Kapital*, 1867.

> *"Philosophy and the study of the actual world have the same relationship to one another as masturbation and sexual love."*
> Karl Marx & Friedrich Engels, <u>German Ideology</u>

> *"Let the ruling classes tremble at a Communist revolution. The proletarians have nothing to lose but their chains."*
> Marx & Engels, <u>The Communist Manifesto</u>

**Masochism** - n. in the philosophy of psychoanalysis, the subjective experience of pain or humiliation as a type of sexual perversion. Named after Sacher Masoch, it is often linked to feminine psychical elements; a pathology of the soul.

*Erotogenic masochism* is the voluntary participation in sexual pain. *Moral masochism* expresses unconscious guilt and exhibits the individual as a victim without any necessary connection to sexual pleasure. *Feminine masochism* is seen in the subject's willingness to tolerate suffering and can occur in both men and women. In all these forms, agressiveness is turned on the self in some manner.

Text to consult: <u>Gesammelte Werke</u> *(18 vols.)*, Sigmund Freud.

**Materialism** - n. in philosophy, any doctrine which rejects spirituality and spiritual factors and focuses on the primacy of matter. Materialism includes epiphenomenalism. It logically pre-supposes that any and all so-called spiritual details of life are merely effects of the primary material basis of reality.

Materialism has a long tradition. In Eastern philosophy, the doctrine of Charvaka was evident about 590 B.C. This system of materialism has some basis in the *Rig Veda*. It maintained the existence of four elements: earth, air, fire, and water. It emphasized a decidedly empirical approach to knowledge, arguing that what cannot be perceived does not exist. It held that pleasure and pain regulate the life of humanity. It proposed that spiritual afterlife is the result of faulty thinking. It criticized religious priests as charlatans, the creators of an ingenious plan of free subsistence at the expense of others.

In the West, the atomist Democritus (460-370 B.C.) theorized that all experience has a measurable material basis. Atoms, as hard irreducible elements, provide the clues to any kind of phenomena. And the strongest modern consequences to the school of materialism are found in the philosophy of Karl Marx (1818-1883), whose work in economics and political philosophy is magnified by the proposed bankruptcy of theological or spiritual facticity.

**matriliny** - n. female lineage; ancestry through the mother's side.

**mawkish** - adj. having an unpleasant taste; also, sickening sentimentality.

**mea culpa** - Latin, meaning "my own fault".

**meditation** - from the Latin *meditio*, meaning "center". Meditation refers to the contemplative practice of focusing on God, reality, or one's self with the goal of improving one's understanding about life. It characterizes the activity of many Eastern religions, such as Buddhism, Taoism, and Hinduism which are correctly seen as religions of meditation.

Meditation can be practiced in the repetition of a prayer, word, sound or phrase. The somatic effects of meditation as a spiritual exercise are manifested in specific bodily changes such as lowered heart rate and metabolism. Scientific studies have also confirmed meditation's effect on brain waves and respiration to be the opposite of those created by stress. Thus, stress related diseases are therapeutically controlled by regular meditation.

In theological terms, the presence of God as a spiritual focus produces healing effects for persons suffering from anxiety, depression, hypertension, insomnia, and even cancer and infertility. This has been an operating axiom in the theological emphasis on healing through spiritual praxis.

In recent years medical research has validated the meditative practices of East and West and promoted the use of these techniques as a supplement to physiological treatments of human suffering.

Texts to consult: *Light Within: The Inner Path of Meditation*, Laurence Freeman, 1987, and *Total Liberation: Zen Spirituality*, Ruben Habito, 1989.

**megalomania** - n. excessive pride in one's self and one's achievements.

**meiosis** - n. understating something in order to preserve or promote esteem for it.

**melancholy** - n. a state of mental or spiritual unhappiness; sadness.

**melange** - n. a collection or set of unrelated elements; a mess.

**melanotic** - adj. having black pigmentation.

**meliorate** - v. to improve.

**Meliorism** - n. from the Latin 'melior' meaning better. Meliorism is the belief that human action, while limited and imperfect, can improve the world. It was a hope of William James (1842-1910) in his work on pragmatism. James was a pluralist and defended the openness of the universe and its future against monistic and deterministic interpretations of reality. He believed that mind and matter are separate sources of organization, with mind having a clear power over the material order.

> *"The world is not yet with them, so they seem often in the midst of the world's affairs to be preposterous. Yet they are impregnators of the world, vivifiers and animators of potentialities of goodness which but for them would lie forever dormant."*
>
> William James, *Varieties of Religious Experience*

**menage a trois** - n. a household of three, made up of a married pair and a lover of one of the spouses.

**mendacious** - adj. untruthful; given to deception.

**mendacity** - n. a lie.

**mendicant** - n. a member of a religious order who practices both monastic life and outside religious work.

**mensal** - adj. monthly.

**mentalism** - n. also called *psychic monism*; the philosophical view that mind is ultimate reality and that the physical realm is a derivative.

**merdivorous** - adj. characterized by dung eating; coprophagous; preferring an inferior diet.

**meritricious** - adj. attractive in a false way; tawdry; also, relating to prostitution.

**Merleau-Ponty, Maurice** (1908-1961) - a French philosopher of phenomenology and existentialism whose unique insights contributed much to the broadening of both fields. Merleau-Ponty taught at the College of France and occasionally worked with Jean-Paul Sartre and Simone de Beauvoir.

Merleau-Ponty was indebted to Descartes and Husserl for his ontological direction and spent most of his life working out original re-interpretations of their thoughts. Idealism, in his view, was subject to problems stemming from fractures in the unity of consciousness and the world. Purely logical systems of the explanation of experience failed to produce complete understanding of human existence.

From Husserl, Merleau-Ponty acquired the means to provide a descriptive account of the design of consciousness. He also borrowed from Gestalt theory to build out a theory of the person as consciousness. Consciousness is an awareness of objects and the perpetual "perspectiveness" which characterizes one's consciousness of objects. Thus, the world is always an experience of incompleteness. This condition is a requirement for consciousness to work and includes the presentation of situations in which the person chooses courses of action among objects. Moral being is an implicit part of the creative nature of existence among objects.

Merleau-Ponty was also very sensitive to the role of language in human consciousness. For, language is the only tool which allows each person as a perceiving subject to create connections with other persons as perceiving subjects.

Principal works: *The Structure of Behavior*, 1942, *Phenomenology of Perception*, 1945, *Humanism and Terror*, 1947, *In Praise of Philosophy*, 1953, *Signs*, 1960, *The Primacy of Perception*, 1964, and *The Visible and the Invisible*, 1964.

> *"The world is not an object such that I have in my possession the law of its making; it is the natural setting of, and field for, all my thoughts and all my explicit perceptions. Truth does not 'inhabit' only the 'inner man', or more*

*accurately, there is no inner man, man is in the world, and only in the world does he know himself."*

*Maurice Merleau-Ponty, <u>Phenomenology of Perception</u>*

**Mesmer, Franz Anton** (1734-1815) - a Viennese doctor of medicine, Mesmer's name is the root of the word *mesmerism* which is associated with his therapeutic methods. Mesmer believed in the existence of 'animal magnetism', a fluid force much like gravity which permeates the universe and living creatures. He believed that this force could contribute to healing in individuals if properly channeled. Though often connected with theories of hypnotism, mesmerism is now classified with such arts as faith-healing. Mesmer's theories never received wide scientific support.

Texts to Consult: <u>Anton Mesmer,</u> D.M. Walmsley, and <u>Hypnotism: it history, practice, and theory,</u> J.M. Bramwell.

**Meta-ethics** - n. the philosophical concern with the logical integrity of statements in the formulation of ethical systems. It is a separate kind of skepticism regarding the efficacy of the words themselves to convey strict and reliable meanings. This separate skepticism is called 'second order' inquiry and has its beginning in language philosophy. Meta-ethics is a concern with the logical and epistemological quality of ethical statements. Historically, the work of G.E. Moore, *Principia Ethica*, 1903, represents the shift over to this kind of concern.

**Metaphysics** - n. in philosophy, the study of reality, its foundations, origins, nature, and destiny. Metaphysics is sometimes sub-divided into *cosmology* (the study of the universe, its origin, nature, and development) and *ontology* (the study of being, including non-being and death). A.N. Whitehead (1861-1947) regarded the conclusions of all metaphysical investigations to be only probable and never certain. In his view metaphysics must draw from the cumulative data of all disciplines to propose answers to the deepest questions human can ask. Henri Bergson (1859-1941) believed that intuition was necessary to break past the natural world and the limited power of reason.

*"Metaphysics has for the real object of its investigation three ideas only: God, Freedom, and Immortality."*

*Immanuel Kant, <u>The Critique of Pure Reason</u>*

**Metapsychology** - n. (German, *Metapsychologie*; Spanish, *metapsicologia*) in the philosophy of psychology, a reference to Freud's hope of finding conceptual theories which would stand apart but support explanations of empirical psychic reality. Freud tried to show that metapsychology is an improvement of metaphysics.

It considers three points of view: (1) *dynamic*- psychical events are the result of conflicts and combinational forces which create pressures in the individual, (2) *economic* - psychic movements and states consists of different quantifiable energy that can increase, decrease or stabilize, and (3) *topographic* - the reference to levels or areas of

124

investigation as if to comprises 'spaces' where psychic entities are found, e.g. the Unconscious, the Conscious, and the Pre-Conscious.

Texts to consult: *Studies on Hysteria* and *Beyond the Pleasure Principle*, Sigmund Freud.

**metastasis** - n. transference of a disease from one primary focus in the body to another, as in *metastatic* cancer.

**metatrophic** - adj. living on decayed organic matter; saprophytic.

**metempirics** - n. philosophy dealing with issues outside empiricism.

**Metempsychosis** - n. migration of the soul after death, especially to another body whether human or animal. It is a feature of most Indian religions including, Hinduism, Jainism, and Buddhism.

> *"The spiritual perfection which opens before man is the crown of long patient, millennial outflowering of the Spirit in life and nature. The belief in a gradual spiritual progress and evolution is the secret of the almost universal Indian acceptance of the truth of reincarnation."*
> Sri Aurobindo (1872-1950), *Silver Jubilee Commemorative Volume of the Indian Philosophical Congress*, 1950

Aurobindo advocated a philosophy of metempsychosis strikingly similar to Neoplatonism. He believed that reality was a graded or staged hierarchy, starting with matter and ascending to Brahman or the Absolute. In his philosophy, Brahman is connected to the finite world through a type of dynamic spiritual force. This power influences the finite to work towards the infinite as well. In nature, it is a struggle from lower to higher evolutionary forms. In humanity, it is the quest to move from the physical to the mental to the spiritual-divine life. Aurobindo called the passage process "integral yoga", creating a transformation of being in life, mind, and body.

Among Greek philosophers, Pythagoras claimed a theory of metempsychosis, arguing that memories of past lives constitute proof.

**metonymy** - n. a linguistic tool, specifically the substituting of a characteristic or related concept for the thing meant, e.g., 'the bottle' vs. 'drink'.

**miasma** - n. a pervasive influence which corrupts or destroys; the putrid smelling gases which arise from swamps, marshes, and ponds.

**micromania** - n. psychotic depreciation of the self.

**Mill, John Stuart** (1806-1873) - an English philosopher whose fame rests on his ethical work in the construction of utilitarianism: happiness is the achievement of "the greatest good for the greatest number".

Influenced by the empiricist philosophers, Mill regarded inductive reasoning as the actual and productive use of logic. Mill noticed that all deductive arguments have an inductive basis, so experience rather than deductive processes provide ultimate confidence in conclusions.  The causal connections one is able to make are experienced rather than thought.  Mill developed a set of devices known as Mill's Methods to organize inductive conclusions.

Mill advocated democratic government but only if there was a commitment to the education of its population.  As a safeguard, educated people should have more influence than the uneducated.

Principal works: *A System of Logic, 2 vols.*, 1843, *On Liberty*, 1859, *Utilitarianism*, 1863, *The Subjection of Women*, 1869, and *Three Essays on Religion*, 1874.

> *"It is better to be a human being dissatisfied than a pig satisfied; better to be a Socrates dissatisfied than a fool satisfied.  And if the fool, or the pig, is of a different opinion, it is because they only know their side of the question."*
> *J.S. Mill, Utilitarianism*

**Millenarianism** - n.  in Christianity, the literal interpretation of Chapter 20 in the Book of Revelation that Christ will rule the earth for 1,000 years before the resurrection of the dead.  Millenarianism has strong connections to apocalyptic teachings.  It is popular with Mormons, Anabaptists, and Adventists but there seems to little basis for it elsewhere in Scripture or Christian tradition.

**minacious** - adj.  threatening.

**Mind-Body Problem** - n. in philosophy, the concern with the puzzling relationship of two very dis-similar entities (mind as non-material and body as material) and how they might be explained to attach to each other.

*Interactionsim* holds that the mind influences the body and that the body can act upon the mind.  Examples are found in illness and depression, happiness and health.

*Parallelism* argues that the mind and body do not interact.  Their actions are independent and run parallel in time and space.

*Epihenomenalism* argues that mind is an effect of complex material arrangements; biological design.  Mind derives from complex physical processes just as smoke rises from fire.

*Psychic monism* argues that matter is illusory and that mind is primary.  Matter or the body is the consequence of a spiritual primacy or foundation in the universe.

**minx** - n.  a wanton girl or woman, one with real seductive powers.

**mirabile dictu** - Latin, "wonderful to relate", including "strange to tell".

**Mirror Stage** - n. (German - *Spiegelstufe*; Spanish, *fase del espejo*)  in psychology, a phase between six and eighteen months when the child's  encounter with mirror reflection of itself.  Theory focuses on the relationship of the mirror reflection with development of the ego. Accordingly, the child supposedly anticipates mastery of its body perceived; related to narcissistic identification.

**misanthrope** - n.  one who hates humanity.

**miscegenation** - n.  a marriage or cohabitation between persons of different races.

**miscreance** - n.  inauthentic religious faith; heresy.

**misogamy** - n.  hatred of marriage.

**misogyny** - n.  hatred of women.

**misology** - n.  hatred of logic;  an aversion to rational discourse.

**misoneism** - n.  hatred of change or innovation.

**misopedia** - n.  hatred of children.

**misprision** - n. contempt;  also, wrongful performance of duty, especially governmental duty.

**misprize** -v.  to hold in contempt;  to despise.

**Mithraism** - n.  Mithras was a Persian sun-god.  Belief in this god was extremely popular with the soldiers of Alexander the Great.  Monuments to the god are very common at the old frontier boundaries of the Roman Empire.  Mithras' slaying of a great bull and the spilling of its blood were said to produce vegetable life on earth, thus this mythos is commemorated in worship and the sacrifice of bulls is supposedly a basis for immortality.  Therein lies the appeal of Mithraism to men in combat.  Initiation was elaborate, limited to men, and involved passage through seven stages symbolizing movement through the cosmology of the seven heavens.  (In Mithraism lie the roots of modern bullfighting.)

**mnemonics** - n.  the study of memory;  the art of memory.

**mobocracy** - n.  rule by the irrational mob.

**modiste** - n.  one who sells what is fashionable, especially for women.

**mogigraphia** - n.  writer's cramp.

**mogilalia** - n.  any defect in the ability to speak.

**moiety** - n.  one of two;  half.

**moil** - n.  hard work;  also, confusion.

**Moira** - n.  in Greek philosophy, a reference to fate;  what is alloted;  representing forces which influence the life of the individual, simultaneously announcing the limits of the power of the gods.  These forces are represented in the names - Terror, Strife, Rumor,

Death, Chaos, and Blind Vanity. Moira obtains a primary role in the type of life lived and cannot realistically be objected to. This point was re-inforced by the recognition of limits with even the gods themselves.

**Moksha** - n. in Indian philosophy, Sanskrit for "deliverance". The term appears in the *Upanishads* as well as the *Bhagavad-Gita*. It holds slightly different meanings for Hindus, Buddhists, and Jains. Primarily it suggests autonomy and self-control.

> *"Not going naked, nor matted hair, nor dirt, nor fasting, nor sleeping on the ground, nor rolling in the dust, nor sitting motionless can purify the one who has not overcome desire."*
>
> > - *The Dhammapada*, 500 B.C.

> *"When all desires of the heart cease, then one becomes immortal; then one attains to union with absolute being."*
>
> > - *Katha Upanishad*, ca. 600 B.C.

**molescent** - adj. soft.

**mollify** - v. appease.

**monandry** - n. the view or custom of having one husband at a time.

**Monasticism** - n. from the Greek 'monazein' (to be alone). Monasticism is important in both Eastern and Western traditions. It focuses on self-mastery through contemplative life, withdrawal from urban influences, and a commitment to work, meditation, and physical simplicity. Typically, although there is a focus on being alone, monastic life usually means community membership with established rules of community life. In the West, St. Antony of Egypt (251-356 A.D.) created the first monasteries in the desert. For St. Antony the aims of the monk's life are centered on personal sanctification, especially through the vows of chastity, poverty, and obedience. Later St. Benedict of Nursia (481-548 A.D. ) became the chief influence on monastic philosophy in the West, i.e., the Benedictines.

**monition** - n. warning; indication of danger.

**monocarpic** - adj. bearing fruit once, resulting in death.

**monocracy** - n. government or rule by one person.

**monoecious** - adj. having both male and female sex organs; hermaphrodite.

**monology** - n. the practice or act of a person speaking to one's self.

**monophagia** - n. the practice of eating only one food.

**monophobia** - n. the fear of being alone.

**Montaigne, Michel de** (1533-1592) - a French philosopher of skepticism, Montaigne criticized almost every known system of philosophy, religion, and science, casting doubt on any possibility of certainty.   Strangely enough, he also served as mayor of Bordeaux and member of the local parliament.

As a cynical skepticist, Montaigne held that people do not know or value truth and goodness.  Human beings are basically vain and immoral, especially in their 'civilized' state.  People who live in primitive settings are actually much more dignified.  Even the life of animals seems better than the degraded existence of modern man.  So, Montaigne advocated a simple and natural existence to reduce the ambition and egoism that are so destructive to personal peace and happiness.

These views led Montaigne to advocate the role of faith and a version of Christianity.  He abandoned the pretense that human reason can decipher reality and thought all rational puzzles pointed eventually to the acceptance of faith.

Principal work: *Essays, 3 vols.*, 1588.

*"Wonder is the foundation of all philosophy, inquiry its progress, ignorance its end. . . . Ignorance that knows itself, that judges itself and condemns itself, is not complete ignorance: to be that , it must be ignorant of itself."*
                              Michel de Montaigne, <u>Essays</u>


**monotheism** - n. in theology, the belief in one god and typically represented by the theological views found in Judaism, Christianity, and Islam.

Text to Consult: <u>*Philosophers Speak of God*</u>, C. Hartshorne & W. Reese, 1976.


**montane** - adj.  being mountainous; eminent.


**Moore, George Edward** (1873-1958) - an English philosopher sometimes labeled a realist, Moore was raised in a religious home but had a very degrading experience at the age of 12.  He was religiously forced to spread the word of Jesus.  This caused him much personal torment and destroyed his interest in religion.  Subsequently, Moore's philosophical interests were directed toward a construction of realist philosophy at the expense of idealism.

Moore was noted for his work in ethical theory and argued that the fundamental purpose of ethics is to identify one object: the good.  Central to his definition of the good were the roles of human affection and aesthetic enjoyment.

Principal works: *Principia Ethica*, 1903, *Ethics*, 1912, and *Philosophical Papers*, 1959.

*"No one, probably, who has asked himself the question has ever doubted that personal affection and the appreciation of what is beautiful in Art or Nature, are good in themselves; nor, if we consider strictly what things are worth having 'purely for their own sakes', does it appear probable that any one will think that anything else has nearly so great a value as the things which are included under these two heads."*
                              G.E. Moore, <u>Principia Ethica</u>

**moral fatigue** - n. in ethics, the observation that moral and ethical philosophies in the life of the individual and society may undergo sustained pressure and, thus, exhibit a weakening of will, collectively or individually. Moral fatigue is the slackening of commitment and the loss of spiritual strength in upholding certain moral positions. This fatigue may be the sign that a revision of ethics is necessary in the life of the state or the individual. Or, it may indicate that the original inspiration and vision of the moral goals need to be re-vitalized.

**morbific** - adj. producing disease.

**mordacious** - adj. the tendency to bite.

**mordant** - adj. being sarcastic or harsh in manner.

**moribund** - adj. being in death throes; near death.

**morpheme** - n. in language, the smallest syntactically meaningful element, as in the use of 's' to show plurality.

**mortiferous** - adj. having the power to cause death.

**mortify** - v. to bring about the death of something; to eliminate vitality.

**mukti** - n. in Hinduism, a reference to "liberation". It represents the final release from worldly existence.

**mundify** - v. to set free, especially from noxious or irritating concerns (matter).

**munificent** - adj. generous; very giving, even lavish.

**myopia** - n. the condition of lacking breadth of understanding; the absence of foresight; defective vision, especially an inability to see laterally.

**mysophilia** - n. the love of filth, dirt.

**mysophobia** - n. extreme fear of dirt or infective bacteria.

**Mysticism** - n. in philosophy, the term refers to any ideology which is centered on the spiritual realm more than the ordinary world. Generally, mysticism seeks to find a union or mental oneness with the foundation of experienced reality, be it God or the Divine, Brahman or Truth. It employs intuitive reason more than discursive processes, banking heavily on the emotional affirmation of core spirituality in persons and things. In fact, mysticism in both Eastern and Western traditions is suspicious of purely rational explanations of reality.

*"The estate of Divine union consists in the total transformation of the will into the will of God, in such a way that every movement of the will shall be always*

*the movement of the will of God."*
*- St. John of the Cross (1542-1591), <u>Ascent of Mt. Carmel</u>*


**mythomania** - n.  an extreme need to lie or exaggerate the ordinary.

**Nagarjuna** (100-200 A.D.) - n. in Buddhism, the philosophical founder of the Middle Way School, related ideologically to Zen principles.  Nagarjuna's way to nirvana was to apply rigorous criticism to all rational philosophies.  Implicit within this strategy was the assumption that all words and ideas bind us down, trapping us in constructs of reality that actually manage to blind us.

*Sunyata* is the notion of "emptyness".  Nagarjuna argued that *sunyata* is a riddance of this world's entrapments.  Of course, encased within this strategy of emptyness lies a paradox, for it is a concept to be grasped and the grasping of concepts is wrong for the goal of liberation.  Even *nirvana* is an illusion.  There is nothing more important in the thrust of Zen Buddhism than transcendence of illusions.

Principal works: *Twenty Verses on the Great Vehicle* and  *Treatise on the Middle Doctrine*.  Text to consult: <u>*Nagarjuna's Philosophy*</u>, K. Venkata Ramanan, 1979.

**Naive realism** - n.   the view that what one sees and experiences is the sum total of reality.  Basically, it represents a failure of critical reason.  Naive realism under-estimates the complexity and mystery of the objective world.  The view is particularly common in those who are poorly educated or mentally dull.  It involves an exaggerated confidence in common sense.

**nanoid** - n.  dwarf.

**naos** - n. temple.

**Narcissism** - n. from Narcissus, exclusive love of one's self, to the detriment of social effectiveness.  Narcissus was unable to resist admiring his reflection whenever possible.

In Freud, narcissism explains the object-choice in homosexuals, who see themselves and each other as the correct sexual object.  Narcissism as 'auto-eroticism' finds its parallel in the homosexual or lesbian who seeks lovers who resemble his or her self.

The healthy development of love, which is a turning toward living things in the human environment, is reversed in the pathological individual.  This theory carries us to further insights on the development of love.  Psychoanalysis, thus, poses the distinction between *primary* and *secondary* narcissism.

Texts to Consult: <u>*Three Essays on the Theory of Sexuality*</u>, S. Freud and *'Le stade du miroir comme formateur de la fonction du Je'*, Jacques Lacan (Trans. as 'The Mirror-Phase', New Left Review, 1968, 51, 71-77.

**narcolepsy** - n. an overwhelming need to sleep; sleep beyond normal biological demands.

**narcomania** - n. an uncontrollable desire for drugs which soothe the body and relieve pain.

**narcosis** - n. a state of unconsciousness caused by chemicals, e.g. LSD, opium.

**narcosynthesis** - n. treatment of mental pathology with the use of drugs.

**nascent** - adj. the quality of beginning; coming into being.

**natant** - adj. floating in water.

**Naturalism** - n. in philosophy, the view that reality has no supernatural order. Nature is the whole of reality, and any explanations about reality must be connected to the natural world. Reference to objects and events must be limited to space-time references in order to be valid. Non-natural orders are fictions of the mind.

**natural theology** - n. pursuit of the knowledge of God independent of traditional revelation; use of nature as a paradigm for an understanding of God. An early example exists in the philosophy of William Paley.

**naupathia** - n. seasickness.

**necrolatry** - n. worship of the dead.

**necromancy** - n. witchcraft, especially in relation to the dead; sorcery work with the dead.

**necromimesis** - n. the subjective belief that one is dead.

**necrophagia** - n. the eating of corpses; the feeding on carrion.

**necrophobia** - n. an extreme fear of death.

**Need for Punishment** - n. (German, *Strafbedurfnis*; Spanish, *necesidad de castigo*) in psychology, behavior that turns out to be the quest for unpleasant or humiliating experiences, from which a pathological enjoyment is derived. It raises metapsychological problems of interpretation, but it is generally connected with the death instinct. It is sometimes included in personality portraits where melancholia exists. Then too, some theoretical treatments include suicide as self-punishment.
    Text to Consult: *The Ego and the Id*, Sigmund Freud.

**nefarious** - adj. being particularly evil, wicked, or mean; having flagrant disregard for goodness.

**Nemesis** - n. a goddess of ancient Greece, identified with forests and fertility and the personification of divine revenge. Nemesis was especially opposed to human arrogance and its associated moral consequences: temerity (recklessness), excess, insolence, and the failure to live up to one's duties.

The holy ground of Nemesis was called *nemos* (a clearing in the woods), a place where mortals could not encroach. Thus, *adyton,* the notion of trespassing, was connected to her realm of being as a moral aspect of her co-existence with mortals. Over time, she was associated with *nomos* (law), because the Greeks recognized the ability of humans to lose shame for satisfying their irrational desires. Without shame punishment became an essential deterrent to human wrong-doing. Nemesis operates as the balance in human affairs, the protectress of that which is good and holy over and above the *hubris* (pride) of mortals, through her power to inflict suffering for moral evil. Her punishments were complex and manifested themselves in the spiritual lives of immoral individuals by deeper and deeper feelings of isolation and unhappiness.

Text to consult: *Paideia: Ideals of Greek Culture*, Werner Jaeger, 1939, 1973.

**neologism** - n. a word or phrase that is new and perhaps crude or inappropriate.

**Neoplatonism** - n. the philosophical views of Plotinus (204-270 A.D.). As the name implies, it is a reformation of Platonism, a 'new Platonism'. It had a profound impact on the metaphysics of Christianity through St. Augustine. Plotinus argued that all of reality is a series of emanations from the One (God). Near the center is the first emanation *nous* (mind), and the second emanation is *psyche* (soul). At the outer edges of reality one finds matter. Beyond matter there is only nothingness. The theocentric nature of Neoplatonism suggests as things become more intelligible, they become more spiritual. Reason and spirituality are mixed together as are matter and chaos. Matter derives its structure from the higher emanations.

> *"The One is perfect because it seeks for nothing, and possesses nothing, and has need of nothing; and being perfect, it overflows, and this its superabundance provides an Other."*
>
> - Plotinus, *Enneads*, Vol. 2, 1

**neoteric** - adj. novel; recently begun.

**nepenthe** - n. something which removes suffering, grief, etc.

**nepotism** - n. rule by family; bestowal of office on one's relations.

**nescience** - n. a state of ignorance.

**Nestorianism** - n. the Christological views of Nestorius (d. ca. 451 A.D.). It argues that there were two separate Persons in Christ, one being God and the other being human. This view stands opposed to the traditional view that Christ was one single Person having the attributes of both God and humanity. In modern times, Nestorianism has survived in the mountains of Khurdistan among descendants of the original Nestorian communities as Assyrian Christians.

134

**Neurath, Otto** (1882-1945) - an Austrian philosopher and sociologist, Neurath made important contributions to the field of linguistic analysis. He was also very interested in social and political problems, working hard to make improvements in education and government. One of Neurath's beliefs was that education was the key to social harmony and that it could be made more effective by the development of a visual learning process. This was funded on the assumption that there is a materialist basis of knowing.

For Neurath, a principal obstacle to learning was the ambiguity and uncertainty of meaning in language. He sought a way of using only pictorial signs, his "Vienna Method", to provide easy acquisition of knowledge that was stripped of encumbrances and easily remembered. Neurath promoted an educational approach that was simple, encyclopedist, and general. He believed that an excellent instructor could simplify the most complex theories and focus clearly on the most important ideas only.

Principal works: *Scientific World View*, 1929, *Empirical Sociology*, 1931 and, *Foundations of the Social Sciences*, 1944.

*"We are like sailors who must rebuild their ship on the open sea, never able to dismantle it in dry-dock and to reconstruct it there out of the best materials. . . . Vague linguistic conglomerations always remain in one way or another as components of the ship."*
            Otto Neurath, "Protocol Sentences" in <u>Logical Positivism</u>, A.J. Ayer

**nexus** - n. link; connection.

**nidification** - n. the act of nest-building; the process of providing a secret or protected place for the young.

**nidus** - n. a breeding place; a nest or home.

**Niebuhr, Reinhold** (1892-1971) - an American philosopher-theologian born in Wright City, Missouri, Niebuhr gained an important place in public debates of the 40's and 50's. His expertise ranged from philosophy to economics to social policy and psychology. Simultaneously, he saw himself as a 'mongrel among thoroughbreds', a Midwesterner among Easterners, a master's degree among doctorates.

Labelled a 'Christian Realist', this meant for Niebuhr a theological realism, a realism measured against spiritual and idealistic facts, especially as found in the ethics of Jesus. His idea of 'vertical dialectic' emphasized the creative and self-transcendent properties of mankind along with a finite, contingent creatureliness.

In *Moral Man and Immoral Society* Niebuhr outlines the uses of power in social groups, the manner in which it corrupts individuals striving to to good, and the way in which idealism runs into trouble when reality presents morally ambiguous situations, situations which cannot be toppled by mere intellectual desire for social justice.

Principal works include: *Moral Man and Immoral Society*, 1932, *Reflections on the End of an Era*, 1934, *Christianity and Power Politics*, 1940, *The Nature and Destiny of Man, 2 vols.*, 1941-43, *The Irony of American History*, 1952.

> *"Nothing that is worth doing can be achieved in our lifetime; therefore we must be saved by hope. Nothing which is true or beautiful or good makes complete sense in any immediate context of history; therefore we must be saved by faith. Nothing we do, however virtuous, can be accomplished alone; therefore we are saved by love. No virtuous act is quite as virtuous from the standpoint of our friend or foe as it is from our standpoint. Therefore we must be saved by the final form of love which is forgiveness."*
> Reinhold Niebuhr, *The Irony of American History*

**Nietzsche, Friedrich W.** (1844-1900) - a German philosopher, whose extraordinary social and self-criticism produced one of the most penetrating understandings of human existence in modern times. Sometimes called "the father of existentialism", Nietzsche has been widely misinterpreted primarily because of his rich use of metaphors and the seemingly contradictory statements throughout his writings.

A highly spiritual thinker, Nietzsche's analysis of human problems discerned three levels of crises: the physical, the psychological, and the ontological. For modern humanity, the central crisis is ontological. The absence of apparent ontological meaning and purpose in people's lives leads them to construct cheap substitutions of meaning in the areas of physical and psychological existence.

An antagonist of psychology, Nietzsche characterized the 20th Century as the age of nihilism and psychology rather than reason and morality. Moreover, the insanity which is the domain of psychology has self-deepening features because it does not recognize the legitimacy of ontological reflection. Psychologically, all human beings seek power over their domain and other persons. This is a consequence of anxiety regarding the security of life. And, having missed the essential signs directing life toward an ontological apprehension of reality, people seek power only in its obvious but unsatisfying forms, i.e. physical achievements and psychological satisfaction.

Nietzsche features the philosophy of nihilism to explain the absence of true spiritual power in the lives of individuals. Moreover, the annihilation of all morals through the "Death of God" insures a world divided between a few moral champions (the master morality of high calibre individuals) and herds of moral cowards (the slave morality of low calibre individuals).

In the 20th Century, Nietzsche's views were adulterated to serve the political ambitions of Nazism. It should be noticed that similar misuses were made of Plato and the Gospel of John. Ultimately, Nietzsche preferred to categorize people according to a moral typology, often reserving some of his severest criticism for Germans: *"How much dreary heaviness, lameness, dampness, sloppiness, how much beer there is in the German intellect!" F.W. Nietzsche, Twilight of the Idols* .

Nietzsche's work sets up many important observations for the development of modern existentialism, especially the theme that one must choose one's own way through a process of deep and personal self-knowledge.

136

Principal works: *The Birth of Tragedy*, 1872, *Human, All Too Human*, 1878, *Beyond Good and Evil*, 1886, *Thus Spoke Zarathustra*, 1885, *The Genealogy of Morals*, 1887, and *Twilight of the Idols*, 1888.

> *"Creation - that is the greatest redemption from suffering, and life's easement. But that the creator may exist, that itself requires suffering and much transformation. . . . For the creator himself to be the child new-born he must also be willing to be the mother and endure the mother's pain. . . . All feeling 'suffers' in me and is in prison: but my willing always comes to me as my liberator and bringer of joy. . . . Willing liberates: that is the true doctrine of will and freedom."*
>
> F.W. Nietzsche, <u>Thus Spoke Zarathustra</u>

**Nihilism** - n. in philosophy, the view that traditional values are without substance or foundation; the belief that life is senseless and useless; the denial of an objective ground for moral truths. Nihilism can also be applied to the arenas of politics, epistemology, and theology such that the perception of order and harmony as constituent qualities find no predictable history.

In philosophy, an early advocate was Philipp Mainlander (1841-1876), *The Philosophy of Redemption,* 1876. His arguments for theological nihilism, the death of God, run like this: 1) God is a unity but the world is a plurality, so God cannot be part of this scene, 2) God is joy but the world is dominated by suffering, so God is not part of this scene, 3) Non-existence is better than existence, because unity and joy are not part of this world, 4) It is logical to admit that life is an awareness of suffering and chaos, so death is a redemption from this life. From Mainlander, a student of Schopenhauer, the exposition of nihilism is taken up by Friedrich Nietzsche (1844-1900) who attempts to combat it with the theory of transvaluation and the introduction of 'courage' as the cardinal virtue.

Text to consult: <u>Irrational Man</u>, William Barrett, 1958.

**Nirvana** - n. Sanskrit for 'blown out' or 'extinguished'. Buddhist philosophy uses this term to identify the elimination of worldly desires. In classic Buddhist fashion, whatever one says to describe the term will fail to describe the term. In the Hinayana school, nirvana means extinction. In the Mahayana school nirvana means total bliss, although the Mahayana teachings of Nagarjuna (100-200 A.D.) argue that nirvana is itself merely another illusion among the countless illusions of this world. For Nagarjuna, *Treatise on the Middle Doctrine,* if nirvana exists then it is subject to non-existence. Whatever is subject to non-existence is an illusion.

> *"Nirvana, or self extinction in Brahman, clearly implies extinction of the ego, the false self, in the Higher Self - the source of all knowledge, of all existence, and of all happiness."*
>
> - Swami Prabhavananda, <u>The Spiritual Heritage of India</u>, 1963

**Nirvana Principle** - n. (German, *Nirwanaprinzip*; Spanish, *principio de nirvana*) in psychology, a view ascribed to Barbara Low, British psycho-analyst, which claims it is the tendency to reduce internal pressures of excitement and desire. It is often connected theoretically to masochism and the death instinct.

**niveous** - adj. being snowlike, pure.

**nocent** - adj. harmful; dangerous.

**nocturnal** - adj. occurring at night; active at night.

**nocuous** - adj. harmful.

**noegenesis** - n. first hand knowledge; knowledge acquired by intellect itself.

**noema** - n. Greek for "that which is thought". In the philosophy of Edmund Husserl (1859-1938), the term signifies the element of thought as material rather than as act. For Husserl, act is represented by 'noesis'.

**noesis** - n. thinking as act.

**noetic** - adj. relating to the mind.

**nomology** - n. the study of physical laws and/or the rules of reasoning.

**nonparous** - adj. the quality of not having given birth to any children.

**nosography** - n. the description of diseases.

**nosological** - adj. relating to the classification of disease, as in the assignment of mental problems to certain categories of psychopathology.

**nosophobia** - n. morbid fear of disease.

**nostomania** - n. extreme homesickness.

**noxious** - adj. distasteful; harmful to life in body or mind.

**nuance** - n. a subtle distinction.

**nudnik** - n. a tiresome individual.

**nyctophobia** - n. morbid fear of darkness.

**obdurate** - adj.  hardened against tender feelings.

**obeisance** - n.  respect;  submission;  homage.

**obfuscate** - v.  to confuse.

**objurgate** - v.  to scold or put down harshly.

**oblate** - n.  someone who is dedicated to monastic life.

**oblate** - adj.  being flattened at the poles or ends.

**obliquity** - n.  deviation from normative values, as in moral philosophy.

**oblivescence** - n.  a state of forgetfulness.

**obscurantism** - n.  deliberate introduction of vagueness;  concealment of understanding.

**obsequence** - n.  eagerness to please or satisfy.

**obsequious** - adj.  being servile or excessively submissive.

**obsolescence** - n.  the condition of being useless or technically out of date.

**obstreperous** - adj.  unruly, noisy;  marked aggressiveness.

**obtest** - v.  to call forth as a witness.

**obtrusive** - adj.  annoyingly pretentious or showy;  forward in manner.

**obtuse** - adj.  blunt;  lacking sharpness of form;  also, stupid.

**obumbrate** - v.  to cloud over.

**obviate** - v. to make unnecessary.

**occlusion** - n.  a complete obstruction or blockage of a passageway.

**ochlesis** - n.  illness caused by over-exposure to dense population.

**ochlocracy** - n.  government by the masses.

**ochlophobia** - n.  morbid fear of crowds.

**odalisque** - n.  a female slave in a harem;  concubine.

**Oedipus Complex** - n. (German, *Odipuskomplex*; Spanish, *complejo de Edipo*)
in psychology, the attachment of the child to a parent, involving a supposed death of the rival, the parent of the opposite sex.  It plays a role in the formation of the personality and the adjustment to sexuality.

**oeillade** - n.  quick visual contact;  affectionate glance.

**officious** - adj.  meddling interference.

**oligolalia** - n.  poverty of language;  a mental condition complicated by a small vocabulary.

**oligophrenia** - n.  feeblemindedness;  low mental inventory.

**oligopoly** - n.  a market in which there are many buyers and few sellers.

**oligopsony** - n.  a market in which there are many sellers and few buyers.

**omnifarious** - adj.  of all sorts or all varieties.

**onanism** - n.  from Onan (Gen. 38:9);  masturbation.

**oneiric** - adj.  having to do with dreams.

**onerous** - adj.  being troublesome;  involving an excessive burden.

**oniomania** - n.  in psychology,  the neurotic need to shop or buy things;  an irrepressible urge to spend money.

**ontogeny** - n.  the record of development of a particular organism, being.

**ontological force** - n.  in ethics, reference to the spiritual effects of an act on the life of the agent.  The power of acts to shape the spiritual well-ness of the agent.

**Ontology** - n.  in philosophy, the study of the origin, nature, and purpose of being;  the study of existence, Being vs. Non-being.  Ontology is a subranch of metaphysics, stemming from the Greek *ontos* meaning 'existence' or 'being', and *logos* meaning purpose, reason, or study of. Martin Heidegger's work in ontology remains the benchmark for 20th Century definitions of Being.

Text to consult: *The Basic Problems of Phenomenology*, Martin Heidegger, 1975.

**onus** - n. a burden that is particularly disagreeable.

**onycophagia** - n. nail eating, especially as it relates to a nervous condition.

**opacify** - v. to make impermeable to light.

**oppilate** - v. to obstruct or block up.

**opprobrium** - n. conduct which brings about disgrace, even contempt.

**oppugn** - v. to fight against, especially with argumentation.

**orbicular** - adj. circular.

**Ortega y Gasset, Jose** (1883-1955) - an important Spanish philosopher of existentialism whose literary achievements did much to establish philosophical thought in the Latin American world.

Ortega begins with a biological emphasis on Life. From there he builds reflection toward a metaphysical sense of reality. Thus, one finds an interesting bi-polarity in his existentialism which helps to heighten one's enthusiasm for understanding life. He called this view "the metaphysics of vital reason". Things and persons are essential to each other, each complementing the other's existence. The ultimate setting of reality is always a setting of the self with things.

In his epistemology he advocates a position called "perspectivism". All points of view are partial, limited, and specific. Each person is necessarily limited to his or her own experience of knowing reality. Ortega develops this into an awareness of what one's personal choices are to find a satisfying life. The specific nature of one's knowledge of the world leads him to argue that each person has one correct choice to make in forming a meaningful life: a vocation or mission.

Ortega's view of society produced a reaction against the alienating effects of mass society. Only individuals can really plan in a specific direction. Masses of people are not able to strive creatively or structure a truly meaningful existence. An awareness of this has, in Ortega's view, produced the weakened unity of community in governments throughout the world. The individual senses the compromised vitality of life in a mass society, thus moving away from its damaging effects.

Principal works: *Meditations on Quixote*, 1914, *Invertebrate Spain*, 1922, *Dehumanization of Art*, 1925, *The Revolt of the Masses*, 1929, *A Philosophy of History*, 1941, and *What is Philosophy?*, 1957.

> *"The most trivial and at the same time the most important note in human life is that man has no choice but to be always doing something to keep himself in existence. Life is given to us; we do not give it to ourselves, rather we find*

*ourselves in it, suddenly and without knowing how. But the life which is given us
is not given us ready-made; we must make it ourselves, each one his own. Life
is a task. . . . Each individual before doing anything must decide for himself
and at his own risk what he is going to do. But this decision is impossible unless
one possesses certain convictions concerning the nature of things around one,
the nature of other men, and the nature of oneself."*
    Jose Ortega y Gasset, *A Philosophy of History*

**osseous** - adj. consisting of or being like bone.

**ostiary** - n. a gatekeeper or guardian.

**otic** - adj. relating to the ear.

**Otto, Rudolf** (1869-1937) - a German philosopher of religion noted for his conceptional interpretation of religious phenomena, especially the spiritual attitude of the believer:
    1) *numinous* - is the feeling of awe that enters the believer in the presence of the holy place or sacred entity.
    2) *mysterium tremendum* - is the apprehension of mystery that lies beyond all reasoning. This apprehension is a sense of the fathomless nature of reality.
    3) *mysterium fascinosum* - is the spiritual satisfaction of the believer in giving in to the enchantment of religious existence.
    These three elements together comprise Otto's theoretical basis for identifying 'holiness'.
Otto's work incorporates a Kantian basis acquired from Jacob Fries (1773-1843), the Neo-Kantian School of Gottingen.
    Principal works: *The Philosophy of Religion of Kant-Fries and its Application to Theology*, 1909, *Darwinism and Religion*, 1910, *The Idea of the Holy*, 1917, and *Mysticism East and West*, 1926.

*"In every highly developed religion the appreciation of moral obligation and
duty, ranking as a claim of the deity upon man, has been developed side by side
with the religious feeling itself. None the less a profoundly humble and heartfelt
recognition of 'the holy' may occur in particular experiences without being
always or definitely charged or infused with the sense of moral demands."*
    Rudolf Otto, *The Idea of the Holy*

**otiose** - adj. useless.

**Overridingness, Principle of** - n. in ethical theory, the view that certain situations of moral choice may present a dilemma of doing one good and ignoring another on the basis that the greater good justifies the neglect of a lessor good, e.g. lying to protect a friend from serious harm.

**overweening** - adj. being arrogant or presumptuous.

**ovine** - adj. relating to sleep.

**paction** - n.  contract.

**padrone** - n.  an employer who controls the lives of his employees.

**pagination** - n.  the act of assembling and numbering pages, as in a book.

**Paine, Thomas** (1737-1809) - an American revolutionary leader, Paine argued for a democracy in which reason is more important than tradition.  In society, individuals should have equal rights but leadership must reveal both talent and wisdom, implying that few are capable of effective leadership.

Theologically, Paine was a deist.  He professed a love of nature and held it as proof of order and design pointing to a Creator.  Paine extended this belief in natural theology to learning, suggesting that human reason should imitate the work of God.  With regard to the problem of evil, Paine argued that suffering is primarily rooted in social injustice.

Principal works: *Common Sense*, 1776, *The Rights of Man*, 1792, and *The Age of Reason*, 1794.

> *"The true deist has but one Deity; and his religion consists in contemplating the power, wisdom, and benignity of the Deity in his works, and in endeavoring to imitate him in everything moral, scientific, and mechanical."*
> Thomas Paine, <u>The Age of Reason</u>

**paladin** - n.  an independent champion of a cause;  a knight errant.

**palaver** - n.  a prolonged meeting between primitive people or traders;  also, beguiling talk.

**paleontology** - n.  the study of life in past geological ages;  fossil study.

**Paley, William** (1743-1805) - an English philosopher who advanced the role of natural theology in philosophy, Paley recognized the historical decline of traditional religion and theology as effective theories of explanation for natural phenomena.  Even though many held to religion's importance as a kind of logic of causality, the writing was on the wall and Paley and others knew it.  Religion was being pushed into a smaller and smaller domain, the consequence of science's overwhelming power to provide improved explanations. For Paley, if the notion of God was to retain any place in human thought, revelation would have to include scientific facts.

Paley argued that complex designs within nature implied a Designer. The possibility of complex designs emerging by mere chance was, in Paley's view, astronomically small and he believed it was sufficient proof of God's existence.

Paley used the example of a watchmaker: if one finds a watch on a desert island, one logically assumes that other humans have been there and that the watch is the product of a watchmaker. So, the deist view argues that even though God may no longer have a relation to this world, the world is still the result of God's design and creation.

Principal works: *The Principles of Moral and Political Philosophy*, 1785, *The Evidences of Christianity*, 1794, and *Natural Theology*, 1802.

*"In what way can a revelation be made but by miracles? In none which we are able to conceive."*

William Paley, *Evidences of Christianity*

**palindrome** - n. a word, phrase, or statement that reads the same way when read forward or backward, e.g. 1991.

**palingenesis** - n. reincarnation; metempsychosis.

**palliate** - v. to moderate by the use of excuses.

**pallid** - adj. without vitality.

**palmary** - adj. worthy of praise; excellent.

**palpable** - adj. evident by sensation; observable.

**panatrophy** - n. the disintegration of a whole body or whole structure.

**pandect** - n. a comprehensive summary.

**pandemic** - adj. found universally; occurring everywhere; affecting a very large portion of a population.

**pander** - n. someone who profits from the weaknesses of others.

**pander** - v. to provide fulfillment for the vices of others.

**pandit** - n. in India, a respected teacher or sage.

**pandour** - n. a soldier of fortune; mercenary; rapacious warrior.

**panegyric** - n. formal praise; often a eulogy.

**Panentheism** - n. in philosophy, the view that God is in everything but not limited to it. Thus, it differs from pantheism in that God's existence is not limited to the material order. The being of all reality is part of the being of God, but the being of God is not limited to the being of all reality. The view attempts to preserve the theological properties of 'transcendence' and 'immanence' simultaneously. Gustav Fechner (1801-1887), German philosopher-psychologist, became a strong exponent of both panpsychism and panentheism in 1839 with the onset of his physical suffering and temporary blindness. A.N. Whitehead (1861-1947) and Charles Hartshorne (1897- ) also defended connections between panpsychism and panentheism.
    Text to consult: *Philosophers Speak of God*, Hartshorne & Reese, 1976.

**panjandrum** - n. an arrogant official; a pompous bureaucrat.

**panlogism** - n. the view that 'logos' is of ultimate importance as a key to structuring a coherent picture of reality.

**panoply** - n. in Ancient Greece, a reference to a hoplite's military armor; a complete covering; a magnificent display.

**Panpsychism** - n. in philosophy, the view that all matter is ultimately 'psychic' or 'spiritual' in nature. Arthur Schopenhauer (1788-1860) presented a panpsychist philosophy by arguing that the world is infused with 'will' that is more or less aware of its motion depending on the level of organized matter. One finds similar expressions in the ideas of A.N. Whitehead (1861-1947) and Charles Hartshorne (1897- ).
    Text to consult: *The World as Will and Idea*, Arthur Schopenhauer.

**pansophism** - n. the claim of having complete wisdom.

**Pantheism** - n. in philosophy and theology, the view that God and the world are one and the same. The term first appeared in the writings of John Toland about 1705. The characteristics of this view, however, go far back into Hinduism. Benedict Spinoza (1632-1677) was a strong advocate of pantheism. Also, F.H. Bradley (1846-1924) promoted a view which included many pantheistic philosophical claims. The basic logic of pantheism derives its forcefulness from the observation that going from nothing to something is merely an addition to a pre-existing non-material Godness which is necessarily infused with Divine properties. If God created the world, how is it possible for reality to be separated from that source of being?
    Text to consult: *Philosophers Speak of God*, Hartshorne & Reese, 1976.

**panzer** - adj. to be heavily armored.

**paraclete** - n. advocate, defender.

**paradisiacal** - adj. having the quality of paradise.

**paragon** - n. an example of true superiority.

**paralogism** - n. defective reasoning; a fallacious argument.

**paramimia** - n. the use of gestures to express thought in an innapropriate way, producing an ambiguous effect.

**paramour** - n. a mistress; an illicit lover.

**parataxic** - adj. characterized by conflict of an emotional nature.

**paregoric** - n. a pain-relieving medical prescription; originally a reference to opium-based pain killers.

**pariah** - n. a social outcast; someone who lives on the margins of society.

**parlance** - n. the appropriate way of speaking of a particular subject; a manner of speaking.

**parlous** - adj. dangerous; perilous.

**Parmenides** (ca. 515-450 B.C.) - a pre-Socratic philosopher who founded a school of philosophy at Elea. His work yielded important advances in the concept of change. Parmenides held that existence or realness implies absoluteness. Being and non-being do not share any mutual contingence by their essence. Something is, or it is-not. For Parmenides, contingency is not a property of real being. Moreover, if some thing were to arise from 'non-being', then non-being as an origination is something and not true 'non-being'.

The problem of making correct distinctions is compounded because humans have sense perceptions. Sense perception is a denial of the logic of 'being' vs. 'non-being', thus sense perception is an illusion.

The work of Parmenides was a challenge to the views of Heraclitus and a resource for the subsequent theories of Plato (see Plato's dialogues: *Parmenides, Theaetetus,* and *Sophist).*

Principal work: *On Nature*

*"There is only one other description of the way remaining, (namely), that (What Is) Is. To this way there are very many sign-posts: that Being has no coming-into-being and no destruction, for it is whole of limb, without motion, and without end. And it never 'Was', nor 'Will Be', because it 'Is' now, a whole all together, One, continuous; for what creation of it will you look for? How, whence (could it have) sprung? Nor shall I allow you to speak or think of it as springing from Not-Being; for it is neither expressible nor thinkable that What-Is-Not Is."*

*Parmenides, On Nature, fragment #7*

**Parousia** - n. in theology, reference or belief in the future coming of Christ. At that time Christ will judge both the living and the dead and finish up the present world order. Though early Christians believed the parousia to be imminent, the exact time and place are not truly specified.  In fact, there is opposition to speculation about the exact details of the parousia.

Its original meaning is 'presence' or 'arrival'.  In Platonism the term 'parousia' implies the presence of form in matter.   In Teilhard de Chardin, 'parousia' is the evolutionary and spiritual anticipation of Christ's return, as the culimination of human spiritual development.

**parricide** - n.  the killing of a father, mother or close relative.

**parsimony** - n.  the exercise of caution in the use of money, to the point of being stingy. In philosophy, the *principle of parsimony* refers to the simplification of theory.  If there are several logically equivalent ways of expressing a theory, then choose the simplest version.

**parthenogenesis** - n.  development of an individual from an unfertilized gamete, occurring among plants and lower invertebrate animals.

**parturient** - adj.  close to giving birth.

**parvenu** - n.  an individual who suddenly becomes wealthy or acquires a position of importance but lacks refinement and social skills;  an upstart.

**Pascal, Blaise** (1623-1662) - a French philosopher of mathematics, logic, and religion, Pascal accepted Descartes mechanistic model of nature.  He argued for certain fixed notions: number, matter, change, space, and time, but concluded that a knowledge of their origins and destiny were impossible.  He also invented a primitive computer from his strong understanding of mathematics and logic.  It was, however, limited by its being made of wood.

Pascal doubted the possibility of proving God's existence but presented an interesting puzzle known as "Pascal's Wager":  1) God exists, or  2) God does not exist. If you wager that God exists, and it is true, then you win all.  If God does not exist, you lose nothing.  If you wager that God does not exist, and it is true, then you win nothing.  If God does exist, you lose everything.  So, the belief in God is better than atheism.

Pascal regarded human existence as corrupt and taught that  contemplative life is the only source of happiness.  Moreover, he emphasized that all reasoning concludes with uncertainty and fails to satisfy our deepest needs for love and spiritual unity.

Principal works: *Essay on Conics*, 1640, *New Experiments Concerning the Vacuum*, 1647, *The Geometric Spirit*, 1658, *Pensees* (Reflections on Religion), 1669.

> *"Men never do evil so completely and cheerfully as when they do it from religious conviction."*
> - *Blaise Pascal, <u>Pensees</u>*

**pathos** - n.  a quality or condition that arouses sympathy or concern, e.g., physical or emotional suffering.

**pathosis** - n.  any corrupted condition;  diseased state.

**Patristics** - n.  the study of the philosophy, theology, and writings of the early church fathers.  It stems from the word 'pater', meaning father.  All important Christian writers up to the 13th Century are referred to as 'Fathers'.  In its strictest usage it ends with writers in the 8th Century.  Patristics examines the defense of traditional dogma and theology.  Thus, it also studies the theological heresies which helped to forge the official theological doctrines of Christianity.

Texts to consult: _Patrology_, Berthold Altaner, 1961, and _Handbook of Patrology_, Patrick J. Hamell, 1968.

**peccable** - adj.  tendency to commit moral error.

**peculate** - v.  to steal or embezzle.

**pediculous** - adj.  infested with lice;  having a lousy quality.

**Peirce, Charles Sanders** (1839-1914) - an American philosopher of pragmatism, Peirce (pronounced 'purse') developed important insights about semiotics, the theory of signs.

Signs are basic to epistemology and involve four important features: 1) the sign or symbol (written or spoken), 2) an object corresponding to the sign, 3) a conceptual interpretation of the sign, and 4) a mind which is capable of using and interpreting signs.

Peirce was a realist and his theory of perception admits the facticity of the external world.  The point of all thought, for Peirce, is to gain satisfactory results in life.  The pursuit of truth is one of approximation.  Truth is never finished (the principle of fallibilism).  Though nothing is completely knowable, we accomplish ever-increasing certitude through aggressive and careful observation of the world.

Ontology and phenomenology aid us in the identification of reality.  Matter, as it appears to us through the senses, is a collection of essences to be described.

Principal works: _Collected Papers_, 1878-1914.

> _"Nothing is 'vital' for science; nothing can be.  Its accepted propositions, therefore, are but opinions at most; and the list is provisional.  The scientific man is not in the least wedded to his conclusions.  He risks nothing upon them. He stands ready to abandon one or all as soon as experience opposes them."_
>
> C.S. Peirce, _Collected Papers_

> _"The person who confesses that there is such a thing as truth, which is distinguished from falsehood simply by this, that if acted upon it should, on full consideration, carry us to the point we aim at and not astray, and then, convinced of this, dares to know the truth and seeks to avoid it, is in a sorry state of mind indeed."_
>
> C.S. Peirce, _Fixation of Belief_

**pejoration** - n.  a worsening.

**pejorative** - adj. having a bad effect, especially in terms of a thing's perceived quality or condition.

**pelagic** - adj. concerning the open sea.

**pellucid** - adj. transparent; easy to comprehend.

**penultimate** - adj. next to the last in a finite sequence.

**penurious** - adj. influenced by greed to the impossibility of sharing; stinginess.

**peradventure** - n. an unplanned event; chance; also, speculation.

**perambulate** - v. to travel or journey on foot.

**perdition** n. an act capable of ruining the spirit or soul; eternal destruction.

**perdurable** - adj. everlasting.

**peregrinate** - v. to move across.

**peremptory** - adj. in dictatorial fashion; without debate or notice.

**perfervid** - adj. extremely intense, especially in regard to the emotions.

**perfidy** - n. a violation of trust.

**perfunctory** - adj. done with little interest.

**perfuse** - v. to spread; to flow.

**pergola** - n. a structure of posts and beams with cross rafters and being open; arbor; patio.

**periapt** - n. something which is wrapped around; an amulet.

**permute** - v. to alter; to change.

**pernicious** - adj. harmful; dangerous.

**perpicacious** - adj. having great insight.

**perpicuity** - n. mental clarity.

**persiflage** - n. useless talk.

**persiflage** - n. useless talk.

**Personalism** - n. in philosophy, the view that the concept of 'person' is the ultimate category of meaning. The person, self, or thinker stands in contrast to the impersonal nature of mechanistic materialism which makes up the bulk of modern life. Personalism emphasizes the importance of moral values, individual persons, and human freedom. This philosophy also poses the reality of God as personal and uncreated. Ethical principles gain their validity from God as Supreme Spirit or Personality. This in turn implies that God is present as a type of worker, attempting to impart moral and religious meaning to the world. E.S. Brightman (1884-1953) was a leading defender of this view. Walt Whitman (1819-1892) also revealed personalist idealism in his writings, and some very good insights are present in the work of Emmanuel Mounier (1905-1950), *What is Personalism?*, 1947, and *Personalism*, 1949.

**pertinacious** - adj. stubborn; unwilling to concede.

**peruse** - v. to examine carefully.

**petrous** - adj. rocky; like stone.

**petulant** - adj. ill-tempered; hostile in attitude.

**pharisee** - n. a sanctimonious hypocrite.

**phatic** - adj. to be focused on feelings and emotional states rather than substantial ideas.

**Phenomenology** - n. in philosophy, study of human consciousness in relation to phenomena, especially its essence and use; a preface to reasoning about reality. In the phenomenology of Edmund Husserl (1859-1938) consciousness is seen as the central fact to deciphering reality. The essence of consciousness is to indicate or point out an objective reality. Consciousness is always consciousness of something. The task of reason is to detail this consciousness, to describe its content and the very activity of structuring pictures of experience. It is along these lines that the work of phenomenology became so important to the research of the existentialists, e.g., Jean-Paul Sartre, Martin Heidegger, Maurice Merleau-Ponty. Phenomenology is almost a technical program for thought analysis, operating as the microscope to further elaborate insights and observation.
Text to consult: *The Problems of Phenomenology*, Martin Heidegger, 1975.

**philander** - v. to make love without commitment.

**phillipic** - n. a verbal condemnation.

**philistia** - n. a reference to cultural philistines; cultural barbarians.

**philistine** - n. an individual who has no appreciation of aesthetic or philosophic values; one who has but the crudest understanding of life and reality.

150

**philogyny** - n. love for women.

**philology** - n. the study of language, especially historical and comparative considerations.

**philoprogenetive** - adj. having a love for children or offspring.

**Philosophy** - n. the love of wisdom. In the ancient philosopher Pythagoras, the goal of wisdom had connection to salvation and religious existence. For Socrates, self-knowledge was the principle goal of philosophy, coupled with a commitment to clarity of linguistic meaning. During the Middle Ages, philosophy was regarded as an accessory to theology and the life of faith or a threat to that faith, depending upon the aggression of philosophy in relation to religious dogma. In the 20th Century philosophy has been concerned with expanding the influence of logic through positivism, has offered valuable insights into psychology through existentialism, and has witnessed the re-emergence of spiritual philosophy through the influence of Eastern philosophy and Western process philosophy.
   Philosophy breaks down into five primary branches of study:
1) *Logic* - the study of reasoning correctly. It includes the study of incorrect reasoning.
2) *Epistemology* - the study of theories of knowledge; its sources, nature, and validity.
3) *Metaphysics* - the study of the nature of reality, literally 'beyond reality'. It is subdivided into *ontology*, the study of being, and *cosmology*, the study of the origins, nature, and development of the universe.
4) *Aesthetics* - the study of beauty or value in things.
5) *Ethics* - the study of human conduct in groups and individuals, with the aim of discerning 'the Good'.

**philtre** - n. a substance, magical or dietary, which arouses sexual passion; a magical substance.

**phlegmatic** - adj. showing a temperament which is sluggish and not easily moved to emotion.

**photobathic** - adj. of the layer of the ocean or sea that light penetrates.

**photobiotic** - adj. requiring light in order to live.

**photophobia** - n. morbid fear of light.

**phreatic** - adj. having to do with ground water.

**phronesis** - n. a special judgment or wisdom in deciding worthy goals and how to achieve them; practical wisdom.

**phyletic** - adj. relating to race or species.

**phylogeny** - n. the historical study of the racial history of an organism; the study of the evolution of a group of organisms.

**phylum** - n.  the first division  in the biological classification of animals;  the origin of a line of organisms.

**physis** - n.  in philosophy, reference to the single underlying reality.

**phytophagous** - adj.  being plant eating.

**phytotoxin** - n.  any poison or toxin produced by a plant.

**piacular** - adj.  the quality of making good for some sin or wrong.

**Piaget, Jean** (1896-1980) - a Swiss philosopher whose intense interest in logic, mathematics, and action led to a lifelong study of the development of knowledge in children.  In a way, Piaget re-examined the whole issue of Kantian categories of thought and worked heavily in the area of epistemology, as well as psychology.

Piaget studied the development of abstract concepts of classes and numbers and more physical concepts of speed, time, space, conservation, and chance, linking these to human action. With regard to language, math, and logic, Piaget believed the child comes to primitive acquaintance through play and only later takes up the conceptual arrangement of these notions.  Play is simply a trial and error use of curiosity to understand one's surroundings.  With the accumulation of experience, the child experiences a rational (ordered) awareness of its world.  Mistakes occur primarily at the frontier of the child's experience, with past successes being the anchor for corrections.  Piaget called this characteristic of thought "reversibility", and believed it to be the basis for deductive reasoning.

In re-working the Kantian notion of time, Piaget concluded that Kant was wrong in setting up time as an *a priori* intuition.  Children often confuse time with notions of size, height, and other visible clues of age.  It is similar to the child's early difficulty with shapes.  Children first distinguish only open and closed configurations and lack an ordered system of perspectives.

Principal works: *The Language and Thought of the Child*, 1923, *The Child's Conception of the World*, 1926, *The Child's Conception of Physical Reality*, 1926, *The Mechanisms of Perception*, 1961, and *Success and Understanding*, 1974.

> *"All in all, it is thus clear that . . . the grasp of consciousness lags behind precocious successes in the field of action and that it progresses from the periphery to the central regions of that action, they (findings) also face us with the new situation of practical success attained by stages with gradual coordinations at distinct levels: in these cases, there is, first of all, a more or less long phase when the action and conceptualization are almost on the same level and when there are constant exchanges between them.  Then (next stage) we find a complete reversal of the initial situation: conceptualization no longer provides action with limited and provisional plans that have to be revised and adjusted, but with an overall programme . . . when practice is guided by theory."*
> *Jean Piaget, <u>Success and Understanding</u>*

**pica** - n. a desire to eat something that is not normally considered food.

**piquant** - adj. savory; a pleasant sharp flavor.

**pique** - v. to cause resentment; to cause irritation.

**piscivorous** - adj. fish-eating.

**pistology** - n. the study of faith.

**placate** - v. to moderate feelings, especially by compromise; to appease.

**Planck, Max Karl Ernst Ludwig** (1858-1947) - a German philosopher of physics, Planck worked out the theory of quantum energy, essential to quantum mechanics. Receiving his Ph.D. at the age of 21, Planck taught at the universities of Munich, Kiel, and Berlin.

Planck studied blackbody radiation in 1897. A blackbody is a body that absorbs the energy that falls upon it, lacking reflective properties, thus it appears black. Some surfaces absorb nearly 98% of energy. Absorption creates higher temperatures, thus blackbodies are also perfect emitters of energy. Planck resolved problems related to the uniform expression of energy exchanges in blackbodies, meaning Planck used the concept of discrete *quanta* to reveal the nature of events in radiation and matter. This work was later useful to Albert Einstein and Niels Bohr in their own discoveries.

Principal works: *Scientific Autobiography and Other Papers*, 1949, and *The Universe in the Light of Modern Physics*, 1937.

> *"There have been times when science and philosophy were alien, if not actually antagonistic to each other. These times have passed. Philosophers have realized that they have no right to dictate to scientists their aims and the methods for attaining them; and scientists have learned that the starting-point of their investigations does not lie solely in the perceptions of the senses, and that science cannot exists without some small portion of metaphysics. Modern Physics impresses us particularly with the truth of the old doctrine which teaches that there are realities existing apart from our sense perceptions, and that there are problems and conflicts where these realities are of greater value for us than the richest treasures of the world of experience."*
>
> Max Planck, <u>The Universe in the Light of Modern Physics</u>

**Plato** (427-347 B.C.) - a Greek philosopher and the most influential thinker in the Western world. The extensive body of philosophical thought which makes up Plato's system is partially portrayed in his Allegory of the Cave: In the Cave (ignorance), there are a number of prisoners who are fated by their chains (conformity) to play a game identifying shadows (appearances) on a wall. Prisoners receive awards by their skill of identification and a kind hierarchy of sorts exists for these captives. One of the prisoners is freed and forcibly removed from the Cave, which he regards as his home. The initial encounter with the light of the outside world has a blinding effect (alienation), and it is difficult for the captive to resist running back to the cave. In time, the prisoner is positively overwhelmed (enlightenment) by the superior appearance (knowledge) of this outside world, and in his excitement, he desires to liberate (education) his friends from their ignorant existence. When he returns to the cave, he experiences the reverse problem. He is blinded (alienated) by the darkness and stumbles in descent. The prisoners are sure their comrade is insane, for he can no longer identify shadows on the wall. He, in turn, insists that they are deceived by their inferior knowledge of reality. Plato, in remembrance of Socrates' execution, explains that the liberated prisoner will be killed by his fellows if he insists that they leave the cave.

Plato's thought is a type of classical idealism, for it maintains that Ideas are the highest order of reality, while matter is subject to the formative effects of the Ideas. The physical world is an illusion due to its perishable nature. Ideas or Forms are eternal archetypes which are imperfectly represented in the whole range of material objects we find around us.

Plato's cosmology includes the notion of a World Soul, the original home of human souls. It also employs the notion of the Demiurge, a type of craftsman deity, which works with forms and matter to fashion the empirical world. Human souls inhabit bodies due to the loss of harmony, a 'falling' from the World Soul. Life is a kind of challenge to re-establish the harmony of the soul and return to the World Soul.

The soul is composed of three elements: reason, spirit, and desire. The confusion and conflict of life reflect the relative imbalance of the soul's elements. The imbalance is a consequence of ignorance, which is for Plato the source of all evil. Morality is a central issue in Plato's philosophy, conveying the importance of correct value formation in order that individuals and societies transmit such values to succeeding generations. Life is thus a 'poiesis', an art or creation.

Wisdom, courage, and temperance are central virtues of the soul, corresponding to the three elements - reason, spirit, and desire. By living according to these virtues, the soul experiences a fulfillment of function and design. Enlightenment ensues, shaping the daily life of the individual.

Socially and politically, the soul is manifested in class structures: *rulers, warriors* and *artisan-merchants*. Rulers represent wisdom; warriors represent courage; and merchants and artisans represent desire. Governments are defined by the spiritual constitution of the state and are ranked in a descending order by Plato: *aristocracy* - guided by reason, *timocracy* - guided by honor and glory in warfare, *plutocracy* - guided by the love of wealth, *democracy* - guided by the views of the masses, *tyranny* - guided by a despot or group of despots *(oligarchy)*.

The process of finding a true understanding of reality takes the individual mind through four stages of development:
1) *Imagination* - the use of fantasy, as with poets and artists; the realm of subjective knowledge.
2) *Belief* - the acceptance of the visible world as the source of truth.
3) *Reason* - the mental movement to the principles of logic and mathematics.
4) *Enlightenment* - the awareness of the unity of the world and its relation to Forms.

Principal works: *The Dialogues: Apology, Crito, Euthyphro, Ion, Protagoras, Gorgias, Meno, Cratylus, Phaedo, Republic, Symposium, Parmenides, Sophist, Theaetetus, Phaedrus, Politicus, Philebus, Timaeus, Critias,* and *Laws.*

*"Surely the soul can reflect best when it is free of all distractions such as hearing or sight or pain or pleasure of any kind - that is, when it ignores the body and becomes as far as possible independent, avoiding all physical contacts and associations as much as it can, in its search for reality."*
Plato, <u>Phaedo</u> 65c

**Platonic year** - n. the time period in which a complete revolution of the equinoxes is achieved, about 26,000 years; procession of the equinoxes.

**Platonism** - n. in philosophy, the views and influence of Plato (427-347 B.C.). Plato's philosophy is recorded in the *Dialogues*, the most important of which are the *Phaedo* (a discussion of immortality; the relation of soul and body, and the role of eternal Forms), *Symposium* (a discussion of eros, the meaning of beauty, and the value of contemplative life), *Protagoras* (a discussion of the notion of the good, the essence of knowledge, and the idea of goodness), and the *Republic* (a discussion of the ideal political state and the psychological nature of humanity).

**Pleasure Principle** - n. (German, *Lustprinzip*; Spanish, *principio de placer*) in psychology, a governing feature of psychic activity; an economic factor in the selection of actions by the agent. The ego's assessment of obstacles to pleasure represents it desire to acquire satisfactions by the most direct route. It is complemented by the tendency to avoid unpleasure.
Text to consult: <u>*Beyond the Pleasure Principle*</u>, Sigmund Freud.

**plebeian** - adj. relating to the common person; crude, coarse, unremarkable.

**plenary** - adj. complete; full.

**pleonasm** - n. the use of words beyond what is necessary; excessive description.

**pleophagous** - adj. eating an assortment of foods; also, being parasitic on a number of hosts.

**Plotinus** (204-270 A.D.) - an Egyptian philosopher and the founder of Neo-Platonism, Plotinus invented the Metaphor of the Sun to describe his beliefs. God, as the One or *Nous* (Mind), is the ultimate source of all reality. From the One flow emanations of reality, beginning with a World Soul, which has ascending and descending features (a motion for proximity or distance from God). The next emanation is the human soul, which possesses a 'fallen' nature. Captive in the bodily form, the soul is doomed to transmigrations until it can find complete salvation. Finally, there is the last emanation, the world of matter, which borders on darkness and nothingness. The soul's captivity in a material body forces it to struggle with the presence of formlessness. A disciplined life is necessary to create union with God, the One.
Principal works: *Enneads, 6 vols.*

*"If we do not possess good, we cannot bestow it; nor can we ever purvey any good thing to one that has no power of receiving good."*
*Plotinus, <u>Enneads</u>, vol. 4*

**Pluralism** - n. in philosophy, the view that the world is composed of multiple types of entities. It includes the view that ideological novelty and difference are proof of variety in reality. It stands in contrast to monism which emphasizes the oneness of substance and dualism which offers a bi-polar perception of reality.

**pluvial** - adj. rainy.

**podalic** - adj. relating to the feet; connected to the base.

**Poiesis** - n. in philosophy, especially Aristotle, the term is a reference to productive science. It literally has to do with making, creating, producing. In the philosophy of James Carse, *Finite and Infinite Games,* 1986, life is a poiema, a created object.

**poignant** - adj. deeply affecting; sharp.

**pogrom** - n. organized extermination or massacre.

**poltroon** - n. a complete coward.

**polyandry** - n. the practice of having more than one husband simultaneously.

**polydipsia** - n. excessive thirst.

**pomology** - n. the study of fruit growing.

**portend** - v. to warn.

**poseur** - n. someone who works at styling life or their ideas in order to impress others.

**post-prandial** - adj. after dinner.

**postrosse** - adj. bent backward.

**potamic** - adj. relating to rivers.

**potation** - n. the act of drinking; an amount of drink taken, usually alcoholic.

**potentiate** - v. to give power; to make vital.

**pother** - n. mental confusion; a burst of unorganized activity.

**Pragmatism** - n. the philosophical view that knowledge is for the sake of life, that knowledge must enhance the practice of living; consistent with the Greek word *pragmatikos*, meaning 'deed' or 'act'.  This school of thought was developed by three American philosophers: Charles Peirce, William James, and John Dewey.  Pragmatism endorses the correspondence theory of truth and is closely aligned with realism as opposed to rational idealism.

> *"The pragmatist clings to facts and concreteness, observes truth at its work in particular cases, and generalizes.  Truth, for him, becomes a class-name for all sorts of definite working-values in experience.  For the rationalist it remains pure abstraction, to the bare name of which we must defer.  When the pragmatist undertakes to show in detail just 'why' we must defer, the rationalist is unable to recognize the concrete from which his own abstraction is taken.  He accuses us of 'denying' truth;  whereas we have only sought to trace exactly why people follow it always ought to follow it.  Your typical ultra-abstractionist fairly shudders at concreteness: other things being equal, he positively prefers the pale and spectral.  If the two universes were offered, he would always choose the skinny outline rather than the rich thicket of reality."*
> *William James, <u>Pragmatism</u>*

**prandial** - adj.  relating to any meal.

**prate** - n.  meaningless talk.

**prattle** - v.  to engage in useless conversation;  to chatter like a child.

**praxis** - n.  practice.

**Prayer** - n.  in theology,  a thought or word directed toward God.  Its efficacy rests on the transcendent and personal reality of God.  It presupposes a relation that is disclosed through the atonement created by Jesus Christ.  Moreover, it is the essence of the search for God, leading  to union and spiritual likeness:

> *"You who are love itself, give me the grace of love.  Give me Yourself, so that all my days may finally empty into the one day of your eternal life."*
> *Karl Rahner (1904-1984)*

**preamble** - n.  an introductory set of remarks or statements.

**prebend** - n.  a financial compensation given to a clergyman, especially when working for a cathedral or college church.

**precatory** - adj.  relating to a request.

**precocious** - adj.  showing early independence or maturity of development.

**predaceous** - adj.  tending to live on others;  tending to ruin or spoil.

**presage** - v.  to warn;  to indicate a foreshadowing of an event.

**preterhuman** - adj. beyond what is human.

**preternatural** - adj. beyond what is natural or ordinary.

**prevaricate** - v. to make misleading statements.

**prevenient** - adj. occurring before.

**prig** - n. a fussy, self-righteous person.

**prima donna** - n. a very vain and undisciplined person.

**prima facie** - adj. apparent.

**primal** - adj. early; original; primitive.

**primogenitor** - n. an ancestor.

**primogeniture** - n. the right to property held by the eldest son; exclusive rights to inheritance.

**Principle of participation** - n. in philosophical anthropology, a view of Lucien Levy-Bruhl (1857-1939). Levy-Bruhl's work on the thought of primitive people revealed a pre-logical consciousness. To describe this consciousness Levy-Bruhl coined the term *principle of participation*. It observes that contradiction in primitive societies is apparently acceptable in that any thing or person can be both itself and not itself. This is achieved through the emphasis on mystical factors in the thinking of primitive people. Life as 'mystery' allows non-logical judgment. Primitives are able to believe both sides of a problem that Westernized persons would regard as contradiction. Correspondence to reality or truth as we know it does not define or organize the thoughts of primitive societies.

**pristine** - adj. being of original form or purity.

**privy** - adj. confidential.

**probity** - n. integrity; honesty.

**procellous** - adj. stormy; unstable; chaotic.

**prochronism** - n. the mistake of assigning an earlier date than the true one.

**proclivity** - adj. a natural inclination.

**proctology** - n. the study of rectal problems and disorders.

**procumbent** - adj. lying face down.

**prodigal** - adj.  being extravagant;  wasteful.

**prodigious** - adj.  being extraordinary.

**prodigy** - n.  a very talented child;  an amazing event or deed.

**prodrome** - n.  a warning signal, especially of disease or decline.

**proem** - n.  introduction; preface.

**proffer** - v.  to present for consideration.

**profligate** - n.  a person completely given over to uncontrolled sensual hedonism;  an immoral person.

**profluent** - adj.  to flow out smoothly.

**progeny** - n.  children; offspring; successors.

**prognathous** - adj.  with projecting jaw.

**Projection** - n. (German, *Projektion*; Spanish, *proyeccion*) in psychological theory, the relocation of a psychological condition in some external object or person.  It is usually representative of a defense action and is often associated with paranoia.

In Gestalt theory, projection is determined to be the sending  of a biased interpretation onto external objects and persons.  A carpenter views the world by the interests, habits and experiences of that life.  A businessperson sees the world as moments and units of profit and loss.  A lawyer sees a legal dimension to all of reality.

**prolepsis** - n.  in logic, the anticipation of a future conclusion as if already in existence.

**prolicide** - n.  killing one's children or offspring.

**prolix** - adj.  tediously wordy.

**prolocutor** - n.  one who presides;  chairperson.

**prolusion** - n.  an introductory and sometimes experimental essay.

**promulgate** - v.  to make known publicly.

**pronto** - adj.  without hesitation.

**propaedeutic** - adj.  preparatory; introductory.

**propensity** - n.  a strong inclination or leaning.

**prophylaxis** - n.  a preventative for disease.

**propinquity** - n.  nearness.

**propitious** - adj.  favorable.

**propter hoc** - Latin meaning " because of this".

**prorogue** - v. to suspend;  to postpone.

**prosaic** - adj.  of the everyday world;  dull.

**proscribe** - v.  to prohibit or forbid.

**prosodemic** - adj.  being of disease spread by personal contact.

**prosthesis** - n.  an artificial replacement for a missing body part, especially a limb.

**Protagoras** (490-410 B.C.) - a Greek philosopher and member of the Sophist school, Protagoras argued that all knowledge is subjective or relative to the individual.  This condition is continued in societies and accounts for the different cultural attitudes toward moral issues as well.  He held that everything is in a state of flux and that judgment could only be specific and never absolute.

Protagoras' fame rested on his reputation as a tutor for aspiring politicians, lawyers, and charlatans in the art of argument.  In fact, he became quite wealthy by his teaching skill, as he taught his disciples how to attack all sides of an issue.

Principal works: *On Truth, On the Gods,* and *Antilogic.*

*"About the gods, I am not able to know whether they exist or do not exist, nor what they are like in form; for the factors preventing knowledge are many: the obscurity of the subject, and the shortness of human life."*
Protagoras, <u>On the Gods</u>

Text to consult:  <u>*A History of Greek Philosophy*</u>, vol. 3, W.K.C. Guthrie, 1979.

**protean** - adj.  versatile.

**protract** - v.  to extend outward.

**protreptic** - n.  a statement used to persuade.

**provenance** - n.  origin.

**prurient** - adj.  causing or having restless sexual craving.

**psellism** - n.  stuttering.

**psephology** - n. the study of elections.

**pseudodementia** - n. a temporary state of insanity due to emotional influences.

**pseudomania** - n. pathological lying.

**pseudomorph** - n. an unclassifiable form; false form.

**pseudoscience** - n. theories and systems of thought which are plausible but have no hard empirical basis for belief.

**psittacism** - n. parrot-like talk; talk that is not comprehended by the speaker.

**psychagogy** - n. the practice of leading souls, especially after death; also meaning a practice of influencing the conduct of others by the suggestion of exciting goals.

**psychasthenia** - n. a neurotic disorder characterized by phobias and acute anxiety; it is manifested as perpetual doubt and a susceptibility to trivial fears.

**psychataxia** - n. inability to concentrate.

**Psychoanalysis** - n. the methods and theories of Freud, with derivative effects in Carl Jung, OttoRank, Alfred Adler, Erik Erikson, Melanie Klein, and others. Psychoanalysis is the picturing of the mental life of the individual with regard to specific theoretical concepts, including *repression, the Unconscious, regression, infant sexuality, defence, projection, the Oedipus complex, wish-fulfillment, the Damming of the Libido, free-association,* and *cathartic method.*

Psychoanalytic treatment of neurosis requires several meetings per week for several years to outline the psychic arrangement of the patient's mind. While it is an important tool in the treatment of mental illness, the results are often questionable, and there is no clear consensus on the handling of sympoms and attitudes in the patient.

In some models, such as Erikson, there is an invariable theory of human development which does not admit the importance of human freedom or question the ethical assumptions in deciding what is normal behavior. In fact, psychoanalysis often assigns 'moral concerns' to religion, simultaneously discrediting it as a legitimate source of meaning and purpose.

Texts to consult: *Psychotherapy and Morality*, Joseph Margolis, 1968, *The Myth of Mental Illness*, Thomas Szasz, 1961, and *Childhood and Society*, E. Erikson, 1950.

**psychogenic** - adj. originating in the mind.

**psycholagnia** - n. intense imaginative preoccupation with erotic ideas.

**psycholepsy** - n. a loss of drive; a sense of hopelessness.

**psychomancy** - n. communication with spirits.

**psychomachia** - n. a conflict within the soul, especially with regard to good and evil.

**psychomorphism** - n. in primitive religion, the attribution of mental states to animals and non-living things.

**psychopannychism** - n. in theology, the view that the soul enters sleep at death and does not awaken until the resurrection of the body.

**psychostasia** - n. in the Ancient world, the belief in and the act of weighing of souls or spirits.

**psychotechnics** - n. the use of psychological theory for controlling human behavior, especially for practical purposes.

**psychotechnology** - n. the study of psychic manipulation, e.g., in business, industry, and other institutional settings.

**psychrophobia** - n. morbid fear of anything cold.

**pudency** - n. modesty.

**puerile** - adj. relating to childishness, immaturity.

**puerilism** - n. childish behavior in an adult; a psychological disorder.

**pugnacious** - adj. belligerent; troublesome.

**pullulate** - v. to multiply or breed quickly; to swarm.

**punctilious** - adj. showing great conformity to codes, rules, conventions.

**pundit** - n. expert.

**purlieu** - n. a favorite place; a haunt; an outlying area.

**purloin** - v. to steal; to acquire wrongfully.

**purport** - v. to imply or claim.

**pursang** - adj. genuine beyond question.

**pursuivant** - n. a follower.

**purvey** - v. to supply.

**purview** - n. scope; a range of vision or understanding.

**putative** - adj.  generally regarded or supposed.

**putrefy** - v.  to make rotten.

**putrilage** - n.  rotten putrid matter.

**pyknic** - adj.  short muscular build.

**pyretic** - adj.  relating to fever.

**pyromancy** - n.  divination by the use of fire.

**pyromania** - n.  obsessive-compulsive incendiarism;  irresistible need to set fires.

**pyrophobia** - n.  morbid fear of fire, especially their occurrence and immediacy.

**pyrosis** - n.  heartburn.

**Pythagoreanism** - n.  in philosophy, a movement started by Pythagoras (570-500 B.C.). Famous for their reverence toward mathematics, Pythagoreans used numbers to outline a type of religious life.  Along with astronomy as number, the analysis of harmony, good health as a measure of harmony,  they developed a geometry.  Pythagoras' work with musical tones in the shortening and lengthening of a vibrating string led to the belief that number is the secret to reality.

Text to consult: *A History of Greek Philosophy*, vol. 1, W.K.C. Guthrie, 1977.

**pythonic** - adj.  being prophetic.

**'Q'** - n. in theology, a reference to the writings which may have contributed to the formation of the Gospels in the New Testament, especially Matthew and Luke. 'Q' derives from the German *"Quelle",* meaning 'source. The 'Q' theory was introduced in the work of Adolf von Harnack and developed by B.H. Streeter.
Text to consult: *The Four Gospels*, B.H. Streeter, 1924.

**QED** - (quod erat demonstrandum) Latin meaning, "which was to be demonstrated"; often found in deductively reasoned work, e.g. Spinoza.

**quadrivium** - n. in medieval schools a curriculum composed of arithmetic, geometry, astronomy, and music.

**quaggy** - adj. marsh like.

**quandary** - n. a practical dilemma; a mental state of doubt.

**quash** - v. to suppress or nullify.

**quaternary** - adj. having four parts.

**quercine** - adj. relating to oak; hardness.

**querulous** - adj. being of a complaining nature; whining.

**quiddity** - n. essence.

**quidnunc** - n. one who seeks to know all the latest gossip; a news monger; an individual who has an insatiable need for speculating and learning of the foibles of others.

**quiescent** - adj. quiet; silent.

**Quietism** - n. in theology, a 17th century spiritual view which emphasizes the importance of withdrawing from the world and its affairs in order to discover God. It advocates an ethic of complete non-violence and absence of effort. It recommends a life of prayer in which even the desire for virtue is an obstacle to entering a pure faith experience.

164

**quietus** - n.  anything which ends a dispute;  that which puts at rest.

**Quine, Willard Van Orman**  (1908-   ) - an American logician in the tradition of Whitehead and Russell.  Quine specializes in the philosophical and meta-linguistic problems of semantics, logic, and epistemology.  Like most modern logicians, he rejects the value of traditional metaphysics, preferring to designate metaphysical issues as 'ontic theory'.  As such, metaphysical reflection must conform to scientific obsrvations of reality.

Principal works include: *Mathematical Logic*, 1940, *Methods of Logic*, 1950, *Word and Object*, 1960, *Set Theory and Its Logic*, 1963, and *Ontological Relativity*.

> *"I see philosophy not as an a priori propaedeutic or groundwork for science, but as continuous with science.  I see philosophy and science in the same boat - a boat which, to revert to Neurath's figure as I so often do, (see page 135) we can rebuild only at sea while staying afloat in it.  There is no external vantage point, no first philosophy."*
> W.V.O. Quine, Ontological Relativity

**quintescence** - n.  the purest example.

**quisling** - n.  a traitor who also collaborates with the enemy.

**quittance** - n.  release from duty or obligation.

**quondam** - adj.  previous; former.

**quorum** - n.  the minimum number necessary to transact a meeting.

**quotidian** - adj.  being ordinary.

**Radhakrishnan, Sarvepalli** (1888-1975) - an Indian philosopher whose strong advocacy of spiritual simplicity and asceticism worked for his popularity as a political leader (President of India, 1962-1967).

Radhakrishnan argued that *maya* (ordinary experience) is a middle zone between unreality and the Absolute, with its origins lying in the Absolute. God is also neither completely transcendent nor completely immanent. The true nature of God inspires a kind of ethical universalism and an attitude of religious tolerance. These things are learned through authentic meditation and the development of an ethical life.

Principal works: *Indian Philosophy, 2 vols.*, 1923, *The Philosophy of the Upanishads*, 1924, *An Idealist View of Life*, 1929, *Eastern Religion and Western Thought*, 1939, and *Religion in a Changing World*, 1967.

> *"The supreme reality is incomprehensible in the sense that it cannot be expressed in logical propositions but it is increasingly apprehensible to the purified mind."*
> S. Radhakrishnan, <u>Eastern Religion and Western Thought</u>

> *"Karma is not so much a principle of retribution as one of continuity. Good produces good, evil produces evil. Love increases our power of love, hatred our power of hatred. It emphasizes the great importance of right action."*
> S. Radhakrishnan, <u>An Idealist View of Life</u>

**raffish** - adj. cheap; vulgar; crude.

**Rahner, Karl** (1904-1984) - a German theologian and Jesuit priest, Rahner became a type of successor to Joseph Marechal, the "Father of Transcendental Thomism". His theology and philosophy also reveal a complexity reminiscent of his teacher, Martin Heidegger.

Rahner's theology regard's human existence as a becoming, drawn forward by the presence of God. It is God alone who can provide people with the fulfillment they seek in every level of their existence. An awareness of spiritual being in one's self liberates the individual from the success and fulfillment which are sought in a material control of life. Rahner's thought introduces this awareness as a type of anthropology of transcendence. This anthropology is, in turn, shaped by a Christology in an evolutionary view of the world. There Rahner sees matter and spirit existing together and argues that

166

*homo sapiens* is both observer and participant in the natural order.  Christ is a subjective expression of God's willingness to self-communicate with mankind.

In his theology of death, Rahner argues that what human life becomes does not perish in death.  A life inspired by faith is everlasting, finding its fulfillment in God.  The finitude so real in death  is mitigated by the transcendent eternal properties of the soul.

Principal works include: *Theological Investigations, 22 vols.,* 1961-1989, *Foundations of Christian Faith,* 1976,  *On Prayer,* 1969, *On the Theology of Death,* 1969, *The Trinity,* 1970, and *Theological Dictionary,* 1965.

> *"If man is thus the self-transcendence of living matter, then the history of nature and of spirit from an intrinsic and stratified unity in which the history of nature develops toward man, continues on in him as his  history, is preserved and surpassed in him, and therefore reaches its own goal with and in the history of man's spirit.  Insofar as this history of nature is subsumed in man into freedom, the history of nature reaches its goal in the free history of spirit itself, and remains an intrinsic, constitutive element in it.  Insofar as the history of man still encompasses within itself the history of nature as the history of living matter, in the midst of its freedom it is still based upon the structures and necessities of this material world.  Because man is not only a spirit who observes nature, but is also a part of it, and because he is to continue its history, his history is not only a history of a culture situated above the history of nature, but is also an active transformation of the material world itself.  And it is only through action which is of the spirit and through the life of the spirit which is the action that man and nature reach their single and common goal."*
>
> *Karl Rahner, <u>Foundations of Christian Faith</u>*

**raillery** - n.  good-natured criticism or ridicule.

**ramification** - n.  outcome;  a branching process.

**ramous** - adj.  having branches.

**rampageous** - adj.  having uncontrolled energy.

**rancor** - n.  deep-seated resentment.

**rankle** - to continue to cause irritation, anger, resentment.

**rapprochement** - n.  the act of reconciliation.

**rarefy** - v.  to thin out;  to make less dense.

**ratiocination** - n.  the process of reasoning;  a logical train of thought.

**Rationalism** - n.  in philosophy,  primarily a reference to the thought of Rene Descartes, Benedict Spinoza, and G.W. Leibniz.

According to rationalism, reason is the principle tool for gaining knowledge and explaining reality. In true rationalist fashion this means that empiricism is a secondary instrument in the architecture of ideas. Sense data, due to the various limitations of perception, are not ultimately reliable in deciphering reality. Even empirical approaches aided by the technology of seeing, i.e., microscopes and telescopes, rely upon reason to order the world around us. Moreover, rationalism, in its strictest type, emphasizes ideas themselves as the raw matter to be used in gaining a truthful definition of reality. It uses mathematics and logic as paradigms for the discovery of knowledge independent of sense data. Principles, laws, and concepts alone constitute knowledge.

Text to consult: *A History of Philosophy*, vol. 4, Frederick Copleston, S.J.

**Realism** - n. in philosophy, the position that objects of knowledge exist independent of our thinking of them. John Locke was a predecessor to modern scientific views of realism. In his empirical emphasis lies the belief that sense data are based in the world, thus coming toward us from an external and independent source.

Realism stands in contrast to Idealism which argues that the external world is secondary to the world of ideas, that the physical world is somewhat of an illusion and that only ideas themselves can be handled as the true, e.g. Plato. Realism works with the scientific method: the objects of sense provide us with a common world of thought that can be compared and tested for accuracy. Realists such as Friedrich Nietzsche (1844-1900), *Thus Spoke Zarathustra*, 1885, complain that afterwordliness and otherworldliness interfere with a picture of reality here and now. In this sense, realists are referred to as 'tough-minded' and idealists referred to as 'soft-minded'.

Associated philosophies include pragmatism and process philosophy.

Texts to consult: *Science and the Modern World*, A.N. Whitehead, 1925, and
*Pragmatism*, William James.

**rebarbative** - adj. being unattractive.

**reboant** - adj. loudly echoing or reverberating.

**recalcitrant** - adj. difficult to handle, treat, or operate.

**recension** - n. revision of a text on the basis of reconsiderations in the resource materials.

**recherche** - adj. rare, refined, exquisite.

**recidivism** - n. the tendency to fall back into previous habits or conduct, especially with regard to criminal actions.

**reciprocate** - v. to return in kind; to give and take equally, more or less.

**recognizance** - n. responsibility for behavior.

**recondite** - adj. esoteric; not easily or commonly understood.

**recreant** - adj. cowardly (also as a noun: a coward).

**recriminate** - v. to make a retaliatory charge against an accuser.

**recumbent** - adj. reclining; resting.

**recusant** - adj. the quality or refusal to comply, especially to established authority.

**redaction** - n. the act of editing, especially in reducing or compressing a work. In theology, *redaction criticism* was coined by Willie Marxsen to note the editorial work of Biblical authors, especially with regard to the Gospels of Matthew and Luke.
    Text to consult: *What is Redaction Criticism?*, Norman Perrin, 1970.

**redintegrate** - v. to restore to a sound state.

**redivivus** - adj. brought back to life.

**redoubtable** - adj. producing fear; formidable.

**reflet** - n. luster; iridescence.

**refluent** - adj. flowing back; ebbing.

**refringent** - adj. to throw back; refractory, as in light.

**refulgent** - adj. shining; brilliant in appearance.

**regicide** - n. killing of a monarch.

**regnant** - adj. to exercise the main power; ruling over.

**regression** - n. a movement backward, usually to a more diseased or inferior condition.

**reify** - v. to make that which is abstract take on physical characteristics.

**rejoinder** - n. an answer to a reply.

**Relativism** - n. in philosophy, the view that no absolutes exist. This doctrine finds its roots in the thinking of Protagoras (490-410 B.C.) who argued that "man is the measure of all things". Relativism appears in both epistemology, as the effect of skepticism, and in ethical theory, as the effect of cultural differences which cause different normative systems to collide.
    Relativism has had particular impact on normative ethical values. This is traceable to a number of causes including:
        1) The decline of religion in the West and now the East.
        2) The mixing of cultures, which demands an acceptance of other values and brings about conflict.
        3) The decline of reason in modern society.

4) The liberal intellectual climate of Western culture, which is reluctant or unable to embrace objectivist thinking because of it commitment to subjectivism.
5) The appeal of the word 'freedom' over the word 'authority'; including a fallacious dissociation of the notion of *freedom* from its logical affiliate *responsibility*.
Texts to consult: *Patterns of Culture*, Ruth Benedict, 1934, *Ethical Relativity*, Edward Westermarck, 1932, and *Ethical Relativism*, John Ladd, 1973.

**remanent** - adj. remaining, enduring.

**remigrant** - n. one who returns; that which returns.

**renascent** - adj. showing new vitality.

**renifleur** - n. a person who is sexually gratified by odors.

**renitent** - adj. to be stubbornly opposed.

**renvoi** - n. expulsion of an alien.

**replication** - n. a reply; an answer.

**reposit** - v. to replace.

**replete** - adj. full.

**reprehend** - v. to find fault.

**requital** - n. a return or repayment; a reward.

**reseau** - n. a network.

**resgestae** - n. acts or deeds performed; facts surrounding a litigated issue.

**resupine** - adj. prone or prostrate due to being bent back.

**retiary** - adj. net-like.

**reticent** - adj. inclined to be silent.

**reticulation** - n. a network; a formation of dots, lines, cross hairs, wires, etc.

**retral** - adj. at or near the back.

**retrocede** - v. to recede; to move away.

**retrograde** - adj. contrary to normal order or progress.

170

**retsina** - n.  a white or red wine with a resinous flavor, especially in Greek wines.

**revenant** - n.  one who returns, especially after a long absence.

**revile** - v.  to attack or abuse.

**rhathymia** - n.  a carefree disposition.

**rhexis** - n.  a break or rupture.

**riant** - adj.  cheerful, happy.

**ribald** - adj.  course, vulgar.

**rident** - adj.  a laughing attitude.

**riparian** - adj.  relating to a natural watercourse or river.

**risible** - adj.  able to laugh.

**risque** - adj.  indecent; borderline actions or words.

**roborant** - adj.  tending to strengthen.

**rogatory** - adj.  concerning the process of questioning.

**roily** - adj.  muddy; sedimentary turbulence.

**Romero, Francisco** (1891-1962) - an Argentine philosopher, Romero was influenced by the views of Wilhelm Dilthey, Jose Ortega y Gasset, and Nicolai Hartmann.  He taught at the universities of Buenos Aires and La Plata.

Romero divided phenomena into four classes: *inorganic* - the physical world of atoms and space, *organic* - the vital world of flora and fauna, *psychic* - consciousness and intentional egoistic transcendence, and *spiritual* - complete non-egoistic transcendence. All four compose a whole in which transcendence is characteristic of development and higher forms of being.

Principal works: *Logic*, 1938, *Philosophy of the Person*, 1944, *Man and Culture*, 1950, *Theory of Man*, 1952, and *What is Philosophy*, 1953.

*"The spiritual act is projected toward the object, and it remains there.  In cognitive, emotional, and volitional activity, the self is concerned with the objectivities for what they are in themselves.*

*In merely intentional activity the subject places the objects and then takes them to himself, whereas in the spiritual act he places the objects and then yields himself to them."*

Francisco Romero, *Theory of Man*

**Rousseau, Jean Jacques** (1712-1778) - a French philosopher and romantic, Rousseau's work helped give form to the French Revolution. In spite of his influence he remained on the edge of society throughout his life, wandering from place to place, and in the end experiencing a deep paranoia of the enemies he had created through his writings.

Rousseau believed that literature, science, and reasoning, as it was taught in the modern world, brought with it "garlands of flowers over the chains which weigh men down." He viewed art and literature as sources of conformity, making people think and act alike in dress, speech, and dispositions.

Rousseau attacked modern politicians for their failure to lead. He argued that ancient leaders lead their citizens toward virtue and morals, whereas, modern politicians lead people toward a pre-occupation with commerce and money. He contrasted this with the state of nature in which humans were essentially good and free of the corrupting influence of modern society.

The goal of Rousseau's thought was to outline a society committed to re-establishing values concerned with the moral development of all its citizens. Law should reflect the general well-being of citizens and avoid special interests and the voice of factions. Subsequently, Rousseau is regarded as the father of liberalism

Principal works: *Discourse on the Sciences and the Arts*, 1750, *Discourse on the Origin of Inequality Among Men*, 1755, *The Social Contract*, 1762, *Emile*, 1762, and *Confessions*, 1782.

> *"Moral liberty . . . alone makes man truly master of himself; for the mere impulse of appetite is slavery, while obedience to a law which we prescribe to ourselves is liberty."*
>
> J.J. Rousseau, <u>Social Contract</u>

> *"Where is there any respect for law? Under the name of law you have seen the rule of self-interest and human passion. But the eternal laws of nature and of order exists. For the wise man they take the place of positive law; they are written in the depths of his heart by conscience and reason; let him obey these laws and be free; for there is no slave but the evil-doer, for he always does evil against his will. Liberty is not to be found in any form of government, she is in the heart of the free man."*
>
> J.J. Rousseau, <u>Emile</u>

**ruction** - n. a noisy quarrelsome disturbance.

**rueful** - adj. bringing about pity.

**rufous** - adj. rust-colored.

**rugose** - adj. wrinkled.

**ruminant** - n. a hoofed animal with four stomachs; a bucolic creature lacking complex existence.

**ruminant** - adj. inclined toward contemplation or meditation.

172

**Russell, Bertrand** (1872-1970) - an English philosopher of logic, mathematics, and society whose productive literary years were so extended that he is difficult to classify, having once defended his pluralistic stance by saying, "I always reserve the right to change my mind."

The work which established Russell's reputation as a philosopher was in the area of logic, mathematics, and language, and was called *logical atomism*. He believed that a perfect language would have logical properties that insure the correspondence between its component parts and facticity, the relation with reality. Logically, language should concern itself with the simplest elements of language to identify their utility in providing exact meaning. This concern led Russell to emphasize *atomic facts*, facts of the simplest kind, and the expression of these atomic facts in *atomic propositions*, the linguistic representation of atomic facts.

Truth and falsity depend upon the careful analysis of words and propositions corresponding to facts. Two or more atomic propositions constitute a *molecular proposition*. The molecular propositions necessitate the use of *truth functions*, symbols which guide us through a kind of arithmetic of truth calculations.

Problems in the application of Russell's theory led to a re-newed interest in empiricism, particularly the ideas of David Hume. This in turn weakened the metaphysical, or abstract focus of Russell's logical atomism. To other logicians, like Ludwig Wittgenstein, the disparity between theory and practice forced a recognition of the propositions of science.

Principal works: *Principia Mathematica, 2 vols. (with A.N. Whitehead)*, 1910, *Our Knowledge of the External World*, 1914, *Principles of Social Reconstruction*, 1916, *Mysticism and Logic*, 1918, *Education and the Social Order*, 1932, *Unpopular Essays*, 1950, *Logic and Knowledge*, 1956, and *Essays in Skepticism*, 1962.

> *"The fundamental argument for freedom of opinion is the doubtfulness of all our beliefs. If we certainly knew the truth, there would be something to be said for teaching it. But in that case it could be taught without invoking authority, by means of its inherent reasonableness. It is not necessary to make a law that no one shall be allowed to teach arithmetic if he holds heretical opinions on the multiplication table, because here the truth is clear, and does not require to be enforced by penalties. When the State intervenes to ensure the teaching of some doctrine, it does so 'because' there is no conclusive evidence in favor of that doctrine."*
>
> *Bertrand Russell, Skeptical Essays,*

**rusticate** - v. to live in the countryside.

**ruth** - n. pity; compassion.

**Ruysbroeck, Jan van** (1293-1381) - A Flemish philosopher of mysticism. At age 60 Ruysbroeck brought together his vast experience in religious reflection to form a community (Groenendael) in the forest near Soines. He taught that the soul finds God through a knowledge of itself, moving from the active life of a terrestrial being to the contemplative life of a terrestrial being.

Principal works: *Adornment of the Spiritual Marriage, The Sparkling Stone, The Book of Supreme Truth,* and *The Espousals.*

*"The image of God is found essentially and personally in all mankind. Each possesses it whole, entire and undivided, and all together not more than one alone."*

Jan van Ruysbroeck, <u>*Adornment of the Spiritual Marriage.*</u>

**Saccus, Ammonius** (175-242 A.D.) - the teacher of Plotinus, who founded the views of Neoplatonism. Saccus also taught Origen, subsequently, he had a profound impact through his students on the formation of Christian philosophy. Christian metaphysics loaned some of its principal framework from Neoplatonism and Platonism. Saccus' work on Platonism seemed to be a reconciliation of the differences between Aristotle and Plato.

**saccadic** - adj. jerky; twitching.

**sacerdotal** - adj. priestly.

**sagacity** - adj. having acute mental apprehension along with great practical wisdom.

**salacious** - adj. given to sexual interests; lecherous.

**sallow** - adj. having a grayish greenish yellow color; sickly.

**salmagundi** - n. a heterogeneous assortment or mixture.

**saltation** - n. a dancing movement.

**salubrious** - adj. being conducive to good health.

**salutary** - adj. bringing about improved health.

**Samsara** - n. in Hinduism, a reference to the cycle of existence or wheel of life - 1) birth 2) growth 3) decay 4) death. In this context death is merely a pause between lives. Life is repeated over and over until the effects of karma (the law of rewards) result in a final and eternal liberation of the soul.

**sanative** - adj. able to cure.

**sangfroid** - n. deep-seated composure, especially in dangerous or strained circumstances.

**sanguinary** - adj.  being bloodthirsty;  combat ready.

**sanguine** - adj.  courageous disposition.

**Santayana, George** (1863-1952) - born in Madrid, Spain;  Santayana remained attached to his Mediterranean roots despite his life in America.  This was due, in part, to his suspicions about the  structure of modern commercial-democratic society, which seemed to be just as much a conflict between his Catholic spirituality and its Protestant counterpart.

Santayana's philosophy is characterized by a spirit of poetic reasoning with interests in social theory, morality, aesthetics, metaphysics, science, and religion.  In his social theory, Santayana noted a hierarchy of organization: *natural society* - cohering on basic human and biological needs; *free society* - institutions going beyond natural needs and addressing the individual needs of persons; *ideal society* - community built upon affection for science, art, and religion.

His moral theory observes three levels or stages of development: *pre-rational* - guidance provided by aphorisms and traditional sayings, being often rich in meaning and inconsistent; *rational* - guidance from the advanced use of reasoning, given to a specific direction and goal; *post-rational* - guidance by images of an after-life, reflecting the growing pessimism characteristic of aging, the lack of confidence in this world.

Principal works: *Sense of Beauty*, 1896, *Life of Reason, 5 vols.*, 1906, *Scepticism and Animal Faith*, 1923, *Realms of Being, 4 vols.*, 1940, and *Dominations and Powers*, 1949.

> *"Scepticism is the chastity of the intellect, and it is shameful to surrender it too soon or to the first comer; there is nobility in preserving coolly and proudly through a long youth, until at last, in the ripeness of instinct and discretion, it can be safely exchanged for fidelity and happiness."*
> George Santayana, <u>Scepticism and Animal Faith</u>,

**sapid** - adj.  tasty; palatable;  also, agreeable to the mind.

**sapient** - adj.  revealing deep wisdom or discernment.

**sarcasm** - n.  satirical comments designed to be painful.

**saprophagous** - adj.  feeding on decaying organic material.

**sarcophagous** - adj.  flesh-eating.

**sardonic** - adj.  having a bitter character;  derisive.

**Sartre, Jean-Paul** (1905-1980) - a French philosopher of existentialism, almost a brand-name existentialist, Sartre popularized the words "existence precedes essence".  The logical equivalent of this phrase is "being precedes meaning".  One exists before one's life is something.  Making it something is dependent upon personal choice.  Failing to make it something is also a personal choice.  For Sartre, the freedom of one's existence implies an openness that is unavoidable. There is no way to scrap this condition or expand a fatalistic view of life. Modern life is a complicated affair and everywhere people live in *bad faith (mauvaise foi);* they deny responsibility for who they are. They live *inauthentically,* attempting to pass off an unsatisfactory existence on some external set of facts.

The life of action is the only reality. Besides the acts one chooses, one is nothing. Even God does not provide a solution, as Sartre accepts the full definition of atheism. There is no God. The human situation is one of *abandonment* or *forlornment.* And, human *anxiety* is the product of an awareness of this abandonment, this finitude of existence. Those who cannot handle the reality of this awareness experience *loneliness, despair,* and perhaps *guilt,* because they adopt ready-made lives. They practice *self-deception.* They try to act as if it is not true that life bears no ready-made script. They get a job. They go to work, and it is perhaps a cheap substitute for choosing the life one really should live according to one's being.

A social consequence of our strange and forlorn condition is that we may fail to see the *intersubjectivity* of persons. Our condition is universal. Everyone experiences what the other experiences, in terms of ontology. It is important to recognize this in order to shut down a sense of self-pity. So, Sartre also focuses on the Nietzschean use of *courage.*

Principal works: *Nausea,* 1938, *The Transcendence of the Ego,* 1936, *Being and Nothingness,* 1943, *Existentialism is a Humanism,* 1946 and *Critique of Dialectical Reason,* 1960.

> *"When, in all honesty, when I've recognized that man is a being in whom existence precedes essence, that he is a free being who, in various circumstances, can want only his freedom, I have at the same time recognized that I can want only the freedom of others.*
>
> *"Therefore, in the name of this will for freedom, which freedom itself implies, I may pass judgment on those who seek to hide from themselves the complete arbitrariness and the complete freedom of their existence. Those who hide their complete freedom from themselves out of a spirit of seriousness or by means of deterministic excuses, I shall call cowards."*
>
> Jean-Paul Sartre, <u>Existentialism is a Humanism</u>

**saturnine** - adj. having a cold gloomy temperament.

**satyriasis** - n. abnormal and uncontrollable sexual desire in the male; having Dionysian preferences.

**satyromaniac** - n. a lustful male.

**saurian** - adj. lizard-like; reptilian.

**scabrous** - adj. difficult; rough; also, promoting scandalous themes.

**scatology** - n. the study of obscene words.

177

**Schleiermacher, Friedrich** (1768-1834) - a German theologian and philosopher, Schleiermacher thought of religion primarily as feeling or intuition rather than reason or ethics. True religion, in his view, stands independent of dogma and is primarily an experience of the infinite.

Schleiermacher defended Christian monotheism, against other religious outlooks, as the highest form of religious experience. He acknowledges that a variety of religious forms exist in different individuals, but Christianity is among the truest.

Principal works: *Religion: Speeches to its Cultured Despisers*, 1799, and *The Christian Faith*, 1822.

> *"Second Theorem: In the uniting of the divine nature with the human, the divine alone was active or self-imparting, and the human alone passive or in process of being assumed; but during the state of union every activity was a common activity of both natures."*
>
> F. Schleiermacher, <u>The Christian Faith</u>

**Schopenhauer, Arthur** (1788-1860) - a German philosopher, Schopenhauer divided reality into four kinds of objects: *physical objects* - located in time and space; the content of scientific thought. *Abstract objects* - the domain of logic and the principles of reason, e.g. rules of inference and the theories of metaphysics. *Mathematical objects* - the geometrical analysis of space and the arithmetic account of time. *Self* - the will and its conscious exertion over life.

Schopenhauer referred to these as objects or forms of the Principle of Sufficient Reason. Moreover, the dynamics of interaction between these objects reveals a deterministic trend in the natural world. Schopenhauer's account of change includes a highest metaphysical force which he calls *will*. *Will* permeates everything, from the highest life form to the lowest objects. It acts in such a way as to be the *will to live*. Everything seeks life over and against other life. Each member of a species is part of the drive for survival, expendable and replaceable. The world is basically a battlefield.

For humanity, the consequences are bleak. Every move we make is directly or indirectly a calculated attempt to escape death. A steady annihilation of the race through disease, war, violence, and time, prevent the attainment of true happiness. Life is fundamentally a struggle to survive, leading to: *aggressiveness, achievement, conflict,* and *self-centeredness*.

Schopenhauer concludes that the only true source of peace comes from philosophical or artistic creativity. He advocates Buddhist principles with an ethic of *sympathy* to escape the destructive power of the universal will.

Principal works: *The Fourfold Root of the Principle of Sufficient Reason*, 1813, *The World as Will and Idea*, 1819, *On the Will in Nature*, 1836, *The Two Basic Problems of Ethics*, 1841 and *Essays of Schopenhauer (T. Saunders, 1951)*.

> *"Great intellectual gifts mean an activity pre-eminently nervous in its character, and consequently a very high degree of susceptibility to pain in every form."*
>
> Arthur Schopenhauer, <u>Essay on Personality</u>

*"Reading is merely a surrogate for thinking for yourself; it means letting someone else direct your thoughts. Many books, moreover, serve merely to show how many ways there are of being wrong, and how afar astray you yourself would go if you followed their guidance."*
*Arthur Schopenhauer, <u>Essays</u>*

**sciolism** - n. superficial knowledge.

**scopophilia** - n. a psychological condition; gratification by looking at erotic images; literally "love of looking".

**scrupulous** - adj. having strong character; principled.

**scrofulous** - adj. having a diseased appearance; spiritually contaminated.

**scrutable** - adj. able to be understood after detailed study.

**scurrilous** - adj. given to gross descriptions; obscenely abusive.

**secern** - v. to make careful distinctions.

**sedition** - n. promotion of resistance or rebellion against lawful authority.

**sedulous** - adj. working with careful persistence; diligent.

**segue** - v. to continue without interruption, especially in music.

**selenocentric** - adj. using the moon as a center.

**selenology** - n. the study of the moon.

**self-abasement** - n. attack on one's self based in feelings of guilt or inferiority.

**self-realization** - n. developing one's talents and abilities as personal sources of meaning and purpose.

**semantics** - n. the branch of linguistics concerned with meanings.

**sematic** - adj. giving warning, especially to other animals by the use of special signals or markings, e.g., rattlesnake's tail, dog's growl, etc.

**semidiurnal** - adj. relating to half a day.

**semiology** - n. the study of signs.

**senescence** - n. the process of aging.

179

**senescent** - adj. the quality of aging.

**sententious** - adj. aphoristic expression; compressed truths, often moralistic and often self-righteous.

**sequacious** - adj. following intellectually, logically; also, being servile.

**sequent** - adj. following.

**sequester** - v. to put into solitude.

**serendipity** - n. accidental encounter with good fortune.

**seriocomic** - adj. semi-serious; semi-comical.

**serry** - v. to push together.

**sesquipedalian** - adj. given to the use of long words.

**Sextus Empiricus** (ca. 225 A.D.) - a Greek philosopher of Skepticism whose philosophical goal was not truth or knowledge but inner peace. The endless conflicts between intellectuals taught Sextus the futility of gaining absolute knowledge of anything.
    *Ataraxia* (peace of mind in day to day life) was the final stage in the process of seeking knowledge. It followed *tropoi* (methods of argument) and *epoche* (the suspension of judgment). For Sextus, the mutilation of one's spiritual life by constant haggling over truth and knowledge simply proved the validity of moving beyond these toward an adjusted philosophy of *eudaimonism* (happiness). It remained, however, that he was still a lover of logic, because paradoxically even to refute logic and knowledge, one must use logic and knowledge.
    Principal works: *Pyrrhonic Sketches, Against the Dogmatists, Against the Intellectuals,* and *On the Soul* (no existing fragments).

**Shinto** - n. the national religion of Japan, *Shinto* means "way of the spirits".
A phrase used conjunctively with Shinto is *"kami-no-michi"*, meaning "the path of the sacred". The *Kojiki* is the ancient manuscript of Shinto. It describes the creation of the world by two 'kami' (sacred ones), *Izanagi* (male-who-invites) and *Izanami* (female-who-invites).
    Shinto teaches that the emperor is the descendant of the sun goddess, *Ameterasu*. Japan itself is perceived as the center of the world, the land of the kami. Along with this belief is the "way of the warrior", *bushido*. Bushido is then the code of the *samurai*. Loyalty to Japan is at the center of Shinto's practices and teachings.
    Text to consult: *On Understanding Japanese Religion*, Joseph Kitagawa, 1987.

**sidereal** - adj. relating to the stars or the heavens; astral.

**Sidgwick, Henry** (1838-1900) - an English philosopher noted mainly for his advocacy of ethical reflection, particularly a defense of utilitarianism. Sidgwick connected ethics to common-sense and three types ethical reflection: *intuitionism* - advocating a pursuit of excellence from obvious principles like compassion, wisdom, and justice; *egoism* - advocating the pursuit of one's personal happiness over other considerations; *utilitarianism* - advocating the greatest good for the greatest number. He used the principles of intuitionism to advance his brand of utilitarianism.

Principal works: *The Methods of Ethics*, 1874, *The Principles of Political Economy*, 1883, and *Outlines of the History of Ethics*, 1886.

**Sikhism** - n. in religion, Sikhism began as a protest to imperfections in Hinduism around 1500 A.D. Nanak (1469-1538) was the founder of Sikhism, advocating a monotheistic doctrine along with an ethical focus on philanthropy, loyalty, truth, honesty, justice, and non-partisan life. Sikhism openly denounces wine, tobacco, idolatry, the Caste system, slander, and hypocrisy. In time, Sikhism abandoned some of its pacifistic beliefs to accommodate military qualities for its own survival in a hostile Muslim environment.

The Khalsa ("pure") Order of Singhs: "The Pure are of God, and the victory is to God." , wear the five K's - (1) *kesh* - uncut hair, (2) *kachh* - military shorts, (3) *kangha* - comb, (4) *kara* - steel bracelet, and (5) *kirpan* - sword.

Sikhism combines elements of Islam with Hinduism to form a unique and durable syncretistic faith. It allows for the equality of men and women, and it reveals a 'process' orientation is accepting the wisdom of gurus after Nanak. In effect, it seems to accept the possibility of a continuing revelation from God.

Texts to consult: *The Sikh Religion: Its Gurus, Sacred Writings, and Authors*, M.A. Macauliffe, 1909, and *The Sikhs*, W.H. McLeod, 1989.

> *"There is pleasure in gold, pleasure in silver, and in women, pleasure in the perfume of sandal; there is pleasure in horses, pleasure in couches and in palaces, pleasure in sweets, and pleasure in meats. When such are the pleasures of the body, how shall God's name obtain a dwelling therein?"*
> *- Guru Nanak, The Sikh Religion, M. Macauliffe*

> *"Accursed the life of him in this world who breatheth without uttering the Name."*
> *- Guru Nanak, The Sikh Religion, M. Macauliffe*

**silvicolous** - adj. belonging to the forest or woodland habitat.

**silviculture** - n. forestry.

**simian** - adj. of or resembling apes and monkeys.

**simony** - n. the sale or trading of sacred things, including heaven itself.

**simulant** - adj. pretending.

**sinecure** - n. an office or position yielding perhaps both honor and profit with little or no work involved.

**sine qua non** - Latin meaning "an indispensable thing"; a requirement.

**sinistrous** - adj. unfavorable.

**sirenic** - adj. dangerously attractive.

**siriasis** - n. sunstroke.

**sitomania** - n. abnormal craving for food.

**skulk** - v. to avoid observation, as with the habit of foxes.

**slake** - v. to relieve by satisfying.

**slattern** - n. a loose woman, especially a prostitute.

**smarmy** - adj. false earnestness; unctuous.

**Smith, Adam** (1723-1790) - a Scottish philosopher of economics, Smith argued against the old view that wealth is the acquisition and retention of money. A nation is better off, reasoned Smith, if it can increase its productivity of goods. Thus, the successful capitalist is one who meets the need for desirable goods. The general welfare of society is improved even if the capitalist seeks only his own well-being, because his work satisfies the needs of others through productivity.

Smith's fame as an economist overshadows his refined personal views of ethics and its relation to a successful life. Building on a moral psychology of sympathy, he advocated moderation and self-control over a life of uncontrolled ambition and self-indulgence. Moral development is a key element in his view of success. Smith reasoned that there are three stages of moral development: *pleasure* - typical of youth and reflecting little restraint due to the absence of informed reasoning; *emulation* - the recognition of superior role models and the opportunity to model one's life accordingly, though often without any real appreciation for the last stage; *virtue* - the authentic recognition of moral qualities which contribute to a happy life, individually and socially.

Principal works: *Theory of Moral Sentiments*, 1759, and *An Inquiry into the Nature and Causes of the Wealth of Nations*, 1776.

> *"In civilized society man stands at all times in need of the cooperation and assistance of great multitudes, while his whole life is scarce sufficient to gain the friendship of a few persons."*
>
> Adam Smith, *Theory of Moral Sentiments*

> *"Capitals are increased by parsimony, and diminished by prodigality and misconduct."*
>
> Adam Smith, *The Wealth of Nations*

**Socialism** - n. in philosophy, the political doctrine that group control of property is desirable, as is the production of goods and the possession of wealth. Socialism is politically allied with communism, being differentiated only in degree. As a philosophy, it stands counter-posed to individualism and personal liberty. The first references to socialism are traced to France in the 1830's.

**sociopath** - n. one who is a danger to society; one with extreme hostilility toward others.

**Socrates** (470-399 B.C.) - a Greek philosopher, Socrates was the teacher of Plato. Originally a philosopher of matter, he gradually abandoned all interest in physics and cosmology. Instead, Socrates became focused on ethical theory as it applied to individuals and society. He attended to the exploration of *self-knowledge* and its relation to human happiness.

For Socrates, the secret to a successful life was *logos* or reason. Reason was the key to psychological harmony. He stressed the relationship between reason and actions. This relationship was to be perfected by the use of *sophia*, wisdom. In turn, this provided the cornerstone for the pursuit of *arete*, virtue: *"Knowledge is virtue."*

Socrates was known for his philosophical method, called "midwifery" or the "Socratic Method", which is characterized by the following elements: *conversation* - the use of a verbal exchange or dialogue; *definition* - the focus on meanings in one's terminology; *dialectic* - the use of counter-argument to deepen the theoretical understanding of some issue; *skepticism* - a professed ignorance of the truth; *induction* - the use of empirical evidence, case examples; *deduction* - conclusions derived from the pre-existing statements of supposed fact.

Principal works: None. The views of Socrates are recorded by Plato the *Dialogues.*

> *"A man who is good for anything ought not to calculate the chance of living or dying; he ought only to consider whether in doing anything he is doing right or wrong."*
>
> *Socrates in Plato's <u>Apology</u>*

**sodality** - n. comradeship.

**solecism** - n. any mistake, but especially grammatical ones.

**solicitous** - adj. filled with concern and anxiety.

**solifidian** - n. one who believes in salvation by faith without works.

**Solipsism** - n. in philosophy, the view that the self alone exists. Solipsism stems from a radical skepticism regarding knowledge of an external world. F.H. Bradley (1846-1924) explained solipsism as a consequence of failure to transcend the self through communion with the Absolute. In logical terms, solipsism is a fallacy of subjectivity, meaning a failure to honor the objective facticity of an external world.

**somnifacient** - adj. causing sleep.

**somniferous** - adj. bringing about sleep.

**somnolence** - n.  sleepiness.

**Sophists** - n. in philosophy, the reference to a group of thinkers known for their skepticism regarding knowledge.  Active in the 5th and 4th centuries B.C., they included: Protagoras, Gorgias, Hippias, and Thrasymachus.  Their positions on theoretical skepticism led directly to ethical skepticism, which emphasized subjectivism and relativism.

**sophrosyne** - n.  moderation;  self-control.

**soporose** - adj.  abnormally sleepy.

**sordid** - adj.  dirty; squalid.

**sororicide** - n.  killing of a sister.

**sot** - n.  a chronic drunkard.

**soteriology** - n.  the theological study of salvation, especially as it relates to Christ.

**spavined** - adj.  in worn-out condition.

**specious** - adj.  superficially correct or good.

**spelean** - adj.  having the habit of living in caves.

**spiel** - n.  an extravagant story.

**Spinoza, Benedict** (1632-1677) - a rationalist metaphysician, Spinoza was born and raised in Amsterdam.  Moving to Voorburg (Netherlands) in 1660, he made a living by grinding and polishing lenses.  During his life he rarely made contact with many other philosophers and lived in relative seclusion as he developed his theories.  His theological opinions fostered a great deal of hatred, and he was once almost assassinated with a dagger (a button blocked the knife's penetration).
      Spinoza presented a pantheistic version of reality:  God and nature are one and the same (*Deus sive Natura).* He removed the idea of a 'relation' with God, making the world and God a unity.  This unity was argued as eternal, so God and matter have no prior cause.  Matter, in turn, exhibits *attributes*: essences perceived by the intellect.  God has an infinite number of *attributes*, but our human reasoning only recognizes two: *thought* and *extension.*
      The universe is also characterized by necessity.  The events of the universe are fixed from eternity.  And, our knowledge of this universe is represented by stages of enlightenment: *imagination* - ideas derived from sense experience, the passive acceptance of sense data; *reason* - the use of mathematical and physical knowledge for the formation of abstract theories; *intuition* - a transcendence of reason and imagination, a comprehensive intellectual grasp of how the whole universe hangs together.

Principal works: *Principles of Cartesian Philosophy*, 1663, *Theological Political Treatise*, 1670, and *Ethics* (published posthumously).

*"Whatever is, is in God, and nothing can exist or be conceived without God . . .*
*God is the indwelling and not the transient cause of all things."*
    Benedict Spinoza, <u>Ethics</u>

**spiritus frumenti** - n. whiskey.

**splenetic** - adj. ill-natured; of the spleen.

**sponsion** - n. promise.

**sporadic** - adj. occasionally.

**spurious** - adj. of questionable origins; counterfeit.

**squalid** - adj. extremely filthy, especially as a result of poverty or neglect.

**staid** - adj. steady in character; being serious or grave.

**stanchless** - adj. incessant.

**stasis** - n. a slowing or stopping of the flow of body fluids; equilibrium.

**stercoricolous** - adj. inhabiting dung.

**stertorous** - adj. characterized by a harsh gasping sound.

**sthenic** - adj. characterized by a strong build.

**stilted** - adj. pompous; above it all; formal.

**stochastic** - adj. involving chance or luck as a complication to prediction.

**Stoicism** - n. in philosophy, the view that indifference to pleasure and pain produces the best adjustment to human existence. Though it advocated a specific outlook with regard to logic and cosmology, stoicism is best known for the emphasis on resignation or acceptance of the circumstances one finds in the world. It emphasizes a simple life, especially since a type of world reason or 'logos' is at the bottom of all events in this world. Representatives of the school included Zeno of Citium (335-263 B.C.), Seneca (3-65 A.D.), and Marcus Aurelius (121-180 A.D.).

**stollid** - adj. unemotional; slow to reveal feeling.

**strappado** - n.  a special form of capital punishment in which the individual is hoisted to a height of 20 feet or more, tied to a rope and then dropped;  also used as a type of torture, contingent on the part of the body connected to the rope and the drop distance.

**stratify** - v.  to form or arrange in layers, classes, or grades.

**stricture** - n.  an abnormal narrowing;  also, adversarial criticism.

**Structuralism** - n.  in philosophy, the view that all cultures and societies possess a common structural foundation upon which secondary differences are built.  The basic categorization of all cultures is possible in terms of psychology, anthropology, religion, economics, and philosophy, thus revealing a foundational order.  Starting with the influence of Claude L'evi-Strauss, ideological support expands with the works of Marx, Freud, Jung, Lacan, Foucault, and Merleau Ponty.  It minimizes differences and individuality by exposing the forms which exist in successive generations of culture everywhere.
        Text to consult:  _The Language of the Self_, Jacques Lacan, 1968, _The Order of Things_ and _The Archaeology of Knowledge_, Michael Foucault.

**stupefacient** - adj.  causing unconsciousness or stupor.

**subjacent** - adj.  underlying.

**sublimate** - v.  to handle or express a primitive instinct in socially refined ways;  to use the energy present in a primitive drive toward a creative act or project;  to divert.

**subrogate** - v.  to substitute.

**sub rosa** - adj.  in secret (in ancient tradition a rose was placed over the meeting table to indicate an oath of secrecy on the part of all participants).

**subterfuge** - n.  a deceptive maneuver;  an evasion.

**succedaneum** - n.  a substitute, especially an inferior one.

**succubus** - n.  a female demon which has sex with men while they are asleep.

**succursal** - adj.  subsidiary.

**sudatory** - adj.  relating to perspiration.

**suffuse** - v.  to spread over.

**Sufism** - n.  in Arabic philosophy, a contemplative type of Islamic mysticism which emphasizes a relationship with Allah through renunciation and love.  Sufism eventually acquired a pantheistic bent and found sympathy with some types of Hinduism in northern

India.  Most likely the name *sufism* derives from the Middle Eastern word *suf*, meaning 'wool'.  Wool was the fabric favored by ascetic philosophers of that world for clothing.
Text to consult: *What is Sufism?*, Martin Lings, 1981.

**sultry** - adj.  with sweltering heat;  strong passion, especially sexual.

**sumptuous** - adj.  luxuriously splendid.

**superable** - adj.  capable of being mastered.

**supercilious** - adj. showing haughty contempt.

**Superego** - n. in the philosophy of Freud and psychoanalysis, that part of the self which acts as a control over the impulses of the id.  The superego includes the notion of a conscience which is built up from the training and conditioning stemming from authority figures such as parents, teachers, and heroic personalities.  It is also a manifestation of threats and warnings regarding dangerous actions, including experiential warnings.
Text to consult: *The Ego and the Mechanisms of Defence*, Anna Freud, 1937.

**supererogatory** - adj.  the quality of doing more than is required or needed; voluntary.

**supernal** - adj.  originating in heaven; of a spiritual character.

**supervenience** - n. in logic, the condition of having something additional or unexpected occur, as in an unexpected logical derivation.

**supine** - adj.  inactive;  also, indolent.

**supplicate** - v.  to pray or beg for humbly.

**supposititious** - adj.  not genuine;  deceptively presented.

**surcease** - v.  to put an end to.

**surmise** - v.  to conclude on a little evidence.

**surrealism** - n.  the use of fantastic dreamlike effects in art, literature, or theater, especially unnatural combinations of elements in experienced reality.

**sybarite** - n.  a person who practices luxurious self-indulgence.

**sychophant** - n.  a flatterer;  one who seeks benefits by providing excessive praise;  a servile individual.

**sylph** - n.  a slender graceful woman or girl.

**sylvan** - adj.  of the woodland or forest.

187

**sylvan** - n.  one who frequents the forest.

**syncretism** - n.  in philosophy, the blending of ideas from opposed systems of thought.  It is an effort to create unity at the expense of philosophical rigor.

**synderesis** - n.  an inborn sense of moral harmony.  It derives from the Greek word 'synteresis' meaning spark of conscience.

**syndetic** - adj.  serving to link or join.

**synergetic** - adj.  a working together;  being cooperative.

**syntality** - n.  the mental and behavioral conformity of a group to the personality of an individual.

**tabescent** - adj.  wasting away.

**Tabula rasa** - n.  from Latin, meaning 'blank slate'.  The term was made famous in the philosophy of John Locke (1632-1704) who used it to defend the epistemology of empiricism.  Locke believed that the mind is blank until experience (sense data) writes upon it.

**tacit** - adj.  implied but unspoken.

**taciturn** - adj.  disinclined to talk.

**Tagore, Rabindranath** (1861-1941) - an Indian philosopher, Tagore had a profound influence on the mixing of Western and Eastern philosophy.  He is recognized as a member of the Renaissance period of Hinduism.  His philosophical position emphasized the need to reconcile opposites as part of a greater truth.  The underlying harmony of the universe teaches us to subordinate our desires and avoid egoism.  At times, he combined the insights of hedonists and ascetics, determinists and free-will advocates, idealists and realists.

Tagore's thought was often expressed in philosophical poetry.  This work characterized the role of emotion in his thought.  Though not a pessimist, Tagore was intellectually challenged to produce poetry capable of producing a philosophy of action as well as contemplation.  He believed that a philosophy which did not work out a doctrine of action was 'escapist' and afraid of mastering real-life problems.

Principal works: *Sadhana*, 1913, *Personality*, 1914, *Creative Unity*, 1922, *The Religion of Man*, 1931, and *Towards Universal Man*, (posthumously) 1961.

> *"Blessed am I, that I have searched for heaven's glorious light.*
> *Blessed am I, that I have loved this lowly earth's delight."*
> *Rabindranath Tagore, (poem) "Prabhat" in* <u>Chaitali</u>

Text to consult: <u>*An Introduction to Rabindranath Tagore*</u>, Vishwanath S. Naravane, 1977

**talisman** - n.  a magical charm.

**Taoism** - n.  a Chinese religion emphasizing a mystical treatment of life.  The *tao* or way is discovered in the unification of one's being.  Life is mastered through silence, letting go, and living in harmony with the natural world.  Part of the secret is a recognition of opposites, *yin* and *yang,* which structure the flow of events in the universe.  The *Tao Te Ching* is the scripture of Taoists, supposedly written by Lao Tzu.

> Text to consult: *What is Taoism?*, H.G. Creel, 1982.

**tectonics** - n.  the science of building construction;  also, a branch of geology.

**Teilhard de Chardin, Pierre** (1881-1955) - a French scientist, priest, and theologian, Teilhard advanced the view that the universe is in both a physical and spiritual evolution, moving toward greater levels of complexity.  The evolutionary process has moved through stages or critical boundaries, including the emergence of life, the appearance of higher animals (including man), and the emergence of rational consciousness.  According to Teilhard, the last stage represents the creative and directed development of the earth, moving toward fulfillment in God.

> Teilhard noted the dissolution of cultures and the emergence of a single technical culture.  The rational consciousness of humanity imposes a *noosphere* over the biosphere.  This *noosphere* is directed toward completion of a cosmic or historical goal: the integration of all human consciousness in the *Omega* point (Christ/God) through love.

> Exiled to China for his ideas, Teilhard became involved in paleoanthropology.  His paleontological work led to the discovery of Peking Man.

> Principal works: *The Phenomenon of Man*, 1955, *The Divine Milieu*, 1956, *The Future of Man*, 1964, *The Hymn of the Universe*, 1965, and *Christianity and Evolution*, 1969.

> Text to consult: *An Introduction to Teilhard de Chardin*, N.M. Wildiers, 1968.

> *"The Primacy of Charity: Since the Christian universe consists structurally in the unification of elemental persons in a supreme personality (the personality of God), the dominating and ultimate energy of the whole system can only be a person-to-person attraction;  in other words, a love attraction."*
> P. Teilhard de Chardin, *Christianity and Evolution*

**telegenic** - adj.  having an appearance or personality that shows well on television.

**telegnosis** - n.  knowledge acquired supernaturally.

**telekinesis** - n.  moving objects without physical contact.

**Teleology** - n.  in philosophy, the study of purposes and causes as principles of explanation.  Teleology is particularly useful to theological speculations about the origins of the universe, e.g., the teleological argument for the existence of God: designs reveal a designer.  'Teleology', as a term, was first used by Christian Wolff in 1728 to denote the science of final causes.

**telesthesia** - n.  sensation from a distance without the apparent use of the senses.

**telic** - adj.   tending toward a specific end.

**telluric** - adj.  of or relating to the terrestrial landscape;  having to do with the earth.

**telos** - n.  an ultimate or highest end.

**temerity** - n.  recklessness;  foolishness.

**tendentious** - adj.  being biased.

**tenebrific** - adj.  causing gloom.

**tenet** - n.  principle;  a belief held to be true.

**tenuous** - adj.  flimsy; without strength.

**tepid** - adj.  lacking conviction or enthusiasm.

**teratogenesis** - n.  the production of biological monstrosities.

**teratoid** - n.  a biological freak.

**teratology** - n.  in biology, the study of malformations and monstrosities.

**teratosis** - n.  an abnormal biological form.

**termagant** - n.  a woman who is overbearing, difficult, stubborn.

**ternary** - adj.  involving three elements.

**terraqueous** - adj.  having to do or constituted of land and water.

**terrene** - adj.  worldly;  of the earth.

**terricolous** - adj.  having the quality of being on or in the earth.

**terse** - adj.  concise;  using as few words as possible.

**testy** - adj.  easily irritated.

**tetrad** - n.  a group of four.

**Thales** (ca. 580 B.C.) - a Greek philosopher who argued that the universe is composed of a single substance (monism): water. He believed it was possible to account for all things with this substance, noting its self-motion, life-producing importance, abundance, and various forms (clouds, rain, lakes, seas, marshes, ice).

Thales was very knowledgeable for his time, predicting an eclipse during a battle between Lydeans and Persians, discovering proofs in geometry, devising systems of measurement for distant objects, and predicting an olive harvest for himself which made him a wealthy man.

Text to consult: *A History of Greek Philosophy*, vol.1, W.K.C. Guthrie.

**thanatology** - n. in philosophy, the study of death; its nature, stages, and consequences.

**thanatos instinct** - n. in psychology, the instinctual tendency toward self-destruction; also called the 'nirvana principle'; opposed to the eros instinct.

**thanatophobia** - n. fear of death.

**thanatopsis** - n. contemplation of death.

**thaumatology** - n. the study of miracles, their nature, origin, and purpose.

**thaumaturge** - n. a miracle worker.

**theanthropic** - adj. being of man and god.

**theanthropism** - n. the unification of human and divine.

**theca** - n. a cover or receptacle, often in relation to the bodies of animals; armor.

**theocentric** - adj. putting God at the center of reality or one's philosophy.

**theogony** - n. tracing the origins of the gods.

**Theology** - n. the study of God and God's relation to the universe; it is divided into dogmatic, philosophical, historical, scriptural, and practical theology, with each of these areas having further classifications.

Text to consult: *Theological Dictionary*, Karl Rahner & H. Vorgrimler, 1965.

**theomania** - a type of insanity in which one believes one's self to be God.

**therianthropic** - adj. being part animal and part human.

**theriomorphic** - adj. being of animal form, especially regarding gods.

**thersitical** - adj. after Thersites, a Greek warrior known for his hyper-critical attitude and who was killed by Achilles for insulting him; thus, meaning loud, abusive, and socially irritating.

**theurgy** - n. the involvement of the gods in human affairs. It was historically practiced by the lesser Neoplatonists but was regarded as a cult which used incantations and ritual to produce beneficent action.

**third sex** - n.  a homosexual.

**Thoreau, Henry David** (1817-1862) - an American philosopher of nature, Thoreau was famous for his life in a hut at Walden Pond near Concord.  There he wrote about life in the wilderness.  His life choices can be interpreted as an endorsement of anarchism, for he believed that freedom was more attainable in the wilderness than in civil settings.  He argued that the spontaneity and creativity of nature is necessary for human spiritual well-being.  As little time as possible should be spent on commerce and political issues.  In fact, Thoreau concluded that to do something for the sake of money is the worst form of wasting time.

Principal works: *Civil Disobedience*, 1849, and *Walden, or Life in the Woods*, 1854.

> *"All men recognize the right of revolution; that is, the right to refuse allegiance to, and to resist, the government, when its tyranny or its inefficiency are great and unendurable"*
>
> H.D. Thoreau, <u>Civil Disobedience</u>

**thrall** - n.  a slave.

**thrasonical** - adj.  being a braggart.

**Thrasymachus** (ca. 500 B.C.) - a Greek philosopher, Thrasymachus sided with the Sophists.  He defended the view that justice is based on strength:  "Might makes right."  Natural justice is the result of the strong over-powering the weak.  He noted that political arrangements override the power of individuals, but politics too expresses the will to power, although in groups.  Thrasymachus is mentioned in Plato's *Republic,* Book I.

Text to consult: <u>A History of Greek Philosophy</u>, vol. 3, W.K.C. Guthrie.

**threnody** - n.  a dirge or lamentation for the dead.

**throe** - n.  a painful struggle.

**Tillich, Paul** (1886-1965) - a German philosopher and theologian who had a powerful influence on religious thought in the 20th century.  Due to Hitler's attack on free-thought, Tillich moved to the U.S. in 1933.  He taught at Union Theological Seminary and the University of Chicago.

Tillich's thought is characterized by existential themes.  His work on anxiety (*angst*) identified three primary sources: the awareness of death, the threat of a meaningless life, and the existence of guilt.  Tillich poses God as a practical solution to human anxiety.  God has the power of offering protection from these threats to being.  Deep awareness of history is linked to the feeling of despair, the reaction to a world in perpetual conflict.

Tillich emphasizes the role of *ontology*, and defines faith as *ultimate concern*.  Yet, he recognizes inferior substitutes: art, science, the state, political movements, material goods, and social status.  These are used to relieve humanity of its anxiety but fail.  This is because these substitutes do not have the Ultimate as their *ultimate concern.*

Since they do not determine the nature of reality, they cannot be Ultimate. Only God is the source of all meaning and being, and thus God or the religious life is the correct approach to being.

Principal works: *The Shaking of the Foundations*, 1948, *Systematic Theology, 3 vols.*, 1951-63, *The Courage to Be*, 1952, *Dynamics of Faith*, 1957, *Theology of Culture*, 1959, and *Morality and Beyond*, 1963.

> *"Anxiety and courage have a psychosomatic character. They are biological as well as psychological. From the biological point of view one would say that fear and anxiety are the guardians, indicating the threat of nonbeing to a living being and producing movements of protection and resistance to this threat. . . .*
> *Courage is the readiness to take upon oneself negatives, anticipated by fear, for the sake of a fuller positivity. Biological self-affirmation implies the acceptance of want, toil, insecurity, pain, possible destruction. Without this self-affirmation life could not be preserved or increased. The more vital strength a being has the more it is able to affirm itself in spite of the dangers announced by fear and anxiety."*
>
> Paul Tillich, <u>The Courage to Be</u>

**timocracy** - n.  a government characterized by the love of honor or glory, e.g., Sparta.

**timorous** - adj.  fearful.

**Tolstoy, Leo** (1828-1910) - a Russian social philosopher, Tolstoy advocated religious anarchy. Influenced by J.J. Rousseau, he believed all governments to be corrupt and coercive toward citizens. Though our relationship towards one and other determines the possibility of a meaningful life, this is only possible when conditioned by a belief in God. He concluded from a study of the Bible, especially the Sermon on the Mount, that there should be five cardinal rules of action: *suppression of all anger, the refusal to judge others, the avoidance of all oaths, the avoidance of all sex outside of marriage,* and *an unconditional love of one's enemies.* Tolstoy denied the divinity of Christ and the notion of the Trinity.

He viewed art as an emotional medium and a vehicle for morality, arguing that is conveyed the highest insights into human existence. Human existence itself being influenced by various types of unseen fate.

Principal works: *War and Peace*, 1873, *Anna Karenina*, 1877, *What I Believe*, 1882-84, and *The Christian Teaching*, 1894-96.

> *"In quiet and untroubled times it seems to every administrator that it is only by his efforts that the whole population under his rule is kept going, and in this consciousness of being indispensable every administrator finds the chief reward of his labor and efforts. While the sea of history remains calm the ruler-administrator in his frail bark, holding on with a boat hook to the ship of the people and himself moving, naturally imagines that his efforts move the ship he is holding on to. But as soon as a storm arises and the sea begins to heave and the ship to move, such a delusion is no longer possible. The ship moves independently with its own enormous motion, the boat hook no longer reaches*

*the moving vessel, and suddenly the administrator, instead of appearing a ruler*
*and a source of power, becomes an insignificant, useless, feeble man."*
Leo Tolstoy, <u>War and Peace</u>

**torpid** - adj. being sluggish or dull.

**torrify** - v. to burn or scorch; to heat up.

**tour de force** - n. French, an accomplishment that has no equal; a deed which reveals the highest level of skill, knowledge, or power.

**tractate** - n. a lengthy essay or dissertation.

**traduce** - v. to slander; to mistreat through false evidence.

**Traducianism** - n. in theology and philosophy, the theory that souls are produced along with bodies; like biological re-generation, souls are also passed along from parent souls in a type of spiritual re-generation. Advocated by Tertullian (155-222 A.D.).

**transcalent** - adj. permitting the passage of heat.

**transect** - v. to cut across.

**transempirical** - adj. lying beyond or outside of sensory knowledge.

**transmogrify** - v. to alter appearance, especially to that which is unsightly or grotesque.

**transpicuous** - adj. easily seen through; easily known or understood.

**travail** - n. adversity; suffering.

**travesty** - n. a terrible and ludicrous alteration; a distortion.

**tremulant** - adj. disordered; shaken.

**trenchant** - adj. very effective.

**trepidation** - n. anxiety; excessive worry.

**tribade** - n. a lesbian.

**tribulation** - n. trouble; suffering.

**trilemma** - n. a situation in which there are three undesirable choices.

**triturate** - v. to reduce to minute particles; to crush.

**trivium** - n.  in medieval schools, the university training in rhetoric, logic, and grammar.

**troglodyte** - n.  a primitive type of people found living in caves;  also, a reclusive person.

**trollop** - n.  a woman available for personal satisfactions;  also, a slovenly woman.

**truckle** - v.  to be servile;  to be submissive.

**truculent** - adj.  very hostile;  capable of inflicting harm with little provocation.

**tryst** - n.  a secret agreement to meet at a certain time and place.

**tumescent** - adj.  engorged or swollen.

**turgid** - adj.  excessively decorated;  pompous.

**tutoyer** - v.  to address a person with familiarity, especially where no familiarity exists.

**Tychism** - n.  in philosophy, the view that events can occur without apparent connection to outside causal forces;  chance is active in the universe.  In the thought of Charles Peirce, chance is an objective fact in the world.  Tychism is taken from the Greek *tyche,* meaning chance.
       Text to consult: <u>*The Collected Papers of C.S. Peirce*</u>, Charles Peirce, 1935, edited by C. Hartshorne & Paul Weiss.

**typhlosis** - n.  blindness.

**tyro** - n.  a neophyte;  a beginner in some art, craft, or discipline;  also, young soldier.

**ubeity** - n.  the state of being in a specific location.

**ubiquitous** - adj.  being everywhere.

**uliginous** - adj.  growing in muddy marshes or swamps.

**ultraism** - n.  the advancement of extreme measures, views, or principles.

**umbra** - n.  a shaded area, especially in reference to a celestial body.

**umbrage** - n.  the feeling that one has been slighted, often accompanied by resentment.

**umbriferous** - adj.  providing shade.

**Unamuno, Miguel de** (1864-1936) - a Spanish existentialist philosopher, Unamuno was influenced by Kierkegaard.  He focused on the *carne y hueso* (flesh and bone) nature of human beings, noting the hunger for immortality within the race.

Unamuno was deeply sympathetic to the individual fate of human existence, which is a sense of uncertainty.  Unamuno himself was torn between the offerings of faith and the demands of reason.  As a Catholic, he loved the Church but could not abandon the power of rational criticism.  Faith affirms immortality and reason denies it.  Thus, Unamuno finds existence to be a dilemma of choices.

Conclusions found in Unamuno's philosophy include: 1) human existence involves a painful awareness of transience and contingency,  2) to handle the anguish which is produced by this awareness, we explore the power of personal spiritual integrity, 3) life is essentially a mystery,  4) love is a property of life which can resolve the feeling of despair stemming from uncertainty, and 5) the goals we establish can only be self-created.

Principal works:  *On Purism*, 1895, *Love and Pedagogy*, 1902, *Tragic Sense of Life*, 1913, and *Saint Emmanuel the Good*, 1933.

*"All this talk of a man surviving in his children, or in his works, or in the universal consciousness, is but vague verbiage which satisfies only those who suffer from affective stupidity, and who, for the rest, may be persons of a certain*

*cerebral distinction. For it is possible to possess great talent, and yet to be stupid as regards the feelings and even morally imbecile."*

*"Suffering is a spiritual thing. It is the most immediate revelation of consciousness, and it may be that our body was given us simply in order that suffering might be enabled to manifest itself. A man who had never known suffering, either in greater or less degree, would scarcely possess consciousness of himself."*

*Miguel de Unamuno, Tragic Sense of Life*

**Unconscious, the** - n. in philosophy, the view that a significant part of the mind's activity exists apart from conscious mental activity. The concept of the unconscious is used by many important thinkers, e.g., Plato - with his doctrine of anemnesis or recollection, Arthur Schopenhauer - the idea of a 'blind will' as the force behind human effort, Carl Jung - the archetypes of the unconscious and their relation to dreams, to fill out the definition of human existence.

Texts to consult: *Memories, Dreams, Reflections*, Carl Jung, 1967, and *Jung*, Anthony Storr, 1973.

**Unitarianism** - n. in theology, the view that God is one and that Jesus is not a supernatural being but merely a human being. Its anti-Trinitarian bias has its origins in Adoptionism, Monarchianism, and Arianism. It does not admit the validity of eternal punishment and champions the goodness of human nature.

Text to consult: *The Philosophy of William Ellery Channing*, R.L. Patterson

**uncouth** - adj. lacking in grace, style, or taste; also, awkward.

**unguinous** - adj. being greasy; slippery; difficult to grasp.

**usury** - n. lending money at an excessively high interest rate.

**Utilitarianism** - n. in ethical theory, a principle using the view that the greatest happiness for the greatest number should guide the formation of ethical decisions. According to utilitarianism, the *utility* of values to produce the greatest degree of satisfaction for the greatest portion of society is the basis of 'the good.'. Advocates include Jeremy Bentham, J.S. Mill, and Henry Sidgwick.

Text to consult: *Utilitarianism*, John Stuart Mill, 1863.

**uxorial** - adj. of or benefiting a wife.

**uxoricide** - n. the killing of one's wife.

**uxorious** - adj. excessively submissive or affectionate towards one's wife.

**vagary** - n. an unpredictable occurrence;  chance.

**valetudinarian** - n. a cripple;  someone who is pre-occupied or obsessed with his or her poor health.

**vapid** - adj. lacking vitality;  dull or lifeless.

**Value theory** - n. in philosophy, the study of measuring worth, especially with regard to human action.  Also designated by the term 'axiology', value theory seeks to clarify various methods for measuring the 'rightness' or 'wrongness' of acts.  Oppositional thinking  occurs in the following  schools of thought: essentialism vs. existentialism, relativism vs. absolutism,  objectivism vs. subjectivism,  as well as cognitivism, naturalism, determinism, etc.  Values are those things which are personally important to us individually and socially.  As such they represent our interests.

**varlet** - n. an unreliable person;  a scoundrel.

**vastitude** - n. the quality of immensity.

**vatic** - adj. relating to the characteristics of a prophet.

**vaticide** - n. the killing of a prophet.

**vaticinate** - v. to foretell the future.

**Veblen, Thorstein Bunde** (1857-1929) - an American philosopher of economics, Veblen was critical of religion, business, and political systems.  Often at odds with college administrators, he taught at the University of Chicago, Stanford, and the University of Missouri.

Veblen argued that modern life is skewed by the philosophy of consumption which is presented by the business community.  He complained that the 'profit-making' values of business destroyed the creative values of workmanship, thus a corruption of social psychology.  He accused the educational system of serving the needs and values of the business community, thus failing to educate.  He believed the philosophy of 'salesmanship' was apparent in religion and politics as well.

Veblen believed that the survival of society would, in the future, depend upon the smooth and efficient operation of it technological structure but hoped to preserve the creative values necessary for the structuring of an enlightened society.

Principal works: *Theory of the Leisure Class*, 1899, *The Theory of Business Enterprise*, 1904, *The Instinct of Workmanship*, 1914, *Higher Learning in America: A Memorandum on the Conduct of Universities by Businessmen (originally subtitled - "A Study in Depravity")*, 1918, and *Absentee Ownership*, 1923.

> *"Modern consumers in great part supply their wants with commodities that conform to certain staple specifications of size, weight, and grade. The consumer (that is to say the 'vulgar consumer') furnishes his house, his table, and his person with supplies of standard weight and measure, and he can to an appreciable degree specify his needs and his consumption in the notation of the standard gauge. As regards the mass of civilized mankind, the idiosyncrasies of the individual consumers are required to conform to the uniform gradations imposed upon consumable goods by the comprehensive mechanical processes of industry."*
>
> Thorstein Veblen, *The Theory of Business Enterprise*

**Vedas** - n. in Indian philosophy, a collection of writings on religious practice and philosophical advice. 'Veda' means knowledge. Vedas include *Samhitas* (hymns), *Brahmanas* (rules for sacrifices), *Aranyakas* (philosophical interpretations of the sacrifices), *Upanishads* (the main outline and details of Hindu philosophy), and *Sutras* (priestly matters, social duties, sexual conduct & pleasures, astronomy, etc.).

Text to consult: *Hinduism*, Nirad Chaudhuri, 1979.

**velitation** - n. a minor dispute.

**velleity** - n. a weak will; a will which nets no result or action.

**venal** - adj. open to influence, especially a corruption.

**venatic** - adj. having connection to hunting.

**venery** - n. hunting, especially as an art or skill.

**venery** - n. the pursuit of satisfaction, especially in sexual pleasure.

**vendue** - n. a public sale or auction.

**ventose** - adj. given to useless chatter; windy.

**venue** - n. the location where an event takes place.

**verbiage** - n. words which do not relate essentially to the respective topic; superfluousness.

**verbose** - adj.  being excessively wordy.

**verdure** - n.  greenness, as in a landscape.

**verecund** - adj.  having no confidence to assert one's self;  being embarrassed.

**veridical** - adj.  truthful.

**verisimilitude** - n.  the appearance of truth.

**verism** - n.  in aesthetic philosophy, the theory that reality is best represented in art through the inclusion of the ugly, the vulgar, and the ordinary as well as the grand and the beautiful.

**vernal** - adj.  having to do with Spring.

**vertiginous** - adj.  inclined toward useless change;  whirling.

**verve** - n.  enthusiasm, especially with regard to a talent or skill.

**vestal** - adj.  pure; unspoiled; chaste.

**viaticum** - n.  the resources for a journey;  the essentials for travel.

**vicinage** - n.  closeness; nearness.

**viduity** - n.  widowhood.

**Vienna Circle** - n.  in philosophy, reference to a group of philosophers, mathematicians, and scientists in the early 20th century (1920's) whose goal was to establish a modern and rigorous form of empiricism, with the associated goal of clarifying the meaning of language.  This group included Rudolf Carnap, Herbert Feigl, Phillip Frank, Victor Kraft, Kurt Godel, Bela von Juhos, Felix Kaufman, Moritz Schlick, Otto Neurath, and Freidrich Waismann.  They worked out of the philosophy of David Hume, since Hume contributed so much to advance the strength of empirical epistemology.

      The label 'logical positivism' is used to describe the Vienna Circle.  Part of their work involved the rejection of traditional metaphysics as meaningless, since metaphsysics has no empirical foundation.  The same concerns were extended in an attempted purification of epistemology and ethics.

      Text to consult: *The Vienna Circle: The Origin of Neo-Positivism*, Viktor Kraft.

**vilify** - v.  to put down; to defame.

**vilipend** - v.  to assign a low value or importance to something.

**virago** - n.  a woman with outstanding qualities of strength and courage;  also, a woman who is hard to be around because of her self-righteous nature.

**virulent** - adj. powerfully poisonous; characterized by intense hostility.

**visage** - n. appearance; face.

**vis-a-vis** - prep. face to face.

**vis-a-vis** - n. counterpart.

**Vishnu** - n. in Hindu philosophy, God. Part of the 'trimurti' or Hindu trinity, Vishnu is the preserver, Brahma is the creator, and Shiva is the destroyer.

**vitiate** - v. to impair or make defective, especially through the addition of some inferior quality or feature.

**vitreous** - adj. transparent like glass.

**Vocation** - n. from the Latin *vocare* meaning 'to call'. Traditionally, this term was used in Christianity to indicate the call to religious life. In modern times, the term is regarded in a more personal way by philosophers like Jose Ortega y Gasset (1883-1955). For Ortega, vocation implies a radical call to pursue one's vitality through authentic selfhood.

**vociferate** - v. to shout.

**volant** - adj. nimble or quick in movement.

**Voltaire, Francois Marie Arouet de** (1694-1788) - a French philosopher, Voltaire once criticized the work of Shakespeare as formless and crude. Much of his thinking was influenced by the views of John Locke.

Theologically, Voltaire was a deist who accepted the freedom of the will and doubted the immortality of the soul. He was a tireless critic of formal religion, regarding ecclesiastical domination as a sign of ignorance and prejudice.

Politically, Voltaire was a parliamentarian and a supporter of the upper classes. His liberalism did not include an admiration for the lower classes, whom he considered incapable of self-rule.

Principal works: *Essay on the Customs and Spirit of the Nations*, 1756, *Candide*, 1759, *Treatise on Toleration*, 1763, and *Philosophical Dictionary*, 1764.

*"After our holy religion which would be the least bad?*

*Wouldn't it be the simplest one? Wouldn't it be the one that taught a good deal of morality and very little dogma? The one that tended to make men just, without making them absurd? The one that wouldn't command belief in the impossible, contradictory things insulting to the Divinity and pernicious to mankind, and wouldn't dare threaten with eternal punishment anyone who has common sense? Wouldn't it be the religion that didn't uphold its beliefs with executioners, didn't inundate the world with blood for the sake of unintelligible sophisms? The one in which an ambiguity, a play on words, or two or three forged charters wouldn't make a sovereign and a god of a priest who is often a*

*man who has committed incest, a murderer, and a poisoner? The one that*
*wouldn't make kings subject to this priest? The one that taught nothing but the*
*worship of a God, justice, tolerance, and humanity?"*
Voltaire, <u>Philosophical Dictionary</u>

**voluble** - adj. talkative; also, fluent.

**voyeur** - n. one who seeks sexual satisfaction and pleasure through seeing; also, one who hunts down that which is scandalous; a prying eye.

**Vulgate** - n. the name given to Latin translations of the Bible, starting with the work of St. Jerome (342-420 A.D.) who made the first translation at the request of Pope Damascus. The *Vulgate* became the basis for the Wycliffe translation into English.

**vulpine** - adj. having the qualities of a fox; being clever or crafty.

**Warsaw Circle** - n. a group of language philosophers whose aims were similar to those of the Vienna Circle. The group included Jan Lukasiewicz (1878-1956), Stanislaw Lesniewski (1884-1939), and Alfred Tarski (1901-1984). Lukasiewicz was the first to develop a three-valued logic: 'true', 'false', and 'possible'. He also developed the Polish notation which has become a standard in logical notation. The teacher of Tarski, Lesniewski worked on problems presented by Russell with regard to the foundations of mathematics. Tarski was known for his aggressive work on the development of metalogic, which included his adaptation of the Correspondence Theory of Truth to metalanguages.

**weal** - n. a healthy, stable society; also, well-being.

**Weber, Max** (1864-1920) - a German philosopher of sociology, Weber was associated with the Neo-Kantian school. He was the older brother of another noted social philosopher, Alfred Weber (1868-1958), whose work distinguished 'culture processes' from 'civilization processes' (see *Principles of Culture-Sociology*, 1921 and *The Tragic and History*, 1943).

Max Weber worked out a theory of *ideal types*: rational individuals who are representative of a certain historical period; individuals whose manner of being is shaped by the specific social organization of an age.

Weber's interest in religion led him to examine the connections between religion, economics, and society. In particular, he described the influence of Lutheranism and Calvinism on the development of capitalist society. He determined that the true meaning of capitalism was the "rational organization of free-labor" rather than the class struggle of Marxism. This 'rational organization' produces the bureaucratic structure of modern capitalism. The structure of corporations, in turn, leads to bureaucratization.

The use of *Verband* (authority) is a trait of bureaucracies, going back even to Roman, Egyptian, and Chinese bureaucratic structures. Following this are the attendant *roles* which members of bureaucracies play. The social dynamic of *Verband* includes an acceptance on the part of members.

*Verband* assumes three basic types which are recognized in a social order: *rational-legal* - the existence of laws and rules establishing authority on a 'rational' model; *traditional* - referring to past institutions; and, *charismatic* - where authority is created by an inspirational personality figure. Significant change is often accomplished by charismatic personalities, since their authority often extends beyond *traditional* and *rational-legal* types.

Principal works: *Capitalism and the Protestant Ethic*, 1905, *The Economic Ethic of the World Religions*, 1915, *Economy and Society*, 1922, *From Max Weber: Essays in Sociology*, 1946, and *On the Methodology of the Social Sciences*, 1949.

> *"Devotion to the charisma of the prophet, or the leader in war, or to the great demagogue in the 'ecclesia' or in parliament, means that the leader is personally recognized as the innerly "called" leader of men. Men do not obey him by virtue of tradition or statute, but because they believe in him. If he is more than a narrow and vain upstart of the moment, the leader lives for his cause and "strives for his work." The devotion of his disciples, his followers, his personal party friends is oriented to his person and its qualities."*
>
> Max Weber, *From Max Weber: Essays in Sociology*

**Weltanschauung** - n. in philosophy, a comprehensive view of the world or reality, especially from a specified logical and metaphysical viewpoint.

**Weltschmerz** - n. a sadness or melancholy, caused by unrealistic expectations for a perfect or ideal life; also, apathy.

**whelp** - n. usually a reference to a young dog; a person who lacks experience.

**whet** - v. to sharpen; also to stimulate.

**Whitehead, Alfred North** (1861-1947) - an English philosopher, Whitehead is the central figure of process philosophy. His original interest was mathematics, which included work with one of his best students, Bertrand Russell, on *Principia Mathematica*. Therein, Russell and Whitehead worked on a demonstration of mathematics' debt to logic.

Gradually, Whitehead lost interest in the abstract considerations of mathematics and language, moving toward questions of metaphysics which he felt were important to the further progress of science. Influenced by the work of Charles Darwin, Max Planck, Niels Bohr, and other scientists, Whitehead wanted a deeper framework for reality which started with a substitution of traditional atomic notions of matter. In Whiteheadian terms, *atoms* are called *actual entities* or *actual occasions*. Whitehead thought that these new names addressed the life-like nature of all reality, even its most primitive basis. It was his intention to emphasize the *organic* nature of reality over the mechanistic models of the past. He wanted to show the vitality of relationships in nature.

Whitehead uses the notion of *actual occasions* to argue for feeling and purpose in the universe. This universe is also marked by *creativity, novelty,* and *becoming.* The things we see are collections of *actual occasions* which Whitehead identifies as *societies.* Whitehead uses the word *prehension* to identify a cohesiveness among *actual occasions* collected together into a *society* or *nexus.* His theory of metaphysical unity also employs the term *concrescence*

Borrowing from Plato, Whitehead introduces the *eternal objects* which act as a kind of polarity for *actual entities. Actual entities* align metaphysically with *eternal objects* through a process Whitehead calls *ingression. Actual entities* derive their specific identity from simple *eternal objects;* in the case of complex objects (*societies*) there are complex *eternal objects.*

In his cosmology, Whitehead designates God as the timeless co-agent of creation. The future represents God's *primordial nature,* whereas the past represents God's *consequent nature.* Guiding values for this co-agency are the good, the beautiful, and the truth.

Principal works: *Principia Mathematica,* 1910, *The Concept of Nature,* 1920, *Science and the Modern World,* 1926, *Religion in the Making,* 1926, *Process and Reality,* 1929, *The Aims of Education,* 1929, *Adventures of Ideas,* 1933, and *Modes of Thought,* 1936.

> *"A race preserves its vigor so long as it harbours a real contrast between what has been and what may be; and so long as it is nerved by the vigour to adventure beyond the safeties of the past. Without adventure civilization is in full decay.*
>
> *"It is for this reason that the definition of culture as the knowledge of the best that has been said and done, is so dangerous by reason of its omission. It omits the great fact that in their day the great achievements of the past were adventures of the past. Only the adventurous can understand the greatness of the past."*
>
> A.N. Whitehead, <u>Adventures of Ideas</u>

**white supremacy** - n. a political-philosophical doctrine which holds that whites are inherently superior to Negroes. Moreover, within the doctrine's aims is the requirement that Negroes be subordinate to whites in all areas of life.

**William of Ockham** (1290-1349 A.D.) - an English philosopher, Ockham is mainly remembered for his *Principle of Parsimony,* often called "Ockham's Razor": *what can be said in few words should not be said or expressed in many words.* Basically, do not extend things unnecessarily.

Ockham's position with regard to nominalism was that there is no 'beyond' with regard to things and universal terms used. The mind of man is the limited domain within which universals exist. Human reflection is limited to the objects of experience and does not imply some extra context outside of the sensory world.

Principal works: *Summa Logicae,* and *Treatise on Predestination and God's Foreknowledge of the Contingent Future.*

> *"That no universal is a substance outside the mind can be evidently proved."*
>
> William of Ockham, <u>Summa Logicae</u>

**Wisdom** - n. in philosophy, the Anglo-Saxon term for *sophia.* Wisdom is the possession of excellent judgment in the affairs of day to day existence. Essentially, it is the maximization of opportunities to construct a satisfying life. In Plato, wisdom is a cardinal virtue, one from which other virtues flow. It is characterized by a degree of humility toward reality, a pronounced curiosity regarding the workings of the world, and a deep respect for the objective forcefulness that exists within things.

**Wittgenstein, Ludwig** (1889-1951) - an Austrian logician, Wittgenstein made very novel contributions to the understanding of language and logic. In the *Tractatus Logico-Philosophicus* he works to identify the basis of empirical science. Wittgenstein noted the role of language in the statement of facts. Language provides pictures of reality. It approximates facts. Facts in turn are the basic parts of the world we experience. Language which does not provide facts is just nonsense, including the statements of religion, metaphysical thought, and probably most of ethics. Wittgenstein concludes in a kind of mystical fashion that even the work of the *Tractatus* is nonsense, since it is metaphysical in nature, attempting to grasp at foundations of reality.

The later Wittgenstein adopts a more liberal view of language assigning it multiple purposes. Thus, language patterns reveal ceremonial language, instructional language, emotional language, and investigative language.

Wittgenstein defined the idea of philosophy as a 'sense of puzzlement' about reality. The role of logic and language is to reduce this sense of puzzlement by rendering a clear picture of reality.

Principle works: *Tractatus Logico-Philosophicus*, 1921, *The Blue and Brown Books*, 1933-35, *Philosophical Investigations*, 1953, *Philosophical Remarks on the Foundations of Mathematics*, 1956, and *Lectures and Conversations on Aesthetics, Psychology, and Religious Belief*, 1966.

> *"4.05  Die Wirklichkeit wird mit dem Satz verglichen."*
> *(4.05  Reality is compared with propositions.)*
> *"4.06  Nur dadurch kann der Satz wahr oder falsch sein, in dem er ein Bild der Wirklichkeit ist."*
> *(4.06  A proposition can be true or false only in virtue of being a picture of reality.)*
> > Ludwig Wittgenstein, <u>*Tractatus Logico-Philosophicus*</u>

**wittol** - n.  a married man who knows of his wife's infidelity and does nothing about it.

**wowser** - n.  Austral for a showingly puritanical person.

**wroth** - adj.  extremely angry, especially to the point of destruction or violence.

**Wu-wei** - n.  in Chinese philosophy, the idea of emptiness or inaction. It is a central notion in the philosophy of Taoism and also in Zen Buddhism, especially in conjunction with understanding the essence of meditation and enlightenment.

> *"Without going out the door, one can know the whole world. Without looking out the window, one can see the Tao of heaven. The further one travels, the less one knows. So, the sage knows everything without traveling. He names everything without seeing it. He accomplishes everything without doing it."*
> > - Ch'u Ta-kao, <u>*The Tao Te Ching*</u>,

**Xenophanes** (575-478 B.C.) - n.  a pre-Socratic philosopher, aligned with thinkers in the Milesian school.  Xenophanes argued for two primary elements, fire and air.  He also taught that there are an unlimited number of suns in the universe.

**xenophilia** - n.  love of things which are different, especially foreign cultures and ideas.

**xenophobia** - n.  a morbid fear of things which are different, especially foreign cultures and ideas.

**xeric** - adj.  needing only very small amounts of moisture;  being accustomed to dryness.

**xerophilous** - adj.  living in a very hot-dry environment.

**xylography** - n.  in the philosophy of technology, woodcarving.

**yahweh** - n.  a name for God used by the early Jews;  the meaning of the tetragram YHWH.

**yaul** - v.  to deviate from a straight course.

**yenta** - n.  a scandal-mongering female;  an unpleasant woman.

**Yin and yang** - n.  in Eastern philosophy, the reference to complementary principles or forces of the universe. 'Yin' represents the feminine principle:  negative, passive, destructive, weak. 'Yang' represents the masculine principle:  positive, active, creative. All change is the result of interaction between opposed principles or forces.

**Yoga** - n. in Indian philosophy, a practical discipline of union between self and the universal soul.  Deriving guidance from the Vedic scriptures, yoga is theistic and is expressed in different schools, e.g., *karma yoga* - the emphasis on duty, *raja yoga* - the emphasis on mental concentration, *jnana yoga* - the emphasis on knowledge, *hatha yoga* - the emphasis on posture and physical conditioning of the body.

**yogi** - n.  a practitioner of yoga;  a reflective or philosophical person.

**yoni** - n.  in Hindu philosophy, the feminine principle symbolized in Hindu art by the female genitalia.

**zeal** - n.  a striving interest to complete something.

**zealot** - n.  usually a partisan with a fanatical consciousness, including a commitment to militant opposition.

**zeitgeist** - n.  the intellectual, noetic, or philosophical character of a time and culture.

**Zen** - n.  a type of Mahayana Buddhism which emphasizes the importance of purity and sudden enlightenment, especially by intuitive and meditative processes of mind.  The historical origins of Zen are obscure.  A search for the beginning of this religious-philosophic discipline leads to several possibilities, all of them proven only by the existence of tradition as explanation.  One story is that Zen was the creation of an Indian philosopher by the name of Bodhidharma (460-534 ).  Other stories attribute Zen to the Buddha himself.  Still other accounts point to Lao-Tzu (ca. 500 B.C.) due to the striking similarities between Zen and Taoism.  The strongest modern advocate of Zen is D.T. Suzuki (1870-1966), *Manual of Zen Buddhism*.  It is perhaps best and in the spirit of Zen that its exact history is nameless, for Zen is the study of the nameless reality which surrounds us.

Zen is divided into two general schools or sects, Rinzai and Soto.  Rinzai emphasizes sudden enlightenment and is less intellectually oriented, claiming that all perceptual and rational discriminations are illusions.  All striving is useless, including the striving not to strive.  Theoretical paradoxes are somewhat of a commodity in Rinzai Zen, aiding in the encouragement to 'transcend' reality.  Paradox is refined in the Zen use of *koans* (statements designed to frustrate rational analysis of reality).   The Soto sect is a moderate representation of the principles of Zen, more popular, and less rigorous than the Rinzai sect.

Zen actualizes its discipline and teachings through various arts, including archery, swordsmanship, the tea ceremony, and landscape gardening.  This aspect of Zen extends the fruits of Mahayana Buddhism beyond the monastery, giving the hope of liberation to ordinary followers.  The contemplative techniques embodied in the arts of Zen are usually administered by a master teacher or *'Roshi'*.  Vows of absolute obedience are used to preserve the spiritual discipline which Zen aims toward.  Vows of obedience also serve to preserve the institutional authenticity of Zen, since Zen is not considered a philosophy that can be truly mastered without the guidance of a proven teacher.

*"In the case of archery, the archer and the target are no longer two opposing objects,*
*but are one reality. The archer ceases to be conscious of himself . . . completely*
*empty and rid of the self, he becomes one with the perfecting of his technical*
*skill.*
*- Daisetz T. Suzuki, Introduction of <u>Zen in the Art of Archery</u>*
*by Eugen Herrigel*

The pragmatic focus which is found in Zen arts has held a great fascination with Westerners, many of whom are disenchanted with the approaches of Western religion. Yet, the attraction to Zen arts is sometimes a wrong way toward Zen, because the esoteric nature of Zen is not simply mastered by physical conformation. Moreover, Zen masters are often reluctant to accommodate the needs of large numbers of students, such accommodation being a type of striving.

Texts to Consult: <u>Zen and Western Thought</u>, Masao Abe, 1987, <u>Zen and Japanese Culture</u>, D.T. Suzuki, 1959, and <u>The Spirit of Zen</u>, Alan Watts, 1958.

**zenana** - n. in Hinduism, a den of licentious pleasure; a place where women are sequestered.

**Zeno of Elea** (490-430 B.C.) - a student of Parmenides, Zeno worked out refutations of plurality and especially motion. He developed a number of paradoxes to illustrate the weaknesses of common sense:

1) *The Arrow:* for an arrow to exist it must occupy a space. To occupy a space means to be motionless. If an arrow moves, it is not occupying a space. If it is not occupying a space it does not exist. Thus, if it does not exist, it cannot move.

2) *Achilles and the Tortoise:* Achilles, running after a tortoise, cannot catch the tortoise because each time Achilles reaches the point where the tortoise last was, the tortoise has moved on. No matter how fast Achilles runs, each time he reaches the point at which the tortoise last was, the tortoise has moved on. The distance may appear to decrease, but no matter how many times Achilles reaches the point at which the tortoise last was, the tortoise will have moved on, however minutely. Thus, theoretically Achilles cannot catch the tortoise.

3) *The Racecourse:* To travel from start to finish on a racecourse, the runner must travel from A to B. But, first the runner must travel half-way. And before reaching half-way, he must reach half-way to half-way between A and B. This requirement of running half-way to each half-way can be extended infinitely, since there are an infinite series of points between any two points, thus an infinite series of half-way points. Thus again, the runner cannot run from A to B.

Text to consult: <u>A History of Greek Philosophy</u>, vol. 2, W.K.C. Guthrie, 1980.

**zephyr** - n. a soft, gentle breeze usually coming out of the west.

**zoanthropy** - n. a mental pathology in which the victim believes his or her self to be an animal and acts like one.

**zoophobia** - n. a morbid fear of animals, the consequence of early childhood experiences, wherein individual traumas, in relation to animals, are psychologically processed to become a general fear and anxiety of all subsequent encounters with animals.

**Zoroastrianism** - n. though originally the faith of *'Parsis'* ("Persians" in Hindu) at about 500 B.C. (some sources go back to 1500 B.C.), this religion survives primarily in India where some 200-300,000 practitioners live. Its migration to India took place about 800 A.D.

Zoroaster (also called 'Zarathustra') became the namesake of this faith by healing an Aryan ruler's horse, declaring allegiance to *Ahura Mazda,* and making spiritual declarations based on visions and communion with the divine *Ahura Mazda.*

The *Avesta* is the sacred text of Zoroastrians, being a collection of hymns and instructions on worship and daily life. Within the text are the *Gathas* or teachings of Zoroaster:

1. The universe is composed of opposing forces put in place by Ahura Mazda. These forces exist as a balance of good and evil.

2. The conflict between good and evil is visible in human life. Individuals have one lifetime to exercise their freedom, choosing either *asha* (truth) or *druj* (falsehood).

3. Reality, as we experience it, is a test of our spiritual powers. It is not a by-product of the senses. It exists and needs to be taken seriously.

4. Eshatologically, time ends and souls continue their existence in paradise or hell. Although, hell exists to purify the damned; through punishment they are cleansed and return in a new age of innocence.

5. Believers must not spoil the earth with their actions and must enact the virtues of truthfulness, compassion, charity, and justice.

Texts to consult: *A History of Zoroastrianism*, 2 vols., Mary Boyce, 1982, and *Textual Sources for the Study of Zoroastrianism*, Mary Boyce, 1984.

**zymosis** - n. fermentation.

**zymurgy** - n. the study of wine-making and beer-making; fermentation.

# Abridged Index

215

To contact the author, write to:

> Joseph A. van de Mortel
> Philosophy Department
> Cerritos College
> Norwalk, CA 90650

To order additional copies of this reference handbook, use the ISBN on the back cover, and order them through any college or university bookstore or contact McGraw-Hill Inc. through any college or university library.